The Challenges of European Governance in the Age of Economic Stagnation, Immigration, and Refugees

The Challenges of European Governance in the Age of Economic Stagnation, Immigration, and Refugees

Edited by
Henry F. Carey

LEXINGTON BOOKS
Lanham • Boulder • New York • London

Published by Lexington Books
An imprint of The Rowman & Littlefield Publishing Group, Inc.
4501 Forbes Boulevard, Suite 200, Lanham, Maryland 20706
www.rowman.com

Unit A, Whitacre Mews, 26-34 Stannary Street, London SE11 4AB

British Library Cataloguing in Publication Information Available

Library of Congress Cataloging-in-Publication Data

Names: Carey, Henry F., 1953- editor.
Title: The challenges of European governance in the age of economic stagnation, immigration,
    and refugees / edited by Henry F. Carey.
Description: Lanham, Maryland : Lexington Books, 2016. | Includes bibliographical references
    and index.
Identifiers: LCCN 2016041262 (print) | LCCN 2016048866 (ebook) | ISBN 9780739166901
    (hardback) | ISBN 9781498547734 (Electronic)
Subjects: LCSH: European federation. | Regionalism—Political aspects—European Union
    countries. | European Union. | Council of Europe. | European Union countries—Foreign
    relations—21st century. | European Union countries—Politics and government—21st century. |
    BISAC: POLITICAL SCIENCE / International Relations / General. | POLITICAL SCIENCE /
    General. | POLITICAL SCIENCE / International Relations / Diplomacy. | POLITICAL
    SCIENCE / Public Policy / Economic Policy.
Classification: LCC JN15 .C4255 2016 (print) | LCC JN15 (ebook) | DDC 341.242/2—dc23
    LC record available at https://lccn.loc.gov/2016041262

Printed in the United States of America

Contents

Introduction

After Brexit, The Dilemmas of European Governance

Henry F. Carey and Diana White

Timothy Garton Ash, deliberately borrowing from Churchill on democracy, wrote before the June 23, 2016 Brexit referendum that: "The Europe we have today is the worst possible Europe, apart from all the other Europes that have been tried from time to time."[1] Prior to the Eurozone crisis of the Millennium's second decade, academics debated whether European international organizations were more supranational or intergovernmental[2] in their decision-making and more or less effective and democratic in their consequences. Obvious shortcomings were noticed, which led to normative debates on whether greater integration was needed to achieve both positive goals in social and economic policy,[3] or whether incipient imperial overstretch threatened the entire project.[4] Technocratic solutions hardly worked, by tinkering through the supranational European Commission; larger pacts effected through the intergovernmental Council, sub regional policies;[5] and civil society activism.[6] Many expensive supranational policies came to a "dead-end" with the Euro-crisis.[7] Others maintained that the siren songs of exaggerated demise does not gainsay "The Transformative Power of Europe."[8] Within multilevel governance studies, a return to focusing on domestic politics study was already underway to assess the top-down effects of Europeanization, but the flip side of Europeanization, bottom-up approaches, became not only a way to understand policy formulation in both supranational and intergovernmental institutions, but also as forms of reaction and retrenchment.[9] As perceived inefficacy emerged in the economy and policy response, particularly the perceived, gratuitous austerity policies, perceived Euro-legitimacy also eroded, increasing Euro-skepticism and nationalism, creating a negatively reinforcing, nascent "perfect storm." Increasing inequalities with economic stagnation in the peripheries across states, classes, regions, urban-rural and educational divides created the developed world's analogue to dependency theory and caused an apparent return to geographic and ideological polarization in politics. Multilevel governance, based on the supremacy of European law, has induced domestic assertions of intergovernmental veto prerogatives, including the prior unmentionable discourses of exit.

This book is designed to show how EU can be at once both influential and transformative, and in decline, in no small measure, because of the dilemma between

Eurozone, Schengen, and security trajectories. Deals are cut with autocrats to get geo-political results, not only in Turkey, but also in Hungary and Poland, as these countries evolve in unethical, illiberal regimes. The contradiction not only sends mixed signals without, but makes the maintenance and deepening of civil society, liberal freedoms, and the rule of law more problematic within its borders. Europe has come full-circle, initially using economics, as well as new legal regimes, to make the opportunity costs of war too high. Now that the peace has been won, the economies have slowed to the point that radical parties are demanding, and public opinion is increasingly respond-ing, by asking less of Europe, and returning more to the states, each of whom has reas-serted the primacy of national culture and politics over the European liberal project. Europe's cohesion is fraying, with the United States pivoting eastward while Europe faces more internal and external threats than at any time since its regional organiza-tions were founded at the end of World War II.

The emergence of European international governmental organizations (IGOs) as a new model of governance was prompted by the cooperation that ultimately elicited academic theories like Functionalism in the 1960s, Realist Inter-governmentalism in the 1970s, and Liberal Institutionalism in the 1980s. Traditional frameworks in International Relations, such as Realism, the dominant paradigm, had underscored the incentives for negative or zero-sum interactions among states resulting from the competition for power under anarchy. Moreover, after the Cold War ended, there was a continued demand for institutions like NATO. Initially, economic develop-ment contributed greatly to European integration, which spilled over the need for supranational institutions implementing common political goals, correcting market failures, and providing public goods. The perceived success of free trade generally and specifically of European integration have made Liberal Institutionalism a viable competitor to the Realist versions of Inter-governmentalism inspired by Exceptionalist practices in high politics, such as France's partial withdrawal from NATO, the defeat of the European Constitutions by national plebiscites, and the existential crises by the European Union's feared inability to manage the Eurozone common currency and Syria-Iraq-induced refugee crises. IGOs were viewed as being able to accommodate diverging interests through economic functionalism, which can resolve policy differ-ences and national rivalries through free trade. Conflict and mistrust in the past can be overcome, only to face new challenges. As the EU and Council of Europe (CoE) expanded to include former Communist states, paradoxically greater conflict and mis-trust have emerged. NATO's security goals have been challenged by unconventional warfare, ethnic separatism, and counterterrorism challenges that were not envisioned in its founding treaty that had ostensibly excluded out-of-area missions, to guarantee military cooperation among affiliated states. Since the dynamics of these institutions are partly driven by common values and goals, IGOs are essential to understand the forces and processes that drive contemporary trends in governance. Contemporary trends of governance can be understood from a rational choice perspective, pursuing the highest net benefits based on available options and information. IGO integration is a theoretically rational choice for states because through this model of governance, states can reach solutions to collective action problems, reduce conflict, lower the costs of reaching agreements, help cooperation, and facilitate compliance. The prob-lems raised by rationalism are clear: that decision-making, institutions, and regimes emerge from many non-rational factors, from culture, imperfect information, transaction costs, competing and contradictory logics, complexity, resistance, elite-mass dynamics, confusion, and chance.

Different approaches, both questions and answers, are suggested by the other, major interpretive paradigms such as Constructivism, Liberalism, and various Critical and neo-Marxist approaches. For Realism, uncertainty is a source of persistent conflict, since in the anarchy that rules international relations, states are primarily concerned with power and security. Defection from cooperation results in negative-sum consequences, even when collective action would lead to improvements in the utility calculations of each state. For Mearsheimer, for whom uncertainty, anarchy, and fear prevail, states that ignore rational balance-of-power considerations will eventually fall victim to other states. Therefore, states prefer the Realist approach of self-help and continuous power accumulation as a response to collective action problems. The rise of perceived, migrant, refugee, and terrorist threats led to self-help and veto-playing by states to protect themselves, rather than relying on European institutions and organizations. As we shall see, this Realist view challenges integration concepts of Liberal Inter-governmentalism of Andrew Moravcsik that at least appeared to be the transcendent paradigm of European integration theorizing since it challenged the Realist Inter-governmentalism of Stanley Hoffman in the 1960s, as France opted out of most NATO institutions.

For Constructivists, uncertainty in relations can be reduced through the creation of norms. Many international norms have roots in domestic norms but are internationalized through the efforts of norm entrepreneurs, intergovernmental institutions (IGOs), institutions and elites. Norms are tools for the resolution of collective action dilemmas because norms standardize behavior by constraining choice and limiting the range of possible actions.[13]

For Liberal Institutionalists, finally, security is also of upmost importance as for Realists, but can be enhanced through information-sharing and monitoring mechanisms. In complicated multistate situations, institutions can provide the possibility of cooperative outcomes.[14] Liberalism perceives increasing, complex interdependence in the international system, along with the need to mitigate perverse incentives toward free riding in collective action, provide public goods, and correct market failure. In response, more complex international organizations, formal and informal, have evolved. In turn, these IGOs have generated even more complex interactions. However, the conditions for cooperation, such viable monitoring, effective sanctions for noncompliance, and consensus on the rules' requirements, are often scarce.

Thus, Liberalism, Realism, and Constructivism offer competing explanations of events and developments. Realism may fail to explain the liberal peace in postwar Europe, but it does account best for the self-help that European states used to establish boundary restrictions on refugees and migrants imposed, beginning in late 2015, in violation of the Schengen regime, to say nothing of the lack of implementation of the Dublin II accords on migration to begin with. Similarly, the EU's 2016 agreement with Turkey offered $6 billion Euros and Schengen access to Turkey, in return for the latter restricting the flow of migrants, by only allowing one refugee into Europe for every migrant that Europe returned to Turkey. Realism accurately predicts that the EU would ignore the increasing authoritarian regime established by its president Recep Tayyip

Erdogan, so long as the refugee flow is controlled, which was at least the initial consequence of the realist pact.[15] However, Liberalism better explains the persistent efforts
to establish institutions to manage some of these challenges within its legal framework, no matter how stretched. Constructivism better explains the persistent calls for
protection of refugee and migration rights, both specifically and of their human rights
generally, as well as open borders within the Schengen zone.

From the theoretical frameworks from these International Relations concepts have
emerged partly derivative concepts in European regional studies. Historical insights
were gained from Functionalism, producing spillover effects from international institutions, to intergovernmental and supranational decision-making of EU and Council
of Europe (CoE) decision-making. Different understandings resulted from top-down,
Europeanization effects on member states and their societies than from bottom-up
effects from states and their civil societies on these regional organizations, including
both unintended effects from norm hijacking, differential understandings and norm
entrepreneurship, which can either reinforce or distort, but which also redounds
into the international level of analysis with distorted standards, and not just the
unanticipated implementation of noncompliance at the local level.[16] Much depends
on whether a policy is formulated out of crisis decision-making or bureaucratic
standard, or out of technocratic or bureaucratic procedures. Contemporary debates
indicate that many different policy outcomes can result from common institutional
perspectives depending on the different factors at the different governance levels.
States with robust and congruent domestic institutions are more likely to enhance
top-down Europeanization for reasons of either rational choice or sociologically constructed norms. This strong effect utilizes many similar variables in concluding that
"Misfits" result when the logics of domestic institutions and culture allow for veto
points where norm entrepreneurs within states and society prevent the deepening of
European norms.[17]

Characterizing the precise concepts or combinations of them to European governance is no simple task. Moved to greater complexity and adaptability at the cost
of decreased coherence and autonomy, regional organizations such as the European
Union, Council of Europe, NATO, the Office of Security and Cooperation in Europe,
as well as thousands of subregional modes of interstate cooperation have established
a European system of regional governance. The exigencies in which Europe has
found itself have undermined confidence in Europe's liberal identity and project. This
results from expanding beyond its territories of competence, which exposed Europe
to shocks from without like Russia and the Middle East and eroding standards from
within among a more heterogeneous group of states with unequal will and skill to
comply with liberal norms. Economic decline, the rise of right-wing parties with
anti-democratic system orientations, the restrictions of human rights in the face of
terrorism, and the entire Brexit debate made not just retrenchment likely, but also
debilitated mortally the respect for and the power of international law to promote and
protect Europe's most important but controversial regimes. As these rules become
weaker and compliance declines, the general legal order, where many rules still operate effectively, may increasingly become undermined. Clearly, the loss of general confidence that the EU and other European IGOs may diminish are part of a self-fulfilling
prophesy dynamics.

As a series of treaties, the EU, CoE, OSCE, and NATO have to rely on informal institutions to achieve enforcement, which leaves these IGOs open to new interpretations and assertions, as well as to formal institutions, which are interpreted through political processes, vagaries, and arbitrariness. All of these political factors are also true of sovereign states, even if there may be a difference of degree. The EU is relatively new to the human rights and soft power game, as it was originally and remains primarily an economic union that joined the human rights crusade either with the 2009 Lisbon Treaty, or a few years before then with some EU Court of Justice decisions embracing the earlier holdings of the European Court of Human Rights, which is rooted in the longer work of the CoE. And, as with human rights work generally, they are highly political and focused on enemy or despotic regimes, but have never been applied universally in practice, whatever the discourse may have been. More cynically, European norms are ways of stigmatizing others, rather than improving one's record at home. In the name of human rights, NATO at the prodding of European states like France and Italy, have effectively, if unintendedly, destroyed Libya through abandonment, joining a similar process by the United States in Afghanistan and Iraq. Similarly, the EU supports, as does the United States, those civil society groups and NGOs that support the outsiders' agendas, rather than engaging in anything remotely either representative or emblematic of the human rights norms.

These formal and informal institutions in European IGOs are affected by hard and soft power leadership by the United States. Resistance can come, such as during the Franco-German opposition to the 2003 US invasion of Iraq, but which was supported by East European and Balkan states oriented toward the "Anglosphere." Militarily weak, France and Germany were powerless to stop an invasion. Germany economically, largely within the EU, exercises similar unilateral power, sometimes to maintain regimes, as suggested by liberal institutionalism, but also in its enlightened self-interest. Balkan and East European states look to NATO, and especially to the United States, for the hard power to protect them from Russia's security threats. These states can have less favorable views of the hard power of Germany's economic leadership, if not dominance, even if it operates with a significant dose of socially constructed, soft normative power that has emerged from both its respect for *Rechstaat*, the rule of law, and its altered, post-Holocaust identity of human rights leadership and accountability. However the hard power of capitalism, which includes not only German economic interests protected by its Finance Ministry, along with the European Central Bank and IMF Troika, led to harsh austerity policies throughout the Eurozone, especially in Greece, to the point where a plebiscite in Greece rejected austerity, but was subsequently ignored by the Troika. Constructivism thus accounts for one side of Germany's leadership, but not others where realist material interests prevail. Germany's identity as a post-Nazi state and its lack of hard military power, and its commitment to European regional legal processes are important, but not the whole story. In protecting its capital and market dominance, Germany also offers support for neo-Marxist and Critical theory interpretations. Even "post-materialist" democracies rarely can represent the desires, even to the point of impoverishment, of those who are at odds with capital.

Similarly, the sudden change in discourse in early 2016, where states suddenly stopped supporting the European refugee regime; interdicting refugees at their national borders; and calling them "migrants" resulted from various domestic sovereign objections, public opposition to saving refugees, and fear of terrorism. This was followed by the realpolitik agreement with Turkey signed and ratified in spring 2016, which traded refugees from Turkey for migrants returned from Greece, with the hard power of up to $6 billion in payments to Turkey.

The high level of European disharmony reflects its ungovernability and legitimacy crises, both at the regional and national levels, and via elections held in 2015–2016, in the rise of the radical right in twenty-six of the twenty-eight EU countries (Spain and Portugal excepted). The "Brexit" plebiscite and the sudden emergence of the UKIP in Britain epitomize how right-wing parties are both a symptom and a cause of not just Euro-skepticism, but also agencies of Euro decay and potential breakdown. However, seen from the perspective of the long twentieth century, including four decades of the "Iron Curtain" over the Soviet Empire, the severity of these recent crises pale in comparison. Healthy Euro-governance, by contrast, goes largely unnoticed in the din of the news cycle. The successful EU project inducing Romania to prosecute massive numbers of corrupt public officials; the deepening of the European single capital market; the successful, if second-best, management of the Euro-crisis and even the refugee influx; and, though perhaps cynical in overlooking its deeper authoritarianism, the reincorporation of Turkey into the EU accession crisis in return for geopolitical priorities, along with similar trends in Central Europe, suggest a complex, but adaptable, silver lining. Such contradictions can also be seen as institutional decay, but repeatedly, Stanley Hoffman's maxim that the EU keeps defying predictions of its demise by finding solutions that maintain its rational benefits of the world's largest single market and a positive peace among its member states. Its deepening institutionalization to both greater union in some supranational regimes and looser intergovernmentalism in others, sometimes induce greater union and sometimes less, or even devolution to national and subnational realms of governance.

To avoid decay, European institutions in coordination with the national and subnational counterparts, need to adapt in a complex, coherent, and autonomous manner[18] to each new crisis and evolving challenge accruing from supranational, intergovernmental, and accession growth and reactions from national sovereignty. In the middle of the storm, one cannot expect such institutional reforms to evolve instantly. The danger of domestic political impatience is a great threat, which could induce domestic revolts before such institutions can fully adapt to such new circumstances. Multilevel governance means that the domestic political systems are integral parts of these institutions, with all the advantages and disadvantages of decentralized governance. Models, such as Waltz's three images[19] (system, state and leader) and Putnam's two-level games[20] (international and domestic diplomacy) are only snap shots of a more complex, multilevel governance across a range of issues and a small, but critical number of emerging and reemerging, great crises.

There are multitudinous puzzles that emerge in attempting to identify the conditions in which either intergovernmental organizations such as the Committee of Ministers of the Council of Europe or the European Union's Council, are effective or ineffective to utilize their comparative advantage in collective action—if and only if there is a consensus on an issue. The issue of consensus is more subtle with supranational institutions, since there are theoretically assumed unitary decision-makers, though agencies such as the European Parliament, the Parliamentary Assembly of the

Council of Europe, the EU Court and the European Court of Human Rights, and especially the EU Commission and the Council of Europe's secretariat, are theoretically rational actors, but follow the laws when interacting with intergovernmental agencies, individual states, and domestic constituencies.

For example, the EU Council has forged an unlikely near-consensus on climate change and Eurozone austerity, unique in the world in both cases, despite the "high politics" of political opposition in energy industries and popular political movements for debt forgiveness. By contrast, supranational agencies have been the prime movers in reviewing accession and taking unprecedented, if inadequate steps in reforming judiciaries, reducing corruption, and decentralizing government power. This is in stark contrast to the policies on migration and refugees, where neither intergovernmental nor supranational agencies have withstood the effects of state dissent, fearful public opinion, and nationalist domestic political forces.

It can be very difficult to assess causality when the real motives, incentives, and actions can be discerned through different international levels of analysis, interpretive frameworks, and ideological lenses. Do countries like Germany, for example, accept about 800,000 refugees in 2015 and commit to half a million more for the foreseeable future, about one percent of its population, because of Realist material factors, the need for workers in an expanding economy; Liberal Institutional imperatives from the refugee protocol dating to the 1950s; because of its Constructivist commitment to European values and leadership role; because of an illusion of beneficence to cover its demands that German bank loans, however misguided be obeyed; or because it wants the European Union and related regimes to survive and thrive, and if so, for its own sake, or because German leadership has become indispensable, or self-serving? There is truth in all these different interpretations, but explaining what is the most important factor and why would require a degree of rigorous analysis that would be difficult to describe and demonstrate.

How do we define governance generally and multilevel governance in particular? Governance generates over three million Google citations, and tens of thousands of scholarly citations. It involves implicitly and explicitly demarcated efforts to establish international and domestic institutions for managing policy problems to achieve desired goals. Governance concerns not just how institutions are formed as Classical Integration theory did under Karl Deutsch and Ernst Haas, among others, but also how they affect politics transnationally and locally. Implementation shortcomings of international institutions can reflect the problems of international designs from above, as well as by policy drift or resistance from below. Multilevel governance consists of the way states compete in the formulation of transnational institutions, the way the latter establishes top-down programs for states, and how local movements and governing units halt and initiate regional and European practices. The rub is not just that the process is neither teleological nor deterministic, pessimistic or optimistic, or consistent across policy realms. Rather, understanding requires identifying competing movements from the ideological right and left, from the center and the periphery, from bureaucratic elites to social movements, and to southern and northern spheres of influence.

Governance, and related concepts of governability and governmentality, connote a variety of outcomes and processes, international institutions and processes, regime

cooperation, and crisis and policy management. Critical theories like governmentality[21] imply that socialized knowledge requires unmasking, such as the discourse gap between rhetoric on the ultimate effect. Governance effectiveness can decrease as the scope and leverage of the EU has broadened across fields and geography, as opposed to policies that have become increasingly divisive, such as the Eurozone, Schengen, immigration, refugees, migrants, trafficking, corruption, judicial reform, etc. The more general policies of the EU that promote an "ever closer union" encounter a more frequent resistance.

Efforts to promote human rights–based, Europeanized identities can erode consensus when conservative, nationalist and racist, white populations in many countries (the United States as well) oppose entry of immigrants and refugees.[22] Out of necessity, given the polarization among opposing elites, Germany has stepped into the void, but failure to solve perceived existential threats to the EU has not made hegemonic stabilization necessary, it is resented by other European states.

At times, official rhetoric and scholarly analysis elicit opposite evaluations. One person's "democratic deficit," resulting from supranationalism, is another's enhancement of democracy, human rights and the rule of law's efforts to raise human rights standards in member states, in EU institutions and outside of EU frontiers in Europe.[23] EU and CoE powers, in turn, increase the accountability of EU policies by relying upon free rider costs assumed by states or the IGO.

To better understand this complexity of processes and outcomes, a variety of independent and intervening variables have been adduced, along with more complex theories such as hegemonic stability, monitoring, functionalism, supranationalism, (liberal) intergovernmentalism, and all of their variants. Some of these factors fall primarily into the international system, some inside domestic politics, but most of them are multilevel, whether Putnam's two-level games[24] or complex interactions of domestic politics affecting international organizations.

Intergovernmentalism means that IGO decision making structure reflects member states' votes and national interests. The voting structure either is one vote per country, or weighted voting schemes, but with each country casting ballots. The Council of the European Union since the Lisbon Treaty has a weighted voting procedure; places "one vote for one country." Now, Germany has more votes than other states, such as Luxembourg.[25] The General Assembly of the UN still has one vote one country.

Intergovernmentalism describes most international organizations and most regimes as structured by individual countries that pursue their national interests. Intergovernmentalism does hold the possibility of some cooperation where states act in their enlightened self-interest. Yet, Realists hold, and Intergovernmentalists hold that international organizations cannot do what the individual countries allow them to do. IGO constitutions or regimes sometimes require unanimity or operate through consensus. The European Union does not manage all policy areas, though many more than it originally did. The EU is three-fourths supranational, including the EU Court of Justice, the Commission, and the Parliament. Many of the major issues, however, are not governed by the European Union, such as national defense policies, even though integration efforts at defense have been undertaken by the United Kingdom and France, while EU diplomacy and foreign aid has been established as a shared EU competence with its member states since the 2009 Lisbon Treaty. Yet, the EU Commission's regulations do affect, in a sense, the entire economy, such as its antitrust regulations.

Within Intergovernmentalism some have suggested four approaches,[26] suggesting that the expansion of the EU's purview from low to high politics[27] required more controversial, complex forms of Inter-Governmentalism that can clash with domestic politics. The first approach, closest to Classical Realism, is Classical Inter-governmentalism.[28] This state-centric approach says that there is one unitary national interest in IGOs and international regimes. The second, domestic politics approach, says states pursue their national interest but it is not often clearly defined. Not every organ of the state pursues the same thing.[29] This approach looks inside the state, analogous to the interpretive framework of Liberalism, where different forces inside the state debate, make compromises, operate illegally, or legally but sometimes according to standard procedures independent of member state control. The national interest results from processes that include different branches of governments and public consultation and debate.

The third approach is called the path-dependent or locked-in approach.[30] The locked-in approach says that states are still the major actors, but they get locked into their commitments, in which they do not anticipate or realize much greater commitments they have not calculated before. The locked-in approach holds that what one do today is going to look different than what actually happens in the long run. So, one create international institutions, international regimes, international legal processes of review of information, provision and monitoring of judgments, possible sanctions, and penalties imposed on countries, which all evolve over time.

The last model is the Liberal Intergovernmental approach of Andrew Moravcsik,[31] which argues state prerogatives give way to liberal restraints, while accruing benefits from cooperation. International institutions determine how effective a regime is, depending on the exact states to monitor and impose sanctions. States still pursue their national interests, but enlightened self-interests are prioritized to achieve positive-sum outcomes for all sides, even if the distributional gains are unequal. The institution should be developed in a rational efficient way.

These intergovernmental interpretations can be evaluated in terms of institutionalization, regimes, institutions, among other conceptual typologies. It would appear that the EU, in expanding its size, under the impulse of geopolitical forces and economies of scale, has decreased its autonomy and coherence, while enhancing their complexity and adaptability. These IGOs promote democracy and human rights while the perception of the organization suffers a democratic deficit from illiberal aspects of European integration resulting from its elite-driven process, rather than driven from popular demands. The European Commission, composed of Eurocrats, the Council of Ministers, and the European Court of Justice have been the agencies of change, not the European Parliament.

The remainder of this introduction summarizes the contributions to the book. It is divided broadly into EU governance among member and nonmember states as a group and EU governance inside member and nonmember states.

EU GOVERNANCE AMONG MEMBER STATES

This first section of the book addresses interactions among IGO member states on their effect on EU institutions. This effect is expanded onto the process of new member accession and how new member states adapt.

In the opening chapter, Ruth Bevan notes that diverging opinions of EU member states on foreign affairs reveal internal tensions. EU integration theories maintained that market integration alone can alleviate historical animosity.[32] Later IGO political objectives have included increase in political leverage and security. Regionalism seems to prevent overburdening on individual states, while ethnic tolerance, known as the *difference project*, has improved protection of individual freedom and security—so long as the EU is perceived as a success. The EU's help in rebuilding post-totalitarian societies and integrating them into the EU, by applying strict requirements for accession, known as the Copenhagen criteria, is a challenging endeavor on which future accession waves to integrate the remaining European territories and possibly Russia depend on the unlikely prospect of both prior success in earlier accession and Russian renunciation of perceived Europeanization of its sphere of influence in the former Soviet satellite states.

Ridvan Peshkopia observes that despite criticism, the EU has managed to frame its governance objectives clearly. He argues that consociationalism, formal and informal power sharing in is the most effective means to alleviate the differences within the EU as it expands eastwards. To increase political cohesion and competitiveness with established members, consociation is a prerequisite for accession of Eastern European applicants to succeed. The EU has succeeded to structure its governance with consociationalism because this model builds popular support for power sharing in a governing coalition.

Francesca Piccin argues that EU member states are rational actors in their approach to humanitarian aid, so they participate based on the costs and benefits rationalization. EU states provide the EU with exclusive competence that is crucial to understanding European Union Humanitarian Aid Policy (EUHAP). The EU often moderates a limited number of engagements in partnership with the member states. EUHAP transaction costs can also be reduced through flexible delegation division of labor, coordination, and humanitarian principles.

Mikael Rask Madsen analyzes how the European Court of Human Rights asserted once unprecedented supranational adjudicatory powers, interpreting and applying the European Convention on Human Rights in claims of individuals from around the entire world for alleged human rights violations by CoE member states. European human rights were not initially entirely conceived as transcending state sovereignty following World War II. International law and lawyers combined law and politics—as to institutionalize the greater autonomy of human rights institutions in Europe. His chapter argues that lawyers played a fundamental, intermediary role. Nevertheless, the Court's authority is no longer challenged legally, only politically, but still has contributed to the development of a highly persuasive, soft law beyond Europe.

Michael E. Smith observes that with each enlargement, the enlargement demands from applicants increase. Each enlargement increases the number of EU Council votes that member states must ratify, but each enlargement makes consensus more difficult. The current divisions in EU foreign policy are the result of conflicting opinions of member states that may be a precursor of the end of EU expansion. Smith argues that the EU Common Foreign and Security Policy (CFSP) became much more complicated under expansion. The multiple treaties and agreements for states with less multilateral capacity receive stricter political and institutional obligations than those who became

members earlier. Future members face even more stringent requirements during association or accession negotiation, particularly in the Western Balkans, where the wars over Bosnia and Kosovo divided EU member states, but led to a reliance on NATO's belated policy responses, which have kept the peace, but failed to build a sustainable, positive peace of robust structural and political reforms, which do not require UN and EU peacekeepers. The theory is that the stability of the region politically, militarily, and economically requires more IGO oversight over the more eastern applicant states. Multi-dimensional partnerships are coupled with obligations with bilateral agreements, which complicate efforts to promote a common EU policy, human rights, and democratization policies.

Pascal Vennesson analyzes the EU's need for a grand strategy, which he defines as a political entity's security goals and means of their fulfillment. He identifies the gaps between what policymakers want and wish to achieve. The four major, grand strategy options of his typologies are: Euro-neutralism, Euro-Atlanticism, Superpower EU, and Civilian power EU. These four types highlight the policy debates regarding EU security strategy and implementation. Dilemmas and trade-offs arise among different goals that each option offers, such as to prevent the disputes, support coherence, and stay competitive, Foreign affairs, in practice, are a hybrid type, mixing all four strategies, but restricted by the limits and specific characteristics of EU integration.

The final chapter of this first section concerns a relative success of the European Union. Jean-Marc Akakpo argues that the EU has had outstanding leadership managing the most ambitious climate change policy in the world, stronger even than a sovereign country like the United States. He attributes this policy management consensus to an effective Liberal Inter-governmentalism, which is based on the domestic consistencies in the civilian states established in Europe after World War II, to replace the states that focused on militarization and nationalism. Targets set by supranational European institutions have also monitored compliance with European climate regulations, which have reduced any gap between *de jure* laws and *de facto* practices.

EU GOVERNANCE AMONG NONMEMBER STATES

This book's second section exposes some of the shortcomings of the EU in its interactions with nonmember states, such as the unclear role and influence of the EU in foreign policy, peacebuilding and human rights. However, some strengths are also revealed, such as the relatively successful promotion of democracy and integration of Eastern European states into the EU.

Patricia Stapleton analyzes institutional choices in biotechnology regulation resulting from multilevel regulation of food safety among many institutions. She argues that differences between EU and United States regulatory culture produce different responses. While EU citizens are much more aware and fearful of Genetically Modified foods, US counterparts are comparatively unaware of them. These differences are important because they have led to conflicts.

Karl Löfgren and Kennet Lynggaard identify political tensions from the EU legislation on data protection, These expansions of EU rulemaking on a global scale are examined through analysis of banking and data privacy regulatory fields. Increased EU-US regulatory integration is partly a result of the EU's financial integration and its capacity. The United States and EU are involved in regulatory discourse but the EU exercise more influence in financial regulation.

Esther Barbé, Benjamin Kienzle, and Martijn Vlaskamp note that the lack of coherence in EU's foreign policy reduces its global influence. The EU's increased involvement in global institutions has not enhanced its influence due to lack of coherence. The prolonged deliberation among EU delegates needed to reach consensus reduces their influence among nonmember states, compared with international power structures. The colonial past of some EU member states can often obstruct EU negotiations with developing countries

Rebekah Dowd examines top-down Europeanization in EU intergovernmental decision-making of the Justice and Home Affairs Council vote on refugee resettlement of 160,000, primarily Syrian refugees, itself an unprecedented amount in cooperative terms, though a fraction of what Germany took in, one million in 2015 and half of what Turkey had accepted. The landmark 2015 vote to accept quotas was achieved, with Poland providing the decisive vote on the comprehensive plan, in spite of the incipient risk that a Euroskeptic government might get elected partly resulting from this vote, which in fact did occur.[33] Dowd examines four case states—two supporting the mandatory quota proposal (Germany, France), one in opposition (Hungary), and one compounding case state (Poland), which also voted to support the quota. The favorable Polish vote by the government led by the Civic Platform party, which only required the resettlement of 7,000 refugees in Poland, was based on popularity for helping refugees registered in 2014 opinion polls that presaged the plummeting of refugee support policy in Europe in 2015–2016. The other Visegrad countries, Czechia, Slovakia and Hungary, who along with Romania, voted against the plan and criticized Poland for caving into EU economic threats. The Polish Law and Justice Party did win the parliamentary elections the next month, October, and announced in March 2016 that it would not accept any refugees at all regardless of the vote. She concludes that leaders of countries with larger populations that include more foreign-born residents are more willing to accept refugee populations (Germany, France). Leaders representing homogeneous populations under economic pressure focus more on national interests and domestic financial strain as they make international policy commitments (Hungary). States that are experiencing positive economic conditions may be willing to overlook changes to social makeup and vote to support policies mandating higher levels of refugee asylum (Poland).

Finally, Onur Sen and Tariel Sikharulidze analyze EU mediation under the French presidency to achieve a cease-fire in the 2008 War between Russia and Georgia in Transcaucasia. Determinants of success in international mediation have been the focus of many scholars dealing with conflict management. Certain cases of international mediation are more successful than others. In this chapter, the authors answer this general question by focusing on the EU mediation in the Russia-Georgia war of 2008. They test the Ripeness Theory of William Zartman that international mediation is most likely to be successful if it is initiated a mutually hurting stalemate (MHS). They propose that the EU mediation process created a ripe moment without the existence of a MHS.

EU GOVERNANCE INSIDE MEMBER STATES

The third section reveals some of the frictions between the EU and the member states on the implementation of human rights. In addition, these provide an insight into the issues of EU institutions that result from their lack of legitimacy and competing interests inside EU member states.

Sarah D. Phillips observes that EU accession has led to improvements in the disability programs of Eastern Europe but these changes are superficial. During Communist rule, disabilities were viewed as individual flaws in these states. The current EU strategy is one of equal rights and inclusion of individuals with disabilities. Prior to accession into the EU, lawmakers worked to update disability laws but the process of implementation is slow. Education is rarely available to children with disabilities and a few NGOs are helping train disabled employees. EU accession has improved life for the disabled but the changes are superficial. Philips compares disability rights for Bulgaria, Romania, Croatia, and Macedonia. Cultural resentment toward the disabled or special needs is a holdover from Communism, one that still institutionalized rather than integrated into society. While legislative reforms for the disabled give the impression of improvement, better education and employment policies are still needed.

Elisabeth Lambert Abdelgawad asks whether recognizing collective mechanisms in the European Court of Human Rights (ECtHR) has reduced the number of applicants from CoE member states since the ECtHR gives priority to mass and structural cases, as opposed to individuals who bring their complaints jointly, The ECtHR is trying to distinguish itself from the American class-action procedure. The benefit of collective action is that the victims are not individually identified, while the cost of the procedure and difficulty of representation are lowered. So, this structure helps sustain the ability of minorities to seek remedies for discrimination.

Tero Erkkilä and Niilo Kauppi examine the challenges faced by the EU Ombudsman through a historical analysis of this institution from an institutional perspective. Since embracing the institution of the Ombudsman, derived from an eighteenth-century Sweden model, the EU has experienced some problems and setbacks. As one of the least known EU institutions, the Ombudsman's negotiations of complaints have had limited influence because it depends on public recognition. This problem is deepened by the limited contact of EU citizens with their institutions.

Klaus Brummer analyzes the dysfunctional collaboration and interaction between the EU and the Council of Europe with their common organizational interests about particular matters. Organizational interests include preserving the organization, protecting the organizational essence, preserving the autonomy, and relative power of these competing IGOs. Brummer concludes that partnership between these two European organizations is contingent on the compatibility of their interests, which is often more theoretical than real, when bureaucracies seek their own prerogatives and power. Still, a high degree of mutual incorporation of law makes a synergistic relationship possible as time provides ways to overcome apparent interest conflicts.

Liliana Popescu deals with the implications of Europeanization of Romanian foreign policy by using a qualitative analysis of data on Romania's foreign policy change and promotion of Romanian national interests at the EU level. To answer the question, the author notes that policies are Europeanized faster than governmental structures and this is a process of constant adaptation. She defines Europeanization[34] as a process of mutual impact and adaptation between member states and to EU institutions, socialization of member states' elites into EU practices, adaptation of member states' administration to EU infrastructure, and projecting national interests on the EU agenda. (Others see it as a m ore top-down process.) In Romania, the process of adjusting to EU practices is one of adaptation. The governmental structure adapts to the new practices slower than policies. The process is ongoing and is affected by the Eurozone crisis.

Elaine Weiner explores the question why is there a gap in gender equality in established and new member states via qualitative analysis of local institutions spanning thirteen years in Bulgaria and twelve years in Romania. The EU links gender equality to democracy but this realization of legislation related to gender equality is lagging behind in the new Eastern European member states. The imminent challenge of gender equality in Eastern Europe is attaining legitimacy. The findings reveal that the efforts to advance the cause are hindered in Eastern Europe by the superficial nature of gender equality legislation that is put in place. Gender equality processes and legislation in Eastern Europe are examined in depth but the chapter lacks data-specific assessment of gender equality. Women are still struggling to learn which areas under EU authority could advance their status. As with the disabled, a Soviet model persists which encourages "equal opportunities for women" but as second class citizens, both at home and in the workplace, with female workers paid less than their male counterparts, as well as requiring both work and home obligations. Though the EU has linked *de jure* gender equality to accession, implementing gender equality with democratization and economic opportunities, has generated resistance. The EU must modify some of its ideas to fit each societal context, especially those still practicing Eastern Bloc political ideologies and cultural practices, which are dominating toward women.

Shannon Jones aims to address why has the EU has failed to reduce discrimination against the Roma despite its commitment to minority protection. She provides qualitative analysis of legislation related to protecting the rights of the Roma in new member states, supplemented with case studies of Roma discrimination in France and Italy. The Roma are the largest and most repressed minority in the EU. Effective implementation of EU human rights policies is inhibited not by superficial monitoring but the EU's failure to require successful implementation prior to membership. The protection of the rights of Roma is not adequate in new member states because the norm-makers implement superficial legislation in order to collect the benefits of EU membership. Failure to reinforce policies increases incentives to make policy changes without any intent to implement them. The EU can spread democratic norms through transnational advocacy groups. Jones then analyzes how compliance with the EU and CoE rules on Roma minority protection has been explicitly tied to gaining membership status in the EU, but the implementation of the *Framework Convention on Minorities* remains superficial. Ending Roma discrimination continues to be a problem, despite the EU's attempt to take measures. Though the EU uses conditionality and normative persuasion to try to convince EU candidate states, laws protecting the Roma are ignored, with discrimination remaining in practice at a deep cultural level. The EU does not enforce laws, allowing candidate and new member states to discriminate just like the old member states. Much still needs to be done in terms of equality of opportunity for the Roma and equal protection in terms of citizens' rights.

Eleanor G. Morris and Manonh Leila Soumahoro examine whether the EU's theoretical assurance of human rights and free movement mask an actual policy of restriction via comparative analysis of EU policies. The decisions of what countries go to what lists is based on performance benchmarks related to good relations with neighboring states and protection of citizens' rights within the state's borders. The EU's theoretical assurance of human rights and free movement of people is superficial because it masks a policy of restriction. The white and black lists for the Schengen area reflect partiality toward specific minority groups and areas. These restrictions severely affect Roma minority and foreign nationals seeking asylum in the EU. All EU member states are theoretically committed to upholding the rights of refugees and asylum seekers, but mass deportations and discrimination evidence racism and xenophobia.

EU GOVERNANCE INSIDE NONMEMBER STATES

This section reveals some of the challenges facing EU governance. In particular, promotion of peace, resolution of conflict, and election monitoring approaches of the EU are discussed in depth in this section.

Sandra Pogodda, Oliver Richmond, Nathalie Tocci, Roger Mac Ginty and Birte Vogel aim to answer the questions, what type of peace is promoted by the EU and whether the EU has a viable strategy to export peace to countries in conflict. Peacebuilding is one of the major goals of the EU[35] stemming from its role as promoter of democracy, rule of law, human rights, and integration. The EU's liberal peace model falls short of addressing the roots and dynamics of conflict. The EU's involvement in conflict resolution fails to translate into a clear peacebuilding approach. By concentrating more on governmental reforms, the EU approach to conflict resolution is indirect. The EU's peacebuilding strategy isn't consistent because it fails to adequately relay its concepts of peace and authority on a local level.

Jamil Sewell and Douglas Gibler suggest that democratizing states form alliances in order to provide a peaceful environment that will allow for the development of democracy. Democracies form alliances in order to reduce the external threats hostile to liberal regimes. Former Soviet republics sought guarantees from the EU and NATO in order to establish democracy after 1991 and their efforts succeeded. Most theories can't explain why democracies preferred alliances with other democracies during the Cold War but not before. However, this research concluded that if autocracies are not threatened externally, they have the greatest chance for democratization and, once democratized, will sustain the regime.

Marcela Symanski argues that both pro-democracy NGOs (DNGOs) and providers of democracy assistance change their behavior after regime-changing elections. Observations reveal the decline and sometimes dissolution of DNGOs in the first few years afterward. Democracy assistance funding and technical support from abroad declines or disappears almost at a matching pace. She analyzes whether these events combined have an effect on the democratization path. In particular, she questions what the EU, one of the main providers of financial and technical support to democratization in the world, is attempting.

James Ker-Lindsay examines the effect of EU accession on the Greek-Turkish division in Cyprus via the longitudinal case study of the conflict before and after EU accession. In 1994, the EU confirmed that Cyprus will be included in the next EU accession wave. The Turkish Cypriot leader strongly opposed this decision but the EU did not reconsider. This decision was based on stable democratic and economic indicators and hopes that EU accession may help resolve the division. However, the EU's appeasement strategy failed and only the Greek-governed part of Cyprus joined the EU, while the Turkish Republic of Northern Cyprus did not. Once Cyprus joined the EU, the EU laws were suspended in the parts that were not under the control of the ethnic-Greek, Cypriot government. This has posed problems for the EU's desires to promote the Copenhagen criteria in the entire island, but its unwillingness to offer EU membership to Turkey has greatly reduced the incentives that could be offered to negotiate the long-term unification and pacification of the island. Intergovernmental vetoes over Turkish accession by not only Cyprus and Greece, but also France and Germany in the EU Council have made it difficult to achieve the peacemaking that the EU often proclaims for itself.

Zeynep Arkan and Soeren Keil pose the question why the uniformity of the EU's discursive practices matter in enlargement policy in the Western Balkans. The method is qualitative analysis from social constructivist perspective by applying discourse analysis methodology supplemented by two case studies from the Western Balkans. The eventual integration into the EU of the region is addressed by the EU through the Stabilization and Association Process (SAP) and is conditional based on economic and political reforms including democratization, state building, and *acquis communautaire*. From the perspective of social constructivism, the EU presents itself as a unitary actor with a single voice. The EU's actors and foreign policy are fashioned through the discursive practices in and around the union. However, the EU is not a unitary actor with a single voice, even though EU policy exists, which makes dissonance in discourse an inevitability, leading to misperceptions in additions to real misunderstandings and exploitations by those outside its official organs.

Randall Puljek-Shank and Tija Memiševic provide an analysis and a set of recommendations to improve the governance of Bosnia and Herzogovina. They conclude that NGOs and civil society organizations have improved greatly, but still have many challenges ahead of them to promote tolerance, democratization and peacebuilding. Donor funding has often been short-term, focused on stabilization and indifferent to the ethnic intolerance of constituencies. They list a series of "politically risky" initiatives that donors should condition their assistance upon in order to induce greater cooperation among different ethnic parties, NGOs and non-civil society organizations.

Alban Lauka and his colleagues, assessing EU peacebuilding in Kosovo, conclude that the effectiveness of Europeanization by conditionality is undermined by double-standards. They risk undermining the general cohesion of accession conditionality based on the Copenhagen Criteria. This chapter argues that there are instances where the criteria for democracy, market economy, the rule of law and human rights, have been modified for the case of Kosovo, and examines the reasons behind them. On the other hand, the EU has been lax on other criteria, looking the other way on electoral fraud, official corruption, ethnic participation of ethnic Serbs under consociational incentives, and potential provocations from extremist parties to create a Greater Albania. The EU's inconsistent signals, which reflect its own priorities, undermine effective peacebuilding policies.

Finally, Marie Milward explains the motivations of the EU to intervene in the electoral process of emerging democracies. The EU's involvement in the electoral process of emerging democracies is rather puzzling since it involves strategic political intervention into the internal affairs of sovereign states. Regardless of the EU's commitment to democratization, no sovereign country is obliged to invite election observers. Feasibility, internal EU politics, and normative considerations are important explanations for the EU's election observation policy. This study supports the idea that the EU's decisions for election monitoring are based on international security, feasibility, and normative motivations.

NOTES

1. Quoted in Roger Cohen, "Britain's Brexit's Leap in the Dark," *The New York Times* (June 24, 2016), Accessed June 25, 2016; http://www.nytimes.com/2016/06/25/opinion/britains-brexit-leap-in-the-dark.html?_r=0.

2. P. Taylor, "Intergovernmentalism in the European Communities in the 1970s: Patterns and Perspectives, *International Organization*, vol. 36, no. 4 (1982), pp. 741–66.

3. C. de la Porte and P. Pochet, *Building Social Europe through the Open Method of Coordination* (Brussells: Peter Lang, 2002); D. Trubek and L. Trubek, "Hard and Soft Law in the Construction of Social Europe: the Role of the Open Method of Co-Ordination, *European Law Journal*, vol. 11, no. 3 (2005), pp. 343–64; M. Heidenreich and J. Zeitland, *Changing European Employment and Welfare Regimes* (London: Routledge, 2009).

4. M. Höpner and A. Schäfer, "A New Phase of European Integration: Organised Capitalisms in Post-Ricardian Europe," *West European Politics*, vol. 33, no. 2 (2010), pp. 344–68; F. Scharpf, "The Asymmetry of European Integration, or Why the EU cannot be a 'social market economy,'" *Socio-Economic Review*, vol. 8, no. 2 (2010), pp. 211–50.

5. Stefan Gänzle and Kristine Kern (eds.), *A "Macro-Regional" Europe in the Making: Theoretical Approaches and Empirical Evidence* (New York: Palgrave Macmillan, 2016); Tanja A. Börzel and Thomas Risse, "Diffusing (Inter-) Regionalism: the EU as a Model of Regional Integration," Working Paper, no. 7 (Berlin: KFG, September 2009).

6. Mario Thomas Vassallo, *The Europeanization of Interest Groups in Malta and Ireland: a Small State Perspective* (London: Palgrave Macmillan, 2015).

7. Amandine Crespy and Gorg Menz (eds.), *Social Policy and the Eurocrisis: Quo Vadis Social Europe* (New York: Palgrave Macmillan, 2015).

8. This is the a name of the "Research College" headed by two of the most influential Europeanization scholars, Tanja A. Börzel and Thomas Risse at the Free University of Berlin. No irony is intended by this reference.

9. Tanja A. Börzel and Thomas Risse, "Conceptualizing the Domestic Impact of Europe," in K. Featherstone and C. M. Radaelli (eds.), *The Politics of Europeanization* (Oxford University Press, 2003); I. Bache and M. Flinders, *Multi-Level Governance* (Oxford University Press, 2004); I. Bache and A. Jordan, *The Europeanization of British Politics* (Houndsmills: Palgrave Macmillan, 2006).

10. Mattei Dogan, "The Decline of Nationalisms in Western Europe," *Comparative Politics,* vol. 26, no. 3 (April 1994), pp. 281–305.

11. Walter G. Stephan, Cookie White Stephan, and William B. Gudykunst, "Anxiety in Intergroup Relations: a Comparison of Anxiety/Uncertainty Management Theory and Integrated Threat Theory," *International Journal of Intercultural Relations,* vol. 23, no. 4 (August 1999), pp. 613–28.

12. Fred W. Riggs, "Bureaucracy and Viable Constitutionalism," in Abdo I. Baaklini, Helen Desfosses (eds.), *Designs for Democratic Stability: Studies in Viable Constitutionalism* (Armonk, NY: M.E. Sharpe, 1997), p. 96.

13. Martha Finnemore and Kathryn Sikkink, "International Norm Dynamics and Political Change," *International Organization,* vol. 52, no. 4 (1998), pp. 887–917.

14. Robert O. Keohane and Lisa L. Martin, "The Promise of Institutionalist Theory," *International Security,* vol. 20, no. 1 (Summer, 1995), pp. 39–51.

15. Turkey is not just a "democracy with adjectives" but also a state that has three times as many refugees as any other country, as well as one that offers foreign aid to other Middle Eastern states, for the first time in its history. Seen objectively, its human rights record does not compare so unfavorably as both Britain and the United States, even if most of the latter's two sets of violations are largely outside its borders (which from a human rights viewpoint is irrelevant in importance).

16. E. Best, T. Christiansen and P. Settembri, *The Institutions of the Enlargeed European Union: Continuity and Change* (Cheltenham, UK: Edward Elgar, 2008).

17. Frank Schimmelfennig and Ulrich Sedelmeier, *The Europeanizatoin of Central and Eastern Europe* (Ithaca, NY: Cornell University Press, 2005). H. Grabbe, *Europeanization through Conditionality in Central and Eastern Europe* (Bassingstoke, UK: Palgrave Macmillan, 2006).

18. Samuel P. Huntington, *Political Order in Changing Societies* (New Haven, CT: Yale University Press, 1968).

19. Kenneth N. Walz, *Man, the State and War: a Theoretical Analysis* (New York: Columbia University Press, 1959).

20. Robert Putnam, "Diplomacy and Domestic Politics: The Logic of Two-Level Games," *International Organization,* vol. 42, no. 3 (1988), 427–60. Accessed September 8, 2015, from; http://www.jstor.org/stable/2706785.

21. Mitchell Dean, Governmentality: *Power and Rule in Modern Society* (SAGE Publications Ltd: London; SAGE Publications Inc: Thousand Oaks, CA, 2010.

22. See the Pew Research Center's Opinion Survey on anti-immigrant attitudes in Italy, France, Germany, Spain, the United Kingdom, Greece, and Poland, published on May 14, 2014. Richard Wike, "In Europe, Sentiment against Immigrants, Minorities Runs High." Available at; http://pewrsr.ch/1sOxlvh.

23. Andrew Moravcsik, "In Defense of the 'Democratic Deficit': Reassessing Legitimacy in the European Union," *Journal of Common Market Studies,* vol. 40, no. 4 (2002), pp. 603–24; Giandomenico Majone, "Europe's 'Democratic Deficit': The Question of Standards," *European Law Journal,* vol. 4, no. 1 (1998), 5–28; Simon Hix and Andreas Follesdal, "Why there is a Democratic Deficit in the EU: A Response to Majone and Moravcsik," *Journal of Common Market Studies,* vol. 44, no. 3 (2006), pp. 533–62.

24. Robert Putnam, "Diplomacy and Domestic Politics: The Logic of Two-Level Games," *International Organization,* vol. 42, no. 3 (1988), pp. 427–60. Accessed September 8, 2015 from; http://www.jstor.org/stable/2706785.

25. Consilium, "Qualified Majority," Last Modified on May 1, 2015; http://www.consilium.europa.eu/en/council-eu/voting-system/qualified-majority/. The Double Majority Voting

Procedure Requires the Approval of at Least 55 percent of the Member States, but also that these Member States Represent at Least 65 percent of the Total Population of the EU.

26. Michelle Cini, "Intergovernmentalism," in Michelle Cini and Nieves Perez-Solorzano Borragan (eds.), *European Union Politics* (Oxford University Press, 2010), pp. 71–84.

27. Stanley Hoffman, *The European Sisyphus: Essays on Europe, 1964–1994* (Westview Press, 1995).

28. Stanley Hoffman. "Obstinate or Obsolete? The Fate of the Nation-State and the Case of Western Europe," *Daedalus*, vol. 95, no. 3 (1966), pp. 862–915. Accessed on August 21, 2012, from; http://graduateinstitute.ch/webdav/site/political_science/shared/political_science/7183/2nd%20week/Obstinate%20or%20Obsolete.pdf.

29. Lisa Martin, *Democratic Commitments. Legislatures and International* (Cooperation Princeton: Princeton University Press, 2000); Peter Gourevitch, "Domestic Politics and International Relations," in Walter Carlsnaes, Thomas Risse and Beth Simmons (eds.), *Handbook of International Relations*, edited by (London: Sage, 2002).

30. Paul Pierson, "Increasing Returns, Path Dependence, and the Study of Politics," *The American Political Science Review*, vol. 94, no. 2 (2000), pp. 251–67. Accessed at; http://www.jstor.org/stable/2586011 on September 8, 2015.

31. Andrew Moravcsik, "Preferences and Power in the EC: A Liberal Intergovernmentalist Approach in Journal of Common Market Studies," *JCMS: Journal of Common Market Studies*, vol. 31, no. 4 (1993), p. 473. Accessed on August 30, 2015, from; http://onlinelibrary.wiley.com/doi/10.1111/j.1468–5965.1993.tb00477.x/abstract.

32. Ernst Haas, *The Uniting of Europe: Political, Social and Economic Forces* (Stanford, CA: Stanford University Press, 1958).

33. Bart Bachman, "Diminishing Solidarity: Polish Attitudes toward the European Migration and Refugee Crisis," (Migration Policy Institute, June 16, 2016), available at; http://www.migrationpolicy.org/article/diminishing-solidarity-polish-attitudes-toward-european-migration-and-refugee-crisis.

34. Claudio Radaelli, "The Europeanization of Public Policy," in *The Politics of Europeanization*, edited by Kevin Featherstone and Claudio Radaelli (Oxford: Oxford University Press, 2003), pp. 27–56.

35. European Union External Action, "Conflict Prevention, Peace Building and Mediation." http://eeas.europa.eu/cfsp/conflict_prevention/index_en.htm.

Part I

EU GOVERNANCE AMONG MEMBER STATES

Chapter 1

The European Union

Does it Make a Difference?

Ruth A. Bevan

SUBSTANTIVE DEMOCRACY

The EU's *difference project* extends beyond the procedural processes of democratic governance, like regular and competitive free elections, vitally important though these procedural items are. The EU's intent is not just to add one more democratic state to the international roster. As we shall see, it has bolder ambitions than this. Moreover, while the individual member states of the EU certainly follow democratic procedures, on the Union level a "democracy deficit," as it is commonly termed, pertains. This deficit refers to the fact that European integration has been elite, rather than mass, driven, as well as driven by its supranational organs more than the intergovernmental Council, which theoretically follows the will of democratically elected heads of government or state.

A revolution in political organization, the EU no doubt would never have seen the light of day if, since 1957 when the Rome Treaty establishing the Common Market went into effect, the mass electorate had been involved in every detailed step of the way. By analogy today, there is a democracy deficit in Serbia about Kosovo: if Serb voters were asked to choose between Kosovo and the EU, the latter would not win, but Serb politicians have chosen, in effect, the EU over Kosovo. For the average post–World War II European nation-state citizen, the very idea of a united Europe proved baffling, even frightening. Enough setbacks would occur over the following five decades with only elite actors involved to produce Euroskeptics; those who swore that European integration would never jump all the hurdles before it and survive the test of time.

It must be remembered, however, that these elite actors were either democratically elected spokespersons of their respective states or ministerial representatives of such. Furthermore, voting mechanisms within the European Union operated initially on the unanimity principle and have only recently changed, with the Lisbon Treaty, to a qualified majority regarding some issues. The unanimity principle flowed from the basic condition of the social contract in democratic theory: all sovereign units present had to agree to the contract creating the state for the state itself to have legitimacy. Integration required *consensual politics*.

The term *democracy deficit* is thus misleading; it implies that the European Union operates beyond democratic control. This creates a false image.

The European Union has followed indirect democratic procedures, meaning it has worked through the elected representatives of its member states. Herman van Rompuy was unanimously chosen on November 19, 2009, to be the first president of the European Union (as established by the Lisbon Treaty of 2009) and Catherine Ashton as its first foreign minister by the heads of state and government of the twenty-seven member states at a summit meeting in Brussels. Few EU citizens had ever heard of the Belgian Rompuy. France and Germany, the power brokers of the "election," leaned toward a Christian Democrat for the post, thereby upsetting Gordon Brown's support for Laborite Tony Blair. Ashton's selection balanced off British national and party interests. The selection of Rompuy and Ashton poignantly illustrates the EU's democratic elitism, which is another way of saying its *democracy deficit*.

EU citizens have for the most part acquiesced regarding Union procedures and decisions, though there are indications afoot of increased citizen awareness and political activity. The European Union has not failed to make good on its promises: it delivers the goods. The *goods* may be either socio-legal *goods* in the shape of rights and protection of the individual and national security or socioeconomic *goods* in the shape of opportunities, efficient management, production, and growth. More subtle, socio-psychological *goods* relate to the government's general reservoir of social capital within the citizenry—the sense of pride that citizens take in the values and behavior of their state as represented by their elected officials, the prevailing sense of trust, which alone enables representative democracy based upon the delegation of powers to operate and the willingness, therefore, to cooperate with each other, especially in the public sphere. Democratic electoral procedures provide the essential framework within which substantive rights and *public goods* evolve and mature. The EU's *difference* project focuses on the substantive quality of democratic life. Does democratic rule make a difference in the quality of life for the individual? More specifically, does *transnational* democratic rule—meaning the transnational complex composing the European Union—make a difference in the quality of life for the individual? Europeans defend adamantly the personal benefits associated with their social welfare states. Health and well-being studies show that Europeans not only live longer and better than former generations of Europeans but also rank at the top of the wellness and "happiness" charts in comparison to citizens of other contemporary democracies. In the words of a French writer, "Europe has never been as prosperous, as secure or as free. The violence of the first half of the twentieth century has given way to a period of peace and stability without precedent in European history."[1]

A TRANSFORMED EUROPE

European integration has involved a social vision, some date that vision back to Charlemagne's dream of restoring European unity on the continent after the collapse of the Roman empire. Military strife among competitive tribes, city-states and kingdoms, then nation-states in Europe certainly defined its post-Roman Empire history and even threatened its very existence. Europe not only warred within its own geographical domain but it transported war to others in the shape of the Crusades, mercantilism, exploration, and imperialism/colonialism. War constituted a way of life. With technological advances, armaments became more deadly and more efficient in their deadliness with the consequences of war correspondingly becoming more devastating. In the twentieth century, war reached its zenith in Europe: industrial genocide. In the words of Max Horkheimer, with the implementation of a technocratic, rationalized assembly-line method of exterminating human beings, Europe confronted *the limits of Enlightenment.*

Today European integrationists see Europe as a political experiment without any similitude. Political scientists do not know how to classify the EU since it is not a Westphalian state possessing governing sovereignty over a stipulated population and territory. The EU is presently composed of twenty-seven sovereign states. Yet the EU enjoys a delegated sphere of sovereignty over and above these states, the *acquis communitaire*, which gives the EU policy authority in areas affecting the Union as an aggregate. With the passage of the Lisbon Agreement in 2009 and the subsequent election of a president and foreign minister, the EU progressively moves in the direction of accomplishing the 1993 Maastrict Treaty's mandate ("pillar") for a Common Foreign and Security policy. Fifteen of the EU states inhabit Euroland, having adopted the euro as their common currency, fulfilling another Maastricht pillar. The third Maastricht pillar, the former Western European Union (WEU),[2] its military-security force, continues to evolve through the European Union External Action Service (EEAS).[3] Though the EU increasingly assumes the responsibilities of an international actor, it is not a state that can be granted official member status in the United Nations (UN), though it does have observer status.

The European Union promotes regional integration across the globe as economically and political beneficial not only to regional partners but to world prosperity and security. It favors regional integration as an effective instrument of peacemaking and peacekeeping.

The European Union does not advocate, however, total abandonment of the nation-state. The constitutional and populist realities of its own existence do not allow this position. Europeans are now socialized into seeing themselves as Europeans, but they continue to construct their lives as Italians, Danes, Czechs, French, or Poles. They have no intention of abrogating national (or even provincial-local) cultural identities. The European approach is to lock the separatist claims of the nation-state into ever wider concentric circles of universalistic interaction and responsibility with correspondingly augmented social, political, and economic benefits.

In her *Origins of Totalitarianism* Hannah Arendt, a German Jewish refugee of World War II who emigrated to the United States, observes that the Rights of Man, in practical, functional terms, are only as good as the community willing to enforce them. Civil rights depend upon the state, the *civitas.* And how should we understand human rights, those rights inherent in the human being *qua* human being? This concept of human rights, Arendt argues, lacks specificity since it "transcends the present sphere of international law which still operates in terms of reciprocal agreements and treaties between sovereign states; and, for the time being, a sphere that is above the nations does not exist."[4]

The judges in the post–World War II Nurnberg Trials, navigating uncharted political waters for international law, introduced ultimately into international law the concept of "crimes against humanity" in prosecuting Nazi perpetrators of genocide. A revolutionary concept, the doctrine of crimes against humanity challenges state sovereignty. Accordingly, state sovereignty cannot be interpreted as giving the state *carte blanche* for doing what it will. Sovereignty does not include the right of the state to abuse fundamental human rights without international repercussion, including prosecution. From this ruling, the Europeans derived the competence of the European Court to arraign and prosecute state leaders like Pinochet of Chile and Milosevich of Serbia for "crimes against humanity."

Within Germany today there is a vocal minority that rebels against the ongoing reference to the Holocaust. At one point in time a new generation must move forward without such constant reference. This rings true. At the same time, the Holocaust remains an indissoluble aspect of European history. It will not vanish at the flick of a magician's wand. And Europeans confront the fact that they as nation-states participated, passively or actively, in one of the greatest atrocities, if not the greatest, in history. World War II transfigured the world.

EUROPEAN SOFT POWER

The EU seeks to use development aid to cajole wayward states to adopt democratic reforms, to train civilians in the techniques of conflict mediation as in the 2007 Instrument for Stability program (IfS) designed to supplement the 2001 Rapid Reaction Mechanism program, to be an influential player in international organizations like the World Trade Organization (WTO) and the UN for the purpose of creating a more equitable and just international order.

This does not mean that the Europeans eschew a military infrastructure. The Cold War division in Europe geographically cut through Germany (i.e., West Germany and East Germany), making Germany the front line of that war in Europe and, from the postwar Allied (i.e., American-NATO) point of view, requiring German *re-militarization*. (The initial 3-D policy of the Allies toward Germany included de-Nazification, democratization and de-militarization.) Today Germany possesses the largest and most efficient military force in Europe. Presently, it has a significant force in Afghanistan, recently increased by Prime Minister Angela Merkel (January 2010), to bolster the American effort.

The states of the European Union are not without a military presence but that presence is neither superior in quality nor truly regionalized into a European force. Nor is it sustained by a European commitment. In his *Of Paradise and Power: America and Europe in the New World Order*, Robert Kagan observes that, in the 1990's, the European Union did not rise to the stature of an international superpower as it assumed it would but rather declined into "relative military weakness compared to the United States."[5] Kagan attributes European opposition to the United States to the military weakness or *hard power* weakness of Europe. He continues: "Europe's relative weakness has understandably produced a powerful European interest in building a world where military strength and hard power matter less than economic and soft power, an international order where international law and international institutions matter more than the power of individual nations, where unilateral action by powerful states is forbidden, where all nations regardless of their strength have equal rights and are equally protected by commonly agreed upon international rules of behavior."[6]

As Kagan stipulates, the United States *thinks* and *behaves* like a Westphalian state. The European Union, however, is not a Westphalian state. While in the early days of the Common Market, reference, in Europe as well as in the United States, was made to the building of a United States of Europe, this reference proved completely misleading and has been dropped. The United States has had, since the ratification of its Constitution, a fixed locus of central authority (sovereignty) with Constitutionally delegated and reserved loci of authority in the individual states. European regional integration has involved a process unrelated to the construction of the American union as well as a structural experiment in sovereignty that separates it altogether from American federalism.

EUROPEAN INTEGRATION AND GLOBALIZATION

The formation of the European Union relates not to a founding constitutional experience like that at Philadelphia—indeed the EU, has yet to acquire a written constitution—but to the economic process referred to as *globalization.* If economic globalization means the transnational flow of capital and transnational production, then the European Union has been formed through globalization. With the Single European Act (SEA) of 1986, which ended exchange controls and restrictions on capital movements, creating a single market for insurance and banks, Europeanists set about deepening European integration which in turn promoted globalization.[7]

Writing about regional planning, Suzannah Lessard asserts that the "global economy is regional. Only the larger, more diverse entity of the region has the multifaceted strength required to compete in the global market, which is why planners can now say with great force that if one part of a region suffers, the whole suffers and becomes less competitive. . . ."[8]

From the global perspective, the European Union represents a world region. From the EU's perspective, the Union itself is composed of regions. Within the EU disparities exist between core and periphery areas. Portuguese peripheral areas, for example, adjoining economically dynamic Spanish centers have been pulled up through regionalism. Ireland constitutes one of the more dramatic success stories, since EU accession transformed its former backwater economy into the Celtic Tiger.[9] John Loughlin refers to a "competitive regionalism" on a European and world scale as the consequence of this nation-state weakening: "Regions and cities found themselves competing within and across countries both for scarce EU funds and for foreign investors."[10]

European political culture has been shaped by a *process* (regional integration) rather than by a *founding experience.* American political leaders think in terms of Constitutional do's and don'ts, of building majorities and persuading the electorate—in primarily legalistic-institutional terms. As yet, the European Union has no written constitution—its first attempt to pass a written constitution failed due to negative results in referenda held in France and in the Netherlands in 2005.[11] These EU states speak different languages, have unique histories, and enjoy diverse cultural mentalities. To think Europe, as the billboards often encourage Europeans to do, means to think in *fluid* terms, across boundaries.

CONSEQUENCES OF REGIONAL INTEGRATION
FOR EUROPE'S *WELTANSCHAUUNG*

While the European Union is not a state, neither is it merely an alliance as some international affairs analysts have described it. With no political vocabulary suitable for its description, the EU remains a Something, an experiment. The character of the experiment, however, uniquely inclines the EU toward an internationalist perspective predicated upon values adduced from its own historical experiences. Three ingredients of the EU's political culture derived from the process and circumstances of regional integration constitute the pillars of its *difference project*. In other words, the EU believes it can make the difference in the world on the basis of the civilian state, commitment to regionalism, and global public goods.

THE CIVILIAN STATE

European integration has produced what James J. Sheehan calls the "civilian state" in Europe—a political order organized for peace, not war, and one in which "social change was translated into economic production, not battle potential."[12] This civilian state mentality has become the dominant cultural norm among Europeans, which "needs only consumers and producers, who recognize that the community serves their interests and advances their individual well-being. And as consumers and producers, most Europeans have usually been rather satisfied with the Union's accomplishments."[13] Sheehan maintains that Turkey's bid for membership in the EU presents problems not because Turkey is a Muslim state but because it is not a civilian state; it is not synchronized with contemporary Europe.[14] The European *Weltanschaaung* coincides with Fareed Zakaria's depiction of the globalized post-American world order in which economics trumps politics.[15] Sheehan maintains that the Europeans could afford to build up their military infrastructure but that their civilian state mentality precludes their doing so. Lest we be tempted to draw a Manichean dichotomy here between the European Union as the white knight and the United States as the black rogue, Andrei S. Markovits adds this tempering note: "The European views of America have little to do with the real America but much to do with Europe."[16] Markovits argues that the Bush Administration's policies, especially in Iraq, ran so counter to the civilian state mentality of Europe that they "have produced a convergence between elite and mass opinion in Europe and elicited the mobilization of anti-American counter-values in the name of Europe. . . . Hence, anti-Americanism has become an emotional, potent, and very real aspect of European identity formation."[17] Since Barack Obama proffered change in American foreign policy, especially in Iraq, and emphasized multilateralism, especially in its relations with the EU, Europeans embraced the election of Obama as president of the United States in 2008. Obama in office, however, has not catered to Europe.

COMMITMENT TO REGIONALISM

As regional integration has been the means to secure peace and prosperity on the European continent, so Europeans argue that regional integration across the globe will enhance global peace and prosperity. The EU seeks to stimulate further global regional integration in an effort to create global public goods. Regarding China, Mark Leonard writes that "the most remarkable shift in Chinese policy has been China's espousal of regional integration. Chinese scholars have studied the European model to see how they can recast their relationship with their neighbors. . . . Throughout the Cold War period China's interactions with ASEAN states were conducted solely on a bilateral basis. However, over the last fifteen years, its passion for regional integration has come to resemble the European Union's."[18]

From the EU's perspective, regional integration enables developing states to adjust themselves gradually to the rigors of greater competition in the global market place. It begins a dynamic process that leads to increased trade between partners, encourages the diversification of national economies and makes possible economies of scale. An enlarged regional market improves competitiveness and attracts more foreign investment. Regional integration also ensures that macroeconomic and institutional reforms are both credible and implemented. The EU stipulates that regional integration must be compatible with WTO rules (i.e., with the multilateral commercial system). It asserts that "the rule-based, open, multilateral, international trade system is a key factor in EU (and global) prosperity. The EU wants to see these advantages extended. . . ."[19] From the European perspective, the open international market creates global public goods, that is public goods that are strongly universal in terms of countries, peoples, and generations. Security concerns in Europe in the post–World War II period until the collapse of the Soviet Union in 1991 related to the Cold War division of the European subcontinent. Since 1991 security questions relate to the "Mediterranean menace"—population migration and refugees, drugs, crime, and disease that move into Europe through the Mediterranean as the negative externalities of stagnant economies, closed markets and corrupt governments in the states clustered around the Mediterranean. Issues related to environmental degradation should also be included within the Europeans' security vista.

These security issues, related to global social problems and not merely reflective of military threats, have led the EU to be attentive to global development policy and to World Trade Organization (WTO) practices. Already in 1982 the EU Commission declared that "development policy is a cornerstone of European integration. . . . The policy is an important one because of the institutional, financial, technical and trade resources it deploys; because of the number of countries it reaches; because of the novel forms of international cooperation it has pioneered. Today, it is a manifestation of Europe's identity in the world at large and a major plank in the Community's external policies generally."[20]

GLOBAL PUBLIC GOODS

Public goods consist of four categories: regulatory goods, productive goods, distributive goods, and redistributive goods. All such goods involve some degree of political interpretation as well as enforcement. Zoning laws or the positioning of traffic lights might be examples. Distributive and especially redistributive public goods, however, tend to become political footballs. As Cerny stipulates: "Many of these goods are 'collective' or 'public' goods because political decisions have been made (whether or not in response to public demand) to treat them as public for reasons of justice, equity or other normative considerations."[21]

Political definitions of collective goods like those of redistribution in effect mean creating political space for such goods and decommodifying them or taking them outside of the market. Labor policies are a prime example here. The neoliberal economic global order, however, puts constraints upon the ability of the globalized competitive state to effect such decommodification. This is where the European Union seeks to make a difference; it wants to replicate the Union's regulated market within the global WTO–U.N. arena. The EU, for example, seeks to eliminate tariff barriers for developing states (to create a more "level playing field" via the WTO for states of the south), to forgive the debt of states of the south and to create conditions promoting greater social justice. The international regulatory economic order remains a bone of contention between the United States (with England) and the European Union (the continental states).

ENLARGEMENT OF THE EUROPEAN UNION

As Hannah Arendt points out in her *Origins of Totalitarianism*, contrary to popular assumptions, "totalitarian" states do *not* rest upon a cohesive social foundation. Quite the opposite. Such states thrive upon atomized, mass society.[22] In all post-Communist states, then, defunct civil society had to be rebuilt and, concomitantly, the formation of social capital (meaning all those values promoting social cooperation and trust) stimulated. Both of these processes remain ongoing in all post-Communist states.

The very presence of the European Union gave inspiration as well as succor to protest movements like Charter 77 in Communist Czechoslovakia and Solidarity in Communist Poland. Importantly, it provided the ready *alternative*. Certainly in states like Romania and Bulgaria, geographically lying within the shadow of the Soviet Union, this lifeline to the West has changed their historical pattern. On December 25, 1989, Ceausescu was arraigned in court, prosecuted on charges ranging from embezzlement to genocide and sentenced to death. Both Nicolae Ceausescu and his wife Elena were executed by a firing squad on the same day as the court's sentencing. The executions raised questions of motivation, legality and propriety. Were the executions a cover-up engineered by "old" Communist elites now "redesigning" themselves for post-Communist rule in Romania? These questions remain unanswered; however, eighteen years later, in 2007, Romania, like Bulgaria, gained membership in the European Union.

In obtaining EU membership, Bulgaria and Romania, like all other EU aspirant members, had to adhere to entry requirements that became codified in the Copenhagen Criteria 1993 and applied to the Fourth and Fifth Enlargements.[23] East Germany, the brightest star in the Soviet International, became the one exception to this rule. While West Germany's Basic Law (constitution) stated that in the event of West Germany's reunification with East Germany the Basic Law would become null and void and a new constitutional convention assembled, Chancellor Helmut Kohl facilely incorporated East Germany into the Bonn (now Berlin) Republic through the All German Election of 1990. West Germany assumed responsibility for reconstituting the former East German Communist satellite and integrating it into the West German democracy.

The World at War, 1939-45

The Invasion and Partition of Poland

No sooner had Hitler finished dismembering Czechoslovakia and seizing the Memel district from Lithuania in March 1939 than it became obvious that Poland would be considered next. Britain and France quickly issued a joint guarantee to Poland and hoped that with this lever they could persuade the Poles to make concessions like the Czechs at Munich, while still convincing Hitler of the need to be reasonable. However, throughout the spring and summer Hitler's aggressive attitude became more obvious especially after April when he revoked the 1934 German-Polish Non-Aggression Pact and the 1935 Anglo-German Naval Agreement. During this period both the western Allies and the Germans were courting Soviet assistance. The British and French efforts were poorly managed and, in any case, it soon became clear that Stalin wanted virtually a free hand in Eastern Europe in return for his help. The talks came to nothing. Instead, in August, the German diplomacy bore fruit and Foreign Minister Ribbentrop concluded first an economic agreement and then a Non-Aggression Pact with the USSR.

Despite some last minute uncertainty on Hitler's part, the German attack on Poland was free to begin on 1 September 1939. France and Britain each responded with an ultimatum to Germany demanding a withdrawal and when no satisfactory reply was received both countries declared war on Germany on 3 September 1939. Australia and New Zealand immediately followed suit and after some debate South Africa joined the war on 6 September. The Germans claimed that Polish provocation had caused the war and, to prove this, evidence of a Polish attack on a German radio station near the border at Gliewitz was shown to foreign pressmen. In fact the 'attack' was staged by the SS and the bodies in Polish uniforms left at the scene were those of concentration camp inmates.

The Germans deployed 53 divisions for the campaign against Poland leaving, by their own estimate, 10 divisions fit for action on the Western Front. Their six tank and their few motorized divisions were in the attack and together were used to form the

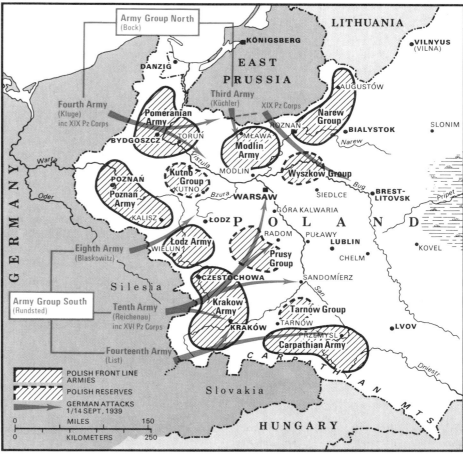

Left: Hitler enters Danzig in triumph in
September 1939. The Danzig corridor was
a constant source of friction between
Nazi Germany and Poland before the war.
Far left: Hitler and his commanders
pictured during the Polish Campaign.

various panzer corps. The German Army
Commander in Chief, Field Marshal Brauchitsch controlled the campaign, largely
without interference from Hitler. In their
preplanning and their retrospective ap-
preciations the German Army described the
campaign in terms of traditional infantry
and artillery battles, allocating the tanks
subordinate supporting roles. Only a few
enthusiasts supported theories emphasizing
the part played by the armored forces. To
support their armies the Germans had an
enormous superiority in the air with about
1600 modern planes facing the 500 largely
obsolescent machines possessed by the
Poles. The Polish mobilization was not
begun until 30 August so the German attack
found the Poles with 23 infantry divisions
deployed and another seven assembling. All
units were short of artillery, there was one
weak armored division and a mass of ineffective cavalry. The Polish forces had been
foolishly placed by Marshal Rydz-Smigly,
their Commander in Chief, in forward
positions near the frontier and, although
they fought bravely, the campaign was
decided within a few days. There was a
Polish counterattack along the Bzura River
from 9–15 September but this only caused
the Germans brief worries. Warsaw fell after
a vicious air bombardment on 27 September
and by 3 October the last significant
resistance had been wiped out.

On 17 September Soviet forces invaded
Poland from the east and on 19 September a
German-Soviet Treaty of Friendship was
announced. This confirmed the arrangements for the partition of Poland that had
been secretly agreed in August. This partition had now been achieved.

The Russo-Finnish War

The Russo-Finnish War, or Winter War as it is sometimes known, is usually remembered for the astonishing resistance of the small and poorly armed Finnish forces against the overwhelming Soviet might. The Finnish strength never exceeded 200,000 and yet they inflicted at least 208,000 casualties (official Soviet figures) on the Soviet forces which eventually employed 1,200,000 men.

The conflict developed from Soviet demands first expressed early in October 1939 for territorial concessions similar to those eventually exacted and shown on the map, although at this stage compensatory changes in the Suomussalmi area were offered by the Soviets. On the Soviet side these demands probably arose from genuine worries about Baltic security similar to those inspiring the contemporaneous moves against the Baltic States. The Finns were naturally reluctant to grant such concessions believing that, if they acceded more demands would follow, and that, in any case, Soviet willingness to negotiate implied that their commitment might be weak.

Negotiations in fact broke down in November and the Soviet attack began on the 30th, employing 26 divisions and a massive preponderance of tanks and artillery against 9 Finnish divisions with few guns, little ammunition and almost no tanks. Despite these advantages, for the first month almost every Soviet attack was resoundingly defeated by the well-trained and confident

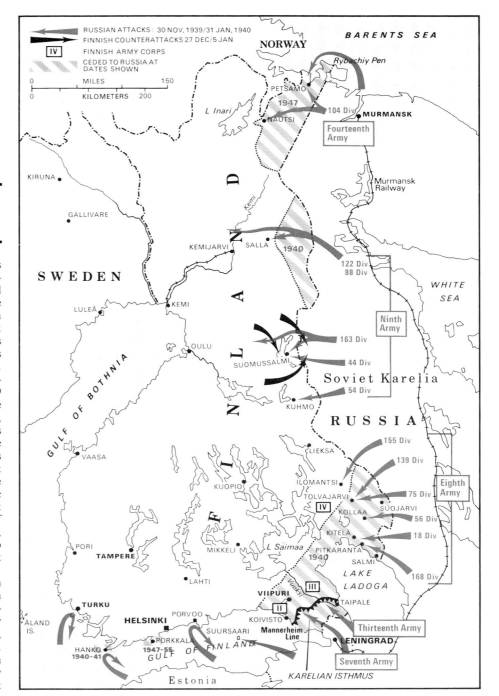

Bottom left: Finnish ski troops consistently outmaneuvered the less mobile Soviet forces during the Winter War.
Bottom: civilians in snow-colored capes take cover during a Soviet air raid.
Right: the Soviet army did not perform well against the Finns in 1939–40 despite its propaganda image.

Finnish forces. The Finns were more mobile in the difficult winter conditions and were able to isolate the clumsy Soviet attack columns and defeat them in detail. By January, however, the Soviets were learning to employ their firepower more effectively in defense and this stiffening was developed by Marshal Timoshenko who was appointed to lead the Soviet forces early in the month. Soviet pressure was stepped up during February and by early March the Finns had been beaten in a series of full-scale battles. An Armistice was agreed on the 11th and became effective on the 13th.

The Russo-Finnish War was important in wider international affairs for several reasons. It began by providing the final humiliation for the League of Nations when the Soviet Union remained unworried by its expulsion after ignoring a League attempt to mediate. Secondly the war illustrated the fumbling weakness of the British and French governments who were unable to decide whether help should be sent to Finland and what form it should take. (An important inducement was the possibility of interrupting supplies to Germany of iron ore from the Kiruna and Gällivare areas.) Although it is now clear that it would have been foolish in the long term to have aroused Soviet hostility by help to Finland, in France Premier Daladier's government fell because of this failure. The more vigorous Reynaud took over. Finally the war was important because of the impression it gave of Soviet inefficiency. This seems to have contributed to Hitler's decision to attack the USSR while it certainly encouraged many much-needed reforms to be carried out within the Red Army.

Russian Annexations 1939–40

The Molotov-Ribbentrop Pact of August 1939 paved the way for Soviet expansion westward. Once Germany had attacked Poland on 1 September 1939, the way was laid open for the Soviet Union to annex Poland's White Russian provinces. On 17 September 1939 Russian Troops entered Poland and encountered almost no oposition. Included in the annexations were the White Russian territories up to and including Bialystok, Brest-Litovsk and Lvov, which had been part of the Russian Empire before 1920, as well as the territory around Wilno, which was largely Jewish and Lithuanian in its ethnic balance.

The Polish annexations were followed swiftly by the Russo-Finnish War, and although the world was amazed by the difficulty the Soviets had in defeating their small neighbor, the war, which began on 30 November 1939, ended in the late winter of 1940 with Soviet territorial gains including eastern Karelia. The annexation of Vyborg gave the Soviet Union total control of Lake Ladoga, a fact which was crucial in the defense of Leningrad during the war against Germany.

Prior to their Finnish annexations, the Soviet Union moved in to control the three Baltic states which before World War I had formed a part of their territory. By the summer of 1940 these nations of Estonia, Latvia and Lithuania were annexed to the Soviet Union, and were later to become separate socialist republics within the USSR. A similar fate was Rumania's, which was one of the successor states of the Austro-Hungarian Empire, and whose territory was composed largely of non-Rumanian speaking people. The territories of northern Bukovina and Bessarabia, the latter being a political football throughout the 19th century, belonging to Rumania and to Russia alternatively, were reannexed by the Soviet Union in June 1940. With these annexations the Soviet Union improved its defenses against Germany.

Norway

The German invasion of Norway and Denmark brought the Phony War to an end. British and French ideas throughout this period had been to avoid costly battles on the Western Front in the style of World War I and instead to rely on the British naval blockade and a strategy of encirclement rather than direct attack. The abortive plans to assist Finland and the related interest in Norway were based on such ideas. The German aims in Scandinavia were to frustrate the Allied plans and, more specifically, to protect imports of iron ore from Sweden. Much of the iron ore traffic passed from Narvik in north Norway by coastal ship to Germany. Hitler became convinced that the Allies were ready to intervene after the *Altmark* incident of February 1940, in which a German ship carrying British prisoners was boarded in Norwegian territorial waters by the British. The Germans had some encouragement from the very small Norwegian Nazi Party led by Vidkung Quisling.

The Germans and the Allies both rapidly improvised plans in the early months of 1940. The Germans moved first by a matter of hours and held the initiative for the rest of the campaign. The German plan was very bold, if not rash, and the naval forces sent to escort the Narvik landing lost very heavily. However, the Germans did succeed in seizing a number of vital airfields at the outset, enabling them to reinforce their assault units rapidly and continue to dominate the coastal waters even when the full strength of the British Royal Navy could be deployed. The Norwegian defense forces were very weak and in many cases arms depots were captured so quickly by the Germans that belatedly mobilizing Norwegian reservists were left without arms. As in other early campaigns of the war the Allied organization was woefully inadequate. The troops were not properly armed, prepared or supplied and German professionalism and air power completed the story. There was a brief Allied revival at Narvik in May but in the light of events in France this foothold was evacuated in June.

Both Denmark and Norway remained under German occupation for the remainder of the war. The Germans gained useful Atlantic bases for striking against the Arctic convoys to the USSR but in the longer term disproportionate German forces were tied up in Norway. In the short term German naval losses helped complicate German planning for an invasion of Britain after the fall of France.

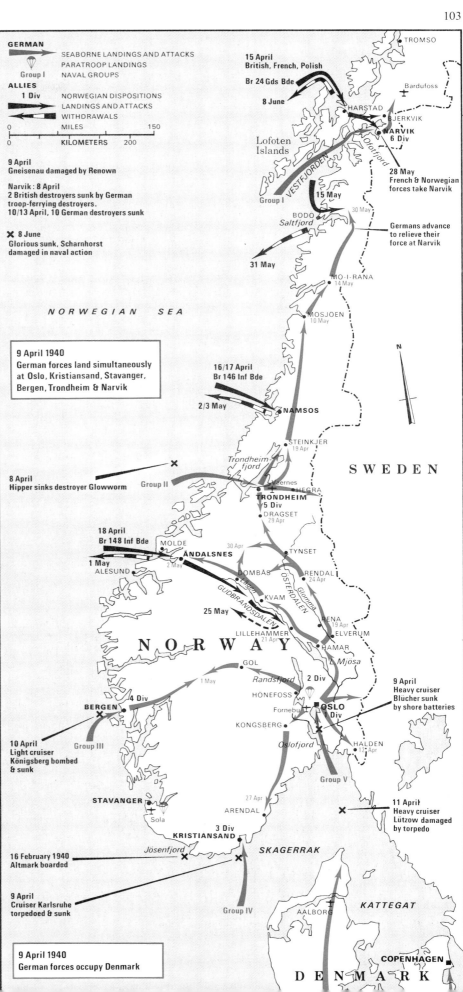

GERMAN
- SEABORNE LANDINGS AND ATTACKS
- PARATROOP LANDINGS
- Group I — NAVAL GROUPS

ALLIES
- 1 Div — NORWEGIAN DISPOSITIONS
- LANDINGS AND ATTACKS
- WITHDRAWALS

0 — MILES — 150
0 — KILOMETERS — 200

9 April
Gneisenau damaged by Renown

Narvik: 8 April
2 British destroyers sunk by German troop-ferrying destroyers.
10/13 April, 10 German destroyers sunk

✕ **8 June**
Glorious sunk, Scharnhorst damaged in naval action

9 April 1940
German forces land simultaneously at Oslo, Kristiansand, Stavanger, Bergen, Trondheim & Narvik

8 April
Hipper sinks destroyer Glowworm

18 April
Br 148 Inf Bde

10 April
Light cruiser Königsberg bombed & sunk

16 February 1940
Altmark boarded

9 April
Cruiser Karlsruhe torpedoed & sunk

9 April 1940
German forces occupy Denmark

15 April
British, French, Polish
Br 24 Gds Bde
8 June

28 May
French & Norwegian forces take Narvik

Germans advance to relieve their force at Narvik

16/17 April
Br 146 Inf Bde
2/3 May

9 April
Heavy cruiser Blücher sunk by shore batteries

11 April
Heavy cruiser Lützow damaged by torpedo

TROMSO
Bardufoss
HARSTAD
BJERKVIK
NARVIK
6 Div
Lofoten Islands
VESTFJORDEN
Ofotfjord
Group I
15 May
BODO
Saltfjord
30 May
31 May
MO-I-RANA
14 May
MOSJOEN
10 May

NORWEGIAN SEA

NAMSOS
STEINKJER
19 Apr
Trondheim fjord
Group II
Vaernes
HEGRA
TRONDHEIM
5 Div
DRAGSET
29 Apr
MOLDE
ÅNDALSNES
TYNSET
1 May
ALESUND
2 May
DOMBÅS
RENDAL
24 Apr
GUDBRANDSDALEN
KVAM
OSTERDALEN
RENA
19 Apr
25 May
ELVERUM
LILLEHAMMER
21 Apr
HAMAR
GOL
L. Mjosa
Randsfjord
2 Div
1 May
HONEFOSS
OSLO
1 Div
KONGSBERG
Fornebu
HALDEN
12 Apr
Oslofjord
Group V
27 Apr
STAVANGER
ARENDAL
Sola
3 Div
KRISTIANSAND
Jösenfjord
SKAGERRAK
Group IV
KATTEGAT
AALBORG
COPENHAGEN
DENMARK

SWEDEN

NORWAY

N

BERGEN
4 Div
Group III

Bottom: French troops lay down their arms after the surrender of Lille to the Germans in May 1940.

The Fall of France, 1940

The period from the end of the Polish campaign until the invasion of Norway and Denmark was known as the 'Phony War' because of the apparent inactivity along the Western Front. In fact many preparations were made.

Hitler initially wanted to attack in November 1939 but after several postponements a decision was made in January 1940 to wait until May. One reason for this hesitancy was difficulty in finding a satisfactory plan. Limited advances into Belgium and Holland were considered, as were variations on the 1914 Schlieffen Plan. None of these seemed adequate because, although they avoided the difficulties of a frontal attack on the French Maginot Line fortifications, they seemed too predictable and easy to counter. The plan finally adopted under the code name Sickle-stroke was largely developed by General von Manstein. He proposed that attacks into Belgium and Holland should be made (by Army Group B) to draw British and French forces forward from their prepared positions on the Franco-Belgian border. At the same time the main German advance (Army Group A), led by powerful tank forces, would move as quickly and secretly as possible through Luxembourg and the wooded and hilly Ardennes area to the Meuse River, cross it and drive to the Channel, cutting off the Belgians and Dutch and all the Allied forces which had advanced to help them.

The British and French took no account of any such possibility in their plans largely because they believed that the terrain in the Ardennes was not suitable for a large-scale advance. Instead they expected a variation on the Schlieffen Plan. The Maginot Line was garrisoned and the remaining forces deployed along the Franco-Belgian border ready for an advance to the line of the River Dyle if the Belgians should ask for help. The best French units and the British were earmarked for this advance. The weakest part of the Allied line was the sector opposite-the Ardennes.

Clearly the Allied plan depended a great deal on co-operation from the Belgians and Dutch but this was never really established before 10 May because the Belgians and Dutch feared to compromise their neutrality and provoke the Germans into attacking. As well as this problem there were other basic weaknesses in the Allied position. General Gamelin, the Commander in Chief, was 68 years old and far from vigorous. His headquarters were badly sited with poor communications and the chain of command,

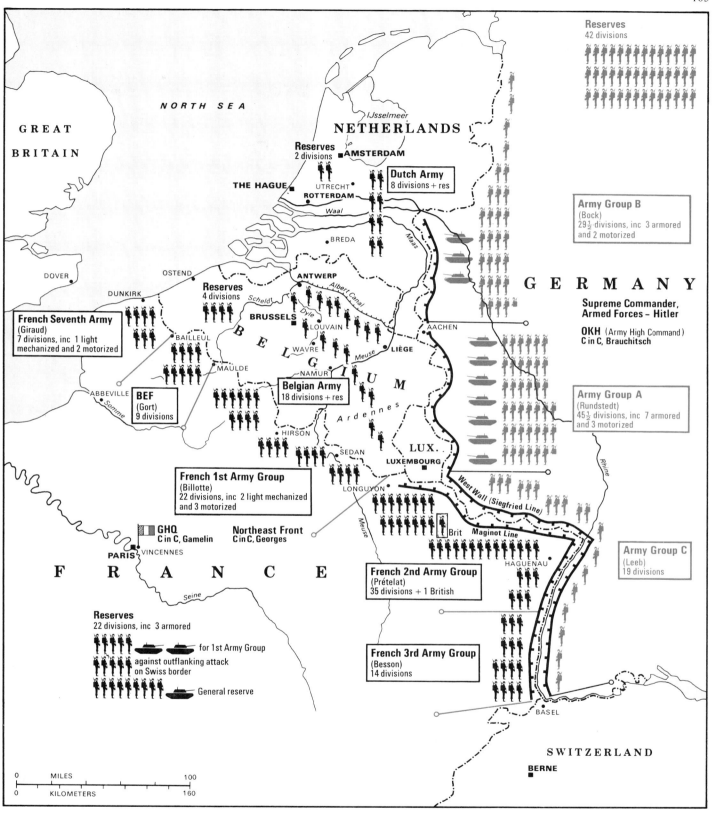

NORTH SEA

GREAT BRITAIN

Reserves
42 divisions

NETHERLANDS

IJsselmeer

Reserves
2 divisions ■AMSTERDAM

THE HAGUE
UTRECHT
ROTTERDAM

Dutch Army
8 divisions + res

Waal

DOVER

OSTEND

BREDA

Maas

Army Group B
(Bock)
29½ divisions, inc 3 armored
and 2 motorized

GERMANY

DUNKIRK

Reserves
4 divisions

ANTWERP
Albert Canal

Scheldt

French Seventh Army
(Giraud)
7 divisions, inc 1 light
mechanized and 2 motorized

BAILLEUL

BRUSSELS
Dyle
LOUVAIN
WAVRE

B E L G I U M

LIÈGE
Meuse

AACHEN

**Supreme Commander,
Armed Forces – Hitler**

OKH (Army High Command)
C in C, Brauchitsch

MAULDE

BEF
(Gort)
9 divisions

ABBEVILLE
Somme

NAMUR

Belgian Army
18 divisions + res

Ardennes

Army Group A
(Rundstedt)
45½ divisions, inc 7 armored
and 3 motorized

HIRSON

SEDAN

LUX.
LUXEMBOURG ■

Rhine

French 1st Army Group
(Billotte)
22 divisions, inc 2 light mechanized
and 3 motorized

LONGUYON
Meuse

West Wall (Siegfried Line)

■GHQ
C in C, Gamelin

Northeast Front
C in C, Georges

Brit

Maginot Line

PARIS ■
VINCENNES

French 2nd Army Group
(Prételat)
35 divisions + 1 British

HAGUENAU

Army Group C
(Leeb)
19 divisions

F R A N C E

Seine

Reserves
22 divisions, inc 3 armored

for 1st Army Group

against outflanking attack
on Swiss border

General reserve

French 3rd Army Group
(Besson)
14 divisions

BASEL

MILES   100

KILOMETERS   160

SWITZERLAND

BERNE ■

through Georges to the Army Group commanders, was unnecessarily complicated. Relations between the British and French were not at all perfect and General Gort's responsibilities to his own government as well as the French command were a potential source of difficulty. The German command arrangements were sensible and workmanlike.

The ground forces of the two sides were fairly evenly matched in numbers. Counting all nationalities the Allies had 149 divisions against 136 German with 3000 tanks against 2700. However there was no comparison in standards of training, leadership, especially at junior levels, or in tactical doctrine and organization. The German armor in particular was far better placed with almost all of their fighting vehicles being formed in panzer divisions and these divisions in turn being grouped together. Most of the strong

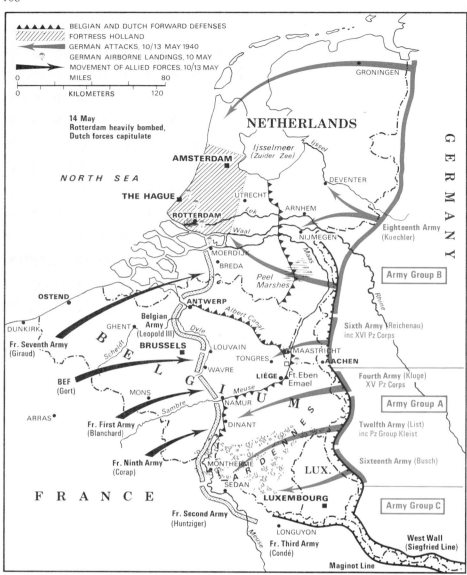

BELGIAN AND DUTCH FORWARD DEFENSES
FORTRESS HOLLAND
GERMAN ATTACKS, 10/13 MAY 1940
GERMAN AIRBORNE LANDINGS, 10 MAY
MOVEMENT OF ALLIED FORCES, 10/13 MAY

0 — MILES — 80
0 — KILOMETERS — 120

14 May
Rotterdam heavily bombed,
Dutch forces capitulate

GERMANY

NETHERLANDS

Ijsselmeer
(Zuider Zee)

Ijssel

NORTH SEA

AMSTERDAM

DEVENTER

THE HAGUE

UTRECHT

ARNHEM

ROTTERDAM

Lek

Waal

NIJMEGEN

MOERDIJK

BREDA

Maas

Peel
Marshes

Eighteenth Army
(Kuechler)

Army Group B

OSTEND

ANTWERP

Albert Canal

Rhine

DUNKIRK

GHENT

Belgian
Army
(Leopold III)

Dyle

Scheldt

BELGIUM

Sixth Army (Reichenau)
inc XVI Pz Corps

Fr. Seventh Army
(Giraud)

BRUSSELS

LOUVAIN

MAASTRICHT

AACHEN

TONGRES

BEF
(Gort)

WAVRE

LIÈGE

Ft. Eben
Emael

Meuse

Fourth Army (Kluge)
XV Pz Corps

MONS

NAMUR

Sambre

Army Group A

ARRAS

Fr. First Army
(Blanchard)

DINANT

Twelfth Army (List)
inc Pz Group Kleist

Fr. Ninth Army
(Corap)

MONTHERME

ARDENNES

LUX.

Sixteenth Army (Busch)

SEDAN

LUXEMBOURG

Army Group C

FRANCE

Fr. Second Army
(Huntziger)

Meuse

LONGUYON

West Wall
(Siegfried Line)

Fr. Third Army
(Condé)

Maginot Line

Bottom: a French truck-mounted antitank gun takes up a camouflaged position. Right: the wreckage left by the retreating British Expeditionary Force at Dunkirk. The British had to leave behind almost all their heavy equipment during the evacuation.

French tank force was wastefully dispersed in small infantry support units and on the day the battle began there was no British armored division in position in France. (One such unit was sent, not fully prepared, immediately fighting began.) Perhaps the most telling German advantage, however, was in the air where the Luftwaffe had over 3000 modern aircraft with well trained pilots and crews to face a mixed bag of less than 2000 Allied machines. (The Allied forces could expect some help and reinforcement from UK-based RAF units.)

The combination of tanks and air power was central to the German success. The aircraft, and particularly the dive-bombing Stukas, acted almost as artillery support to the army both when it was necessary for the tanks to break through solid defenses and also when, in the advance to exploit success, armored columns ran into pockets of resistance after having left their own artillery behind. Few even in the German Army understood the potential of such a system but their leadership was so dynamic that the *Blitzkrieg* or lightning war which they advocated became a byword for military skill and success.

The German attack began on 10 May and for the first few days attention was held, as the Germans had hoped, by events in the

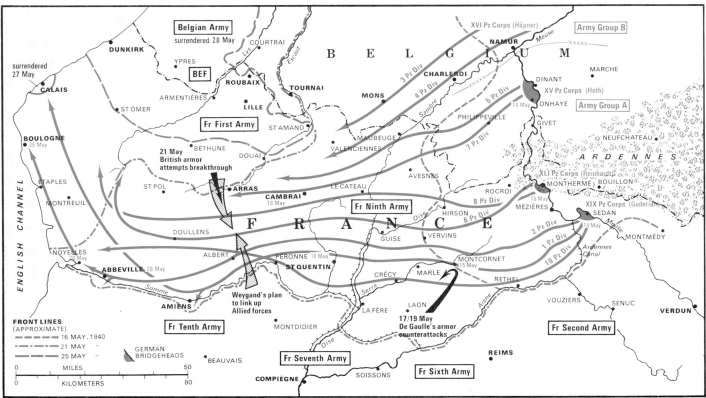

Belgian Army
surrendered 28 May

XVI Pz Corps (Höpner)

Army Group B

DUNKIRK

COURTRAI

NAMUR

MARCHE

surrendered
27 May

YPRES

Lys

Escaut

B E L G I U M

3 Pz Div

CHARLEROI

DINANT

CALAIS

BEF

ROUBAIX

TOURNAI

MONS

4 Pz Div

XXXXX

XV Pz Corps (Hoth)

Army Group A

ST OMER

ARMENTIÈRES

LILLE

5 Pz Div

14 May

ONHAYE

BOULOGNE
25 May

Fr First Army

ST AMAND

Sambre

MAUBEUGE

PHILIPPEVILLE

GIVET

NEUFCHATEAU

BÉTHUNE

VALENCIENNES

7 Pz Div

21 May
British armor
attempts breakthrough

DOUAI

A R D E N N E S

ETAPLES

ST POL

ARRAS

LE CATEAU

AVESNES

XLI Pz Corps (Reinhardt)

MONTREUIL

CAMBRAI
18 May

Fr Ninth Army

ROCROI

MONTHERMÉ

BOUILLON

8 Pz Div

ENGLISH CHANNEL

F R A N C E

Oise

HIRSON

15 May

MÉZIÈRES

XIX Pz Corps (Guderian)

6 Pz Div

DOULLENS

GUISE

VERVINS

2 Pz Div

SEDAN

14 May

NOYELLES
20 May

ALBERT

PERONNE 18 May

1 Pz Div

Ardennes
Canal

MONTMÉDY

ABBEVILLE 20 May

ST QUENTIN

MONTCORNET
15 May

10 Pz Div

Meuse

Somme

CRÉCY

MARLE

RETHEL

AMIENS

Weygand's plan
to link up
Allied forces

LA FÉRE

Serre

LAON

Aisne

VOUZIERS

SENUC

VERDUN

Fr Tenth Army

MONTDIDIER

17/19 May
De Gaulle's armor
counterattacks

Fr Second Army

FRONT LINES
(APPROXIMATE)

Fr Seventh Army

Oise

BEAUVAIS

REIMS

16 MAY, 1940
21 MAY
25 MAY

GERMAN
BRIDGEHEADS

0   MILES   50

0   80
KILOMETERS

COMPIÈGNE

SOISSONS

Fr Sixth Army

Bottom right: lines of British and French troops wait to be evacuated from the Dunkirk beaches in May/June 1940. Still greater numbers were lifted from the harbor at Dunkirk itself.

Low Countries. The Germans began with a number of daring paratroop and ground force attacks on important border defenses in both Belgium and Holland. These made important gains particularly the capture of Fort Eben Emael. The Dutch forces were left totally disorganized by a combination of paratroop drops and air attacks. Their defenses were never properly put into operation and after a particularly vicious air raid on Rotterdam on 14 May the Dutch surrendered. The French Seventh Army attempted to intervene but was thrown back.

Queen Wilhelmina and her government were evacuated to England from where they hoped to continue the fight.

In Belgium the German attacks were soon making good progress both in the north and in the tank advance to the Meuse. The British and French had advanced as planned to the Dyle but found that their positions there were weak and called in reinforcements from the reserve. Despite thus playing into the German hands, by 15 May it was necessary to order the evacuation of the Dyle Line in the face of the German attack. This was even before the German tank advance became an obvious threat.

The German tank forces had quickly penetrated through the Ardennes and on 14 May they secured vital bridgeheads over the Meuse in what were probably the most decisive actions of the whole campaign. The local French forces failed to counterattack. The German armor then began rushing forward to the sea, hindered more by the caution of the higher German commanders than by the British or the French. General Weygand replaced Gamelin as French Commander in Chief and tried to organize a counteroffensive but the only significant response was a limited British attack near Arras.

After this effort there was little the Allied forces could do but retreat to the sea. They were helped in this by a strange order from Hitler and Rundstedt which largely halted the German armored advance from 23–26 May. Most of the Allied force was able to fall back to the Dunkirk perimeter and 338,000 men, including 120,000 French, were evacuated in the nine-day operation (26 May–4 June) at heavy cost in transport ships and covering aircraft.

While the Germans were concentrating on Dunkirk Weygand was trying to organize the remaining French forces for defense of the line of the Somme. The Germans began to attack south on 5 June and the line was soon broken despite brave resistance from many French units. The German advance continued apace and on 16 June Premier Reynaud and his government resigned. The new head of government was Marshal Pétain and on the 17th he announced that France was seeking an armistice. The armistice was signed on 22 June.

France was divided into an occupied and an unoccupied zone. The unoccupied zone was ruled by the Pétain government from Vichy and, although its independence was nominally preserved, on many issues there was complete co-operation with Germany. A comparatively junior army officer and politician, General de Gaulle, escaped to Britain with a small following and proclaimed himself leader of Free France, announcing that France had lost a battle but had not lost the war.

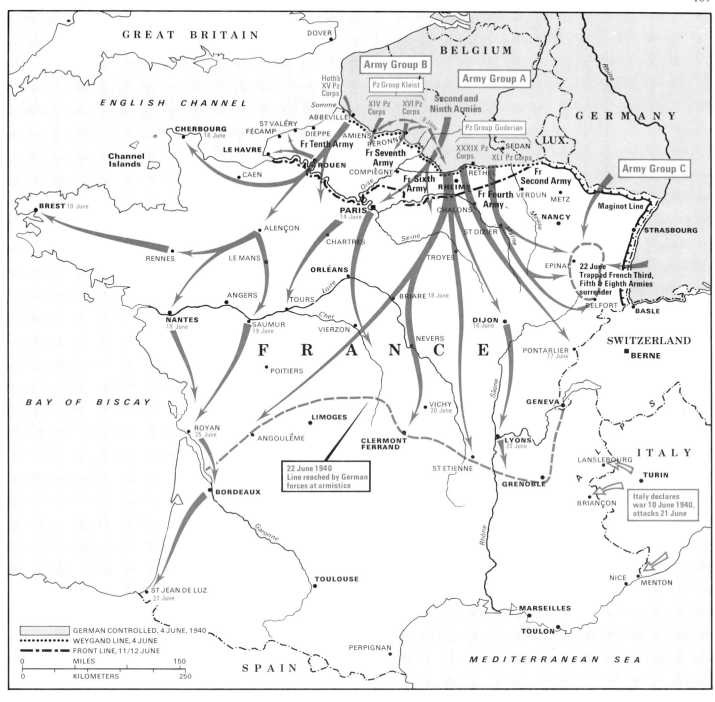

GREAT BRITAIN

DOVER

BELGIUM

ENGLISH CHANNEL

Army Group B

Pz Group Kleist

Hoth's XV Pz Corps

Somme

XIV Pz Corps

XVI Pz Corps

9 June

Second and Ninth Armies

Army Group A

Pz Group Guderian

GERMANY

LUX

Rhine

CHERBOURG 18 June

ST VALÉRY FÉCAMP

DIEPPE

ABBEVILLE

PÉRONNE

AMIENS

Fr Tenth Army

XXXIX Pz Corps

SEDAN

XLI Pz Corps

Army Group C

Channel Islands

LE HAVRE

ROUEN

COMPIÈGNE

Fr Seventh Army

RETHEL

Fr Second Army

VERDUN

METZ

Maginot Line

CAEN

Oise

Fr Sixth Army

RHEIMS

Fr Fourth Army

NANCY

STRASBOURG

BREST 19 June

PARIS 14 June

CHALONS

ST DIZIER

Seine

Meuse

RENNES

ALENÇON

CHARTRES

TROYES

Marne

EPINAL

22 June Trapped French Third, Fifth & Eighth Armies surrender

LE MANS

ORLÉANS

Loire

BELFORT

BASLE

ANGERS

TOURS

BRIARE 18 June

DIJON 16 June

SAUMUR 19 June

VIERZON

NEVERS

PONTARLIER 17 June

SWITZERLAND

BERNE

NANTES 19 June

Cher

F R A N C E

POITIERS

Saône

BAY OF BISCAY

VICHY 20 June

GENEVA

S

ITALY

ROYAN 25 June

LIMOGES

CLERMONT FERRAND

LYONS 20 June

LANSLEBOURG

TURIN

ANGOULÊME

22 June 1940 Line reached by German forces at armistice

ST ETIENNE

GRENOBLE

BRIANÇON

Italy declares war 10 June 1940, attacks 21 June

BORDEAUX

Garonne

Rhône

NICE

MENTON

ST JEAN DE LUZ 27 June

TOULOUSE

MARSEILLES

TOULON

GERMAN CONTROLLED, 4 JUNE, 1940

WEYGAND LINE, 4 JUNE

FRONT LINE, 11/12 JUNE

PERPIGNAN

MEDITERRANEAN SEA

SPAIN

MILES 0 150

KILOMETERS 0 250

Battle of Britain

On 16 July 1940 Hitler issued his Directive 16 to the German Armed Forces. It began, 'I have decided to begin to prepare for, and, if necessary, to carry out, an invasion of England.' It went on to explain that the Luftwaffe must defeat the RAF so that the Royal Navy would be unprotected if it tried to interfere with an invasion force crossing the Channel.

If the British were to survive this threat the RAF had to gain time for the army to reequip after the losses of Dunkirk and if possible to hold the Germans off until bad weather in the fall made an invasion impossible.

The RAF was none too strong for its task but was well organized and led. Air Chief Marshal Dowding, who led Fighter Command, and his principal lieutenant, Air Vice-Marshal Park, were both particularly able and perceptive officers. The British

fighter direction system was well thought out with radar and other information being coordinated and instructions issued from operations rooms in each RAF sector. Although they understood its technical capabilities the Germans failed to appreciate the importance of radar within the British system and did little to attack the radar stations. In a sense this was part of the 'home advantage' which the British had throughout the battle. In order to plan, the Germans needed, and did not get, accurate information on damage done and losses inflicted while the RAF had a more clear-cut task and could husband its resources accordingly. The RAF's principal shortage was of trained fighter pilots and it was, therefore, of considerable importance that defending pilots who were shot down unwounded could immediately return to service. The Germans, of course, had no such second chance and their principal fighter aircraft, the short-range Messerschmitt Bf 109, could only fight over southern England for a very limited time.

All these British advantages would not have cancelled out the greater German strength and the experience of their pilots unless the German High Command had not been found wanting. Reichsmarshal Göring, the Commander in Chief of the Luftwaffe, controlled the German attack and made many wrong decisions. There was no real understanding of the urgency of the invasion timetable – the all-out Luftwaffe attacks only began on 13 August, more than two months after Dunkirk. There was, too, no clear understanding of the exact aim. For a few days in late August and early September the Germans came close to winning the battle, with attacks on No 11 Group airfields, but on 7 September the main German target became London and the RAF was allowed to recover. Although it was not obvious at the time, the last major German effort was on 15 September. There were many later daytime attacks, and the night 'Blitz' on Britain's cities continued well into 1941, but Hitler postponed the invasion on 17 September.

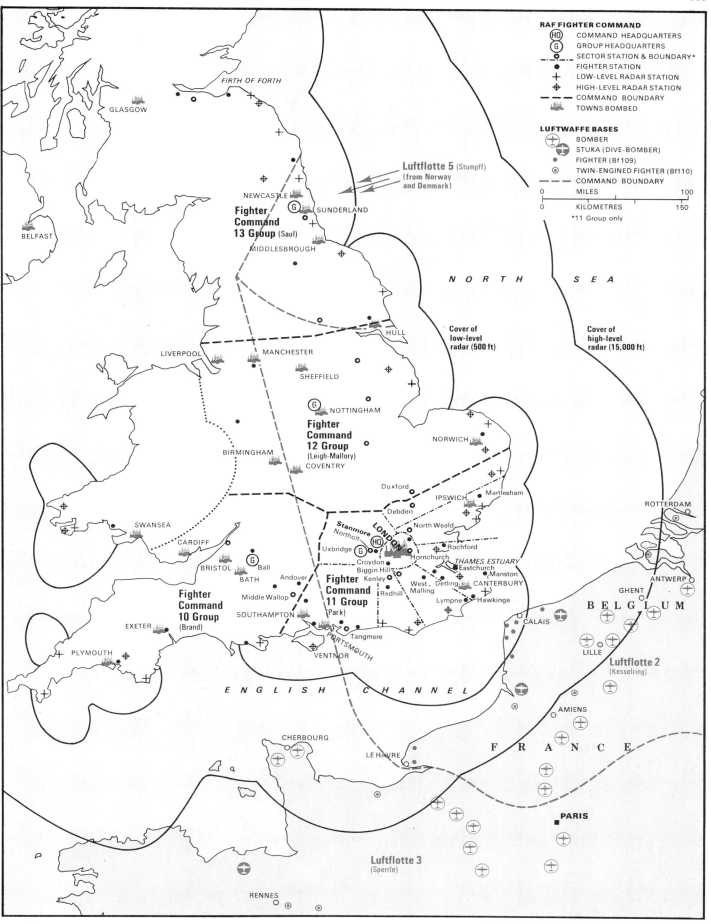

RAF FIGHTER COMMAND

- (HQ) COMMAND HEADQUARTERS
- (G) GROUP HEADQUARTERS
- ⊙ SECTOR STATION & BOUNDARY*
- ● FIGHTER STATION
- + LOW-LEVEL RADAR STATION
- ✛ HIGH-LEVEL RADAR STATION
- – – – COMMAND BOUNDARY
- TOWNS BOMBED

LUFTWAFFE BASES
- ✛ BOMBER
- STUKA (DIVE-BOMBER)
- ● FIGHTER (Bf 109)
- ⊙ TWIN-ENGINED FIGHTER (Bf 110)
- – – – COMMAND BOUNDARY

MILES 0 — 100
KILOMETRES 0 — 150

*11 Group only

FIRTH OF FORTH

GLASGOW

BELFAST

NEWCASTLE

SUNDERLAND

Fighter Command 13 Group (Saul)

Luftflotte 5 (Stumpff) (from Norway and Denmark)

MIDDLESBROUGH

NORTH SEA

HULL

Cover of low-level radar (500 ft)

Cover of high-level radar (15,000 ft)

LIVERPOOL

MANCHESTER

SHEFFIELD

NOTTINGHAM

Fighter Command 12 Group (Leigh-Mallory)

COVENTRY

BIRMINGHAM

NORWICH

Duxford

IPSWICH

Martlesham

ROTTERDAM

Debden

SWANSEA

CARDIFF

BRISTOL

BATH

Ball

Andover

Middle Wallop

Fighter Command 10 Group (Brand)

EXETER

PLYMOUTH

Stanmore
Northolt

LONDON

Uxbridge

Croydon

Biggin Hill

Kenley

Redhill

Fighter Command 11 Group (Park)

SOUTHAMPTON

PORTSMOUTH

VENTNOR

Tangmere

North Weald

Rochford

Hornchurch

THAMES ESTUARY

Eastchurch

Manston

Detling

West Malling

CANTERBURY

Lympne

Hawkinge

ANTWERP

GHENT

BELGIUM

CALAIS

LILLE

Luftflotte 2 (Kesselring)

AMIENS

ENGLISH CHANNEL

CHERBOURG

LE HAVRE

FRANCE

PARIS

Luftflotte 3 (Sperrle)

RENNES

Below: Italian troops, laden with bundles of barbed wire, move through a mountain pass during the disastrous war with Greece in the winter of 1940–41. The Italians were no match for the Greeks in this mountain campaign.

Greece

Although Hitler's plans for 1941 were dominated by the idea of attacking the USSR he also intended to secure German domination of southeastern Europe and the natural resources of that area. The allegiance of Hungary, Rumania and Bulgaria was secured during the winter of 1940–41 but Greece and Yugoslavia presented different problems. Italy had occupied Albania in 1939 and late in October 1940 had begun a war with Greece. Despite Mussolini's blustering confidence the Italians fared badly and by mid-March 1941 had suffered many defeats and had lost control of a large part of Albania. By that time also the Greeks were receiving help from Britain. The combination of defeat for his Italian ally and the prospect of British forces within striking distance of the oil fields of Rumania was clearly unacceptable to Hitler and he confirmed the plan to attack Greece which had been in preparation since late 1940.

To defend Greece the Allies had, in addition to the forces facing the Italians, seven weak Greek divisions, the New Zealand Division, part of the 6th Australian Division and a British armored brigade. The Germans employed three full army corps including a strong armored element. They had overwhelming air support. The British leaders hoped to base their defense on the naturally strong Aliakmon Line and have forces in hand to cover the Monastir Gap but despite this sensible advice the Greek Commander in Chief, General Papagos, insisted that he could not abandon Greek Macedonia and deployed much of his available strength on the weaker Metaxas Line covering that region. The Germans planned to destroy this force in direct attacks and push other units through the Monastir Gap to outflank the defense lines.

The attack began on 6 April and the map shows the speed with which the German plan was completed. By 10 April the Aliakmon Line was being evacuated and General Wavell's decision of 16 April to stop reinforcements being sent from Egypt effectively meant that the fight in Greece was being abandoned.

In a postscript to the Greek campaign German airborne troops landed on Crete on 20 May and despite a fierce struggle had captured the island by the end of the month.

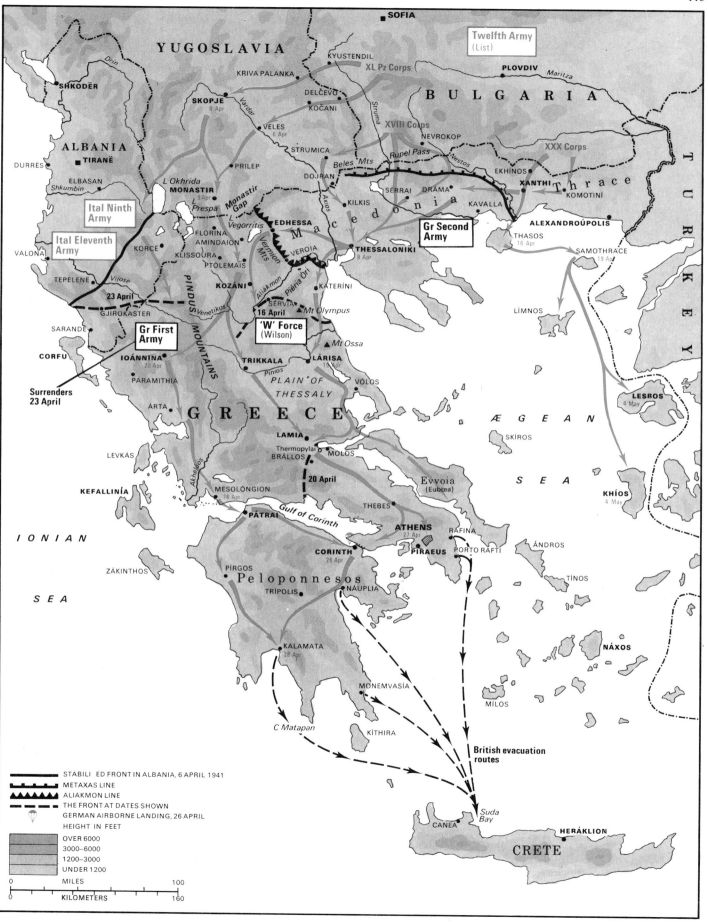

SOFIA

YUGOSLAVIA

KYUSTENDIL

Twelfth Army
(List)

KRIVA PALANKA

PLOVDIV

Maritza

XL Pz Corps

DELČEVO

SKOPJE
8 Apr

KOČANI

B U L G A R I A

Vardar

VELES
6 Apr

Struma

XVIII Corps

NEVROKOP

STRUMICA

Beles Mts

Rupel Pass

Nestos

XXX Corps

ALBANIA

PRILEP

DOJRAN

EKHÍNOS

XANTHI

Thrace

KOMOTINÍ

DURRËS

TIRANË

L Okhrida

MONASTIR
9 Apr

Monastir Gap

Axios

KILKIS

SÉRRAI

DRÁMA

KAVALLA

ALEXANDROÚPOLIS

T U R K E Y

ELBASAN

Shkumbin

L Prespa

Ital Ninth Army

L Vegorritis

FLORINA

EDHESSA

Ma c e d o n i a

THESSALONÍKI
9 Apr

Gr Second Army

THASOS
16 Apr

SAMOTHRACE
19 Apr

Ital Eleventh Army

KORCÉ

AMINDAION

KLISSOURA

PTOLEMAÏS

Vermion Mts

VEROIA

Piéria Óri

KATERÍNI

VALONA

KOZÁNI

Aliakmon

SÉRVIA
16 April

Mt Olympus

LÍMNOS

LESBOS
4 May

TEPELENÉ

Vijosë

23 April

Venetikos

P I N D U S

'W' Force
(Wilson)

Mt Ossa

SARANDÉ

GJIROKASTER

Gr First Army

IOÁNNINA
20 Apr

TRIKKALA

LÁRISA
19 Apr

Pinios

SAMOTHRACE

KHÍOS
4 May

**Surrenders
23 April**

PARAMITHIÁ

M O U N T A I N S

*PLAIN OF
THESSALY*

VOLOS

Æ G E A N

CORFU

ÁRTA

G R E E C E

SKÍROS

S E A

LEVKÁS

Akhelóos

LAMIA

Thermopylai MOLOS
BRÁLLOS

20 April

Evvoia
(Euboea)

I O N I A N

KEFALLINÍA

MESOLÓNGION
26 Apr

THEBES

ÁNDROS

TÍNOS

Gulf of Corinth

PÁTRAI

ATHENS
27 Apr

RÁFINA

PIRAEUS

PORTO RAFTÍ

S E A

PÍRGOS

CORINTH
26 Apr

Peloponnesos

TRÍPOLIS

NÁUPLIA

NÁXOS

ZÁKINTHOS

S E A

C Matapan

KALAMATA
28 Apr

MONEMVASÍA

KÍTHIRA

MÍLOS

**British evacuation
routes**

CANEA

*Suda
Bay*

HERÁKLION

CRETE

STABILISED FRONT IN ALBANIA, 6 APRIL 1941
METAXAS LINE
ALIAKMON LINE
THE FRONT AT DATES SHOWN
GERMAN AIRBORNE LANDING, 26 APRIL
HEIGHT IN FEET

OVER 6000
3000–6000
1200–3000
UNDER 1200

0   MILES   100

0   KILOMETERS   160

Yugoslavia

As the other Balkan countries fell under German influence one by one during the winter of 1940–41 pressure on Yugoslavia to follow suit increased. On 25 March, with the agreement of Prince Paul the Regent, the government gave in and signed the Tripartite Pact but this decision was overturned on the 27th by a largely Serbian-backed coup deposing Prince Paul and his government in favor of King Peter. Hitler responded by immediately ordering his forces to prepare to invade Yugoslavia and also to carry out the attack on Greece which was already planned.

The attack began on 6 April with heavy air raids on Belgrade and against the Yugoslav Air Force which was soon out of the fight. On the same day units of List's Twelfth Army moved into Yugoslavia toward Strumica and Monastir but these were really part of the force attacking Greece. The land attack on Yugoslavia proper began on 8 April when Kleist's First Panzer Group crossed the Bulgarian border. Weich's Second Army joined in on the 9th and on the 11th the remaining Italian, Hungarian and German units began their efforts. There was little resistance to any of the attacks and the country was quickly overrun. King Peter and his government fled and on the 17th an armistice was agreed. The defense was vitiated by a senseless cordon deployment and by internal dissension, particularly Croatian disaffection. The Germans lost less than 200 dead in the whole campaign.

It has often been suggested that, although at the time the Greek and Yugoslavian campaign seemed disasters for the Allied cause they were indirectly beneficial by crucially delaying the attack on the USSR. Modern historical research suggests that this is not so. Any delay was caused rather more by weather and supply problems and, although it certainly took time to redeploy forces from the Balkans to face the USSR, it is not clear that the units involved were essential in the initial stages of the attack. If it had been necessary to move them to their Barbarossa positions quicker this could have been done also.

Below left: a 15cm howitzer, mounted on a Panzer I chassis, operating in Yugoslavia in the spring of 1941.
Bottom left: a formation of Junkers Ju 87 Stukas flies over the Bosnian mountains during an operation against Yugoslavian guerrilla forces.
Bottom: a German half-track fords a river in Yugoslavia during an attack on Partisan forces.

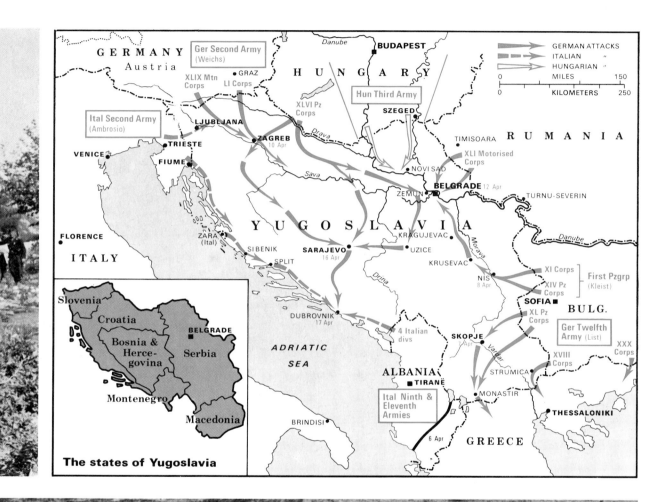

The states of Yugoslavia

War in the Desert, 1940–41

In its repeated changes of fortune the North African campaign was unlike any other of the war. Between the Axis base at Tripoli and the British base in the Nile Delta there was a 1500-mile expanse of waterless and largely roadless desert. Both sides' attempts to build up the supplies and reinforcements necessary for any sustained advance in such terrain were continually hampered by the demands of other theaters and other problems. Thus in 1940–41 the British Middle East Command fought successful campaigns in East Africa and Syria and unsuccessfully in Greece and Crete. At the end of 1941, even as the British were advancing once again, units had to be withdrawn to be sent east to face the Japanese. It was by no means a one-sided process. The Germans soon assumed the dominant role in the Axis partnership, and constraints on their commander, General Rommel, were soon apparent. The German High Command saw North Africa as a distinctly minor theater and allocated forces and supplies accordingly. The proportion of these supplies reaching Rommel was also highly variable. When the German Mediterranean air forces were strong as at the beginning of 1941 or at the same time in 1942, Rommel tended to do well, whereas when the British naval and air forces were strong, particularly those based in Malta, Rommel did badly. Many of Rommel's supply and other problems would have been much less acute with wholehearted

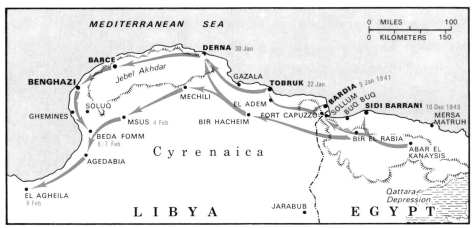

and efficient cooperation from his Italian allies. These general difficulties affected each side almost independently of the prevailing tactical situation but because of the poor land communications and the lack of suitable ports the military dictum, that an army becomes weaker as it advances away from its base and stronger as it retires, was a formula with special relevance to the North African battle. Only if this whole list of constraints and imperatives is taken into account can the unique rhythms of the fighting in North Africa be understood.

Italy declared war on Britain on 10 June 1940 and in September the numerically strong Italian Tenth Army made a short tentative advance into Egypt. By December the much smaller British and Imperial force was ready to attack under the able leadership of Generals Wavell and O'Connor. The Italians were successively hustled out of defensive positions at Sidi Barrani, Bardia

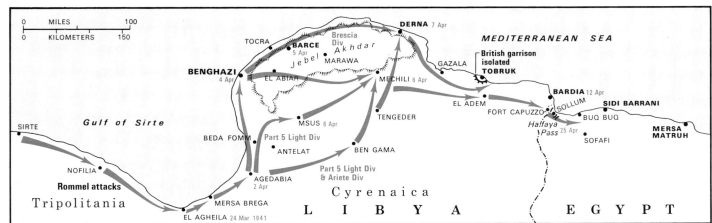

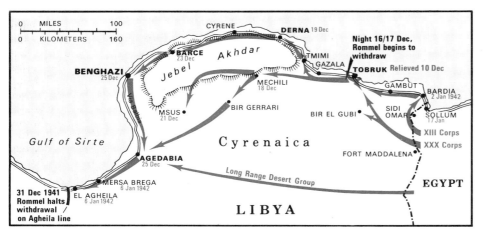

and Tobruk and thrown into abject retreat along the coast road. The Italian defeat was completed when a force sent across the Cyrenaica Plateau cut their retreat at Beda Fomm. In those two months the British forces never had more than two divisions in the fight. Ten Italian divisions were destroyed and 130,000 prisoners taken for the loss of 550 dead and 1400 wounded. Already, however, the British position was deteriorating. Troops had been withdrawn to East Africa and more were about to go to Greece. Even those forces remaining could not all be supplied at the front and so it was not solidly held, the more so because many of the tanks were worn out.

General Rommel arrived in Africa on 12 February 1941 with a small German force and instructions to block any further British advance. He quickly discerned the British weakness and by early April had begun an all-out attack which quickly overwhelmed the depleted British force. However, although the main front line was pushed back into Egypt, Rommel was unsuccessful in desperate attempts to capture Tobruk before his own acute supply problems forced a pause.

During the next phase of the campaign both sides tried to build up their forces and supply stocks for an offensive. A premature British attack in June, Operation Battleaxe, was soundly defeated but Tobruk remained a thorn in the German side. The British were again ready to attack in November 1941 under a new Commander in Chief, General Auchinleck and Operation Crusader accordingly began on the 18th. The British had far greater resources initially but the individual German units were better led and far more professional in their approach. The result, when combined with errors in generalship on both sides, was a prolonged and highly confused battle in the area between Tobruk and the Egyptian frontier. After very heavy losses on both sides Rommel was forced to retreat and because of the lack of suitable defensive positions and the danger of being outflanked he had to go back as far as El Agheila. Once more, however, there were signs of a change: Malta was coming under heavier attack and the British naval forces had recently suffered serious losses; Rommel was receiving reinforcements even as he retreated and British and Australian troops were being withdrawn to reinforce the Far East against the threat from Japan.

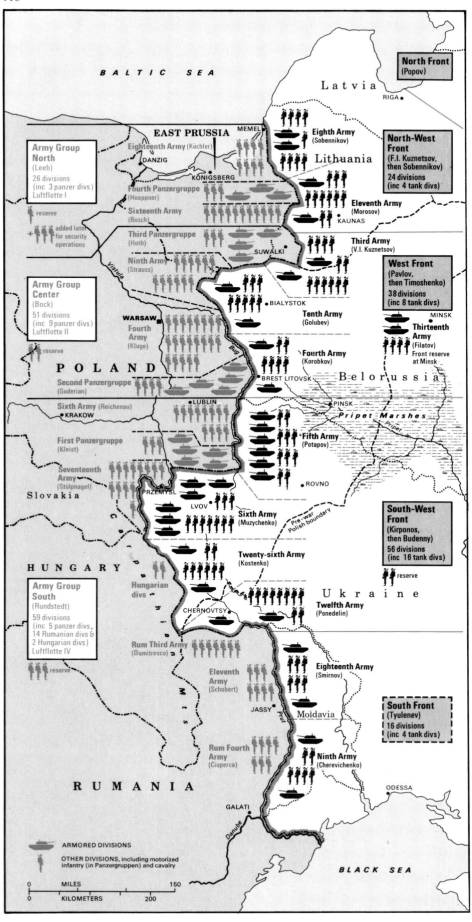

Army Group North (Leeb)
26 divisions (inc 3 panzer divs)
Luftflotte I

reserve

added later for security operations

Army Group Center (Bock)
51 divisions (inc 9 panzer divs)
Luftflotte II

reserve

Army Group South (Rundstedt)
59 divisions (inc 5 panzer divs, 14 Rumanian divs & 2 Hungarian divs)
Luftflotte IV

reserve

BALTIC SEA

Latvia

RIGA

North Front (Popov)

EAST PRUSSIA
MEMEL

Eighteenth Army (Küchler)
DANZIG
KÖNIGSBERG

Fourth Panzergruppe (Hoeppner)

Sixteenth Army (Busch)

Third Panzergruppe (Hoth)

Ninth Army (Strauss)

Vistula

WARSAW
Fourth Army (Kluge)

POLAND

Second Panzergruppe (Guderian)

Sixth Army (Reichenau)
KRAKOW

First Panzergruppe (Kleist)

Seventeenth Army (Stülpnagel)

Slovakia

HUNGARY

Hungarian divs

Rum Third Army (Dumitrescu)

Eleventh Army (Schobert)

JASSY

Rum Fourth Army (Ciuperca)

RUMANIA

GALATI

Danube

Eighth Army (Sobennikov)

Lithuania

Eleventh Army (Morosov)
KAUNAS

SUWALKI

Third Army (V.I. Kuznetsov)

Bug

BIALYSTOK

Tenth Army (Golubev)

Fourth Army (Korobkov)

BREST LITOVSK

LUBLIN

PINSK

Belorussia

Pripet Marshes

Pripet

Fifth Army (Potapov)

ROVNO

PRZEMYSL

LVOV

Sixth Army (Muzychenko)

Pre-war Polish boundary

Twenty-sixth Army (Kostenko)

CHERNOVTSY

Ukraine

Twelfth Army (Ponedelin)

Eighteenth Army (Smirnov)

Moldavia

Prut

Ninth Army (Cherevichenko)

ODESSA

BLACK SEA

North-West Front (F.I. Kuznetsov, then Sobennikov)
24 divisions (inc 4 tank divs)

West Front (Pavlov, then Timoshenko)
38 divisions (inc 8 tank divs)

MINSK

Thirteenth Army (Filatov)
Front reserve at Minsk

South-West Front (Kirponos, then Budenny)
56 divisions (inc 16 tank divs)

reserve

South Front (Tyulenev)
16 divisions (inc 4 tank divs)

ARMORED DIVISIONS

OTHER DIVISIONS, including motorized infantry (in Panzergruppen) and cavalry

| 0 | MILES | 150 |
| 0 | KILOMETERS | 200 |

Operation Barbarossa

In February 1941 a sympathetic German printer showed to Soviet diplomats in Berlin a new Russian phrasebook he had been ordered to print in large quantities, and which included phrases like 'Hands up or I'll shoot!' and 'Are you a communist?' This was just one of several signs that Hitler was preparing to turn against the USSR. He had in fact issued a general directive plan in December 1940 which, drawing on the experience and self-confidence gained in the French campaign, proposed that the initial aim should be nothing less than the complete destruction of the Red Army. This would be facilitated by the circumstance that the Russians, whose prevailing military doctrine was the doctrine of the offensive, had placed almost their entire active army close to the frontiers. Deep penetrations by German armor would be able to cut off the retreat of these Soviet formations. Having accomplished this, the German forces were to press eastward and establish a line running roughly from Archangel to Astrakhan.

22 June 1941 was the date finally fixed for this Operation Barbarossa. In the preceding weeks the Soviet government, despite ominous indications of German preparations, had issued orders that no Soviet preparations should be made, as the Germans might regard these as a provocation to attack. When war came, therefore, Stalin and his colleagues were in the unusual situation of being both unsurprised and unprepared and, long after the British and French had shown the perils of appeasement, stood revealed as the greatest appeasers of all. The Soviet formations were taken, catastrophically, by surprise.

After heavy German air attacks, directed mainly at airfields close to the frontier, and which had the effect of shattering the Red Air Force, German troops advanced across the frontier at dawn on 22 June. Army Group Center made a pincer movement from East Prussia and Poland toward Minsk, cutting off parts of two Soviet armies whose men, after a little confused resistance, surrendered en masse. Meanwhile Army Group South entered the Ukraine and, aided by Rumanian troops, also forced large Soviet concentrations to surrender.

In September Budenny, a cavalryman and crony of Stalin since the Russian Civil

SWEDEN

FINLAND

Lake Oneg

LAKE LADOGA

HELSINKI

HANKO (USSR)
3 Dec 1941 Evacuated by Russia

Gulf of Finland

VIIPURI

Twenty-third Army

Forty-second & Fifty-second Armies

LENINGRAD

VOLKHOV
Eighth Army

TIKHVIN

Fifty-fourth Army

Fourth Army

Fifty-ninth Army

Second Shock Army

NOVGOROD

Eleventh Army

KALININ

MOSCOW

Volga

North-West Front (Voroshilov)

Thirty-fourth Army

Third Shock Army

Twenty-seventh Army

Twenty-second Army

Twenty-ninth Army

Thirtieth Army
Nineteenth Army
Sixteenth Army

Thirty-second Army

Twentieth Army

Twenty-fourth Army

Twenty-eighth Army

Forty-third Army

West Front (Timoshenko)

Fiftieth Army

BRYANSK

Third Army

OREL

Thirteenth Army

KURSK

South-West Front (Budenny)

Fortieth Army

KHARKOV

Twenty-first Army

Thirty-eighth Army

Sixth Army

Twelfth Army

MELITOPOL

Ninth Army

Sea of Azov

Fifty-first Army

Crimea

SEVASTOPOL

BLACK SEA

Army Group North (Leeb)

Eighteenth Army

MEMEL

Fourth Pzgrp
Sixteenth Army

Ninth Army
Third Pzgrp

EAST PRUSSIA

Army Group Center (Bock)

WARSAW

Fourth Army
Second Pzgrp

POLAND

Sixth Army
First Pzgrp

Seventeenth Army

Army Group South (Rundstedt)

Slovakia

HUNGARY

Carpathian Mts

RIGA

SIAULIAI

Eighth Army

Lithuania

KAUNAS

VILNYUS

Third Army

BIALYSTOK

Tenth Army

Fourth Army

BREST-LITOVSK

KOVEL

ROVNO

LWOW

TERNOPOL

Sixth Army

Twenty-sixth Army

CHERNOVTSY

Twelfth Army

Eleventh Army

Moldavia

KISHINEV

Rum Fourth Army

Ninth Army

RUMANIA

BUCHAREST

CONSTANTA

Danube

Eleventh Army

VENTSPILS

Latvia

Estonia

TALLINN

TARTU

L. Peipus

NARVA

LUGA
Luga

PSKOV

OSTROV

REZEKNE

Dvina

DAUGAVPILS

IDRITSA

POLOTSK

VITEBSK

Velikaya

KHOLM

OSTASHKOV

VELIKIYE LUKI

VELIZH

YARTSEVO

VYAZMA

SMOLENSK

BELYY

RZHEV

Neman

NOVI BORISOV

Moscow Highway

MINSK

GORODISHCHE

Berezina

ORSHA

MOGILEV

YELNYA

KALUGA

TULA

ROSLAVL

NOVO BYKHOV

KRICHEV

Sozh

GRODNO

Pripet

PINSK

Pripet Marshes

MOZYR

Twenty-first Army

RECHITSA

BOBRUYSK

GOMEL

Second Pzgrp

STARODUB

NOVGOROD-SEVERSKI

KONOTOP

BAKHMACH

CHERNIGOV

Desna

Belorussia

Ukraine

Fifth Army

Fifth Army

ZHITOMIR

KIEV

Thirty-seventh Army

Second Army

LOKHVITSA

First Pzgrp

POLTAVA

KREMENCHUG

BERDICHEV

KAZATIN

VINNITSA

KAMENETS-PODOLSKY

Dniestr

UMAN

CHERKASSY

PERVOMAYSK

Yuzhni Bug

Seventeenth Army

KRIVOY ROG

DNEPROPETROVSK

ZAPOROZHYE

Eighteenth Army

Dniepr

Eleventh Army

NIKOLAYEV

ODESSA
16 Oct

Prut

Eighteenth Army

Psel

Rum Third Army

PEREKOP

Legend:

STALIN LINE

FRONT LINE, 21 JUNE 1941

" 9 JULY

" 1 SEPTEMBER

" 30 SEPTEMBER

RUSSIAN COUNTERATTACKS

TRAPPED RUSSIAN POCKETS

MILES 200

KILOMETERS 300

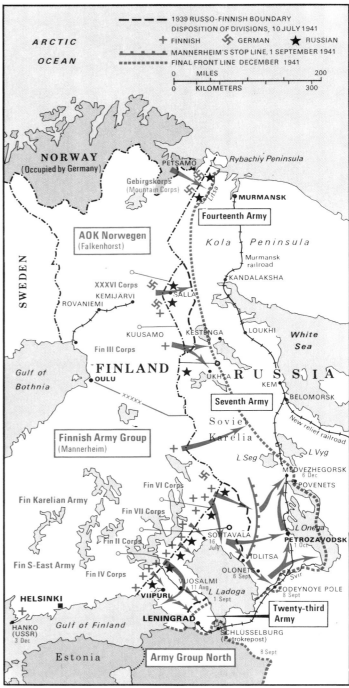

War, allowed his South-West Front (that is – army group) to engage in catastrophic battles rather than retreat in good time. At Kiev alone half a million Red soldiers were taken prisoner, and by mid-November Rostov had been taken by the invaders, as well as the Perekop Isthmus commanding the Crimea. In the center there had been a big tank battle near Smolensk, and a second battle at Bryansk had allowed the Germans to take Orel, Tula and Vyazma. In the north the Baltic states had been occupied and some formations had penetrated east of Leningrad. The much-publicized 'Stalin Line,' had been shown to be virtually non-existent.

The Finnish Front, 1941

After their defeat by Russia in 1940 the Finns were, understandably enough, ready to join Germany in the Barbarossa attack in 1941 with the aim of recovering their lost territory. The Finnish front was strategically important because attacks there would probably help the German Army Group North to reach Leningrad.

With German help the Finnish forces were better prepared than in 1940. The Finnish mobilization system had been overhauled to increase the proportion of the country's manpower called up for military service and training had been improved.

The joint German and Finnish attack began on 19 June 1941. The earliest successes were in the area immediately north of Lake Ladoga and in August there were also important gains on the Karelian Isthmus. These almost reached Leningrad before being halted on Mannerheim's orders. In September, October and November there were further Finnish advances toward Lake Onega and farther north but by December the Finns had gone over completely to the defensive.

Opposite left: German troops take a rest in recently captured Soviet trenches during the early months of Barbarossa.
Below: Cossack cavalry charge across a snowfield. Their main usefulness was in harassing enemy rear areas.
Bottom: a German motor convoy drives through a snowstorm during the first winter of the Russian campaign.

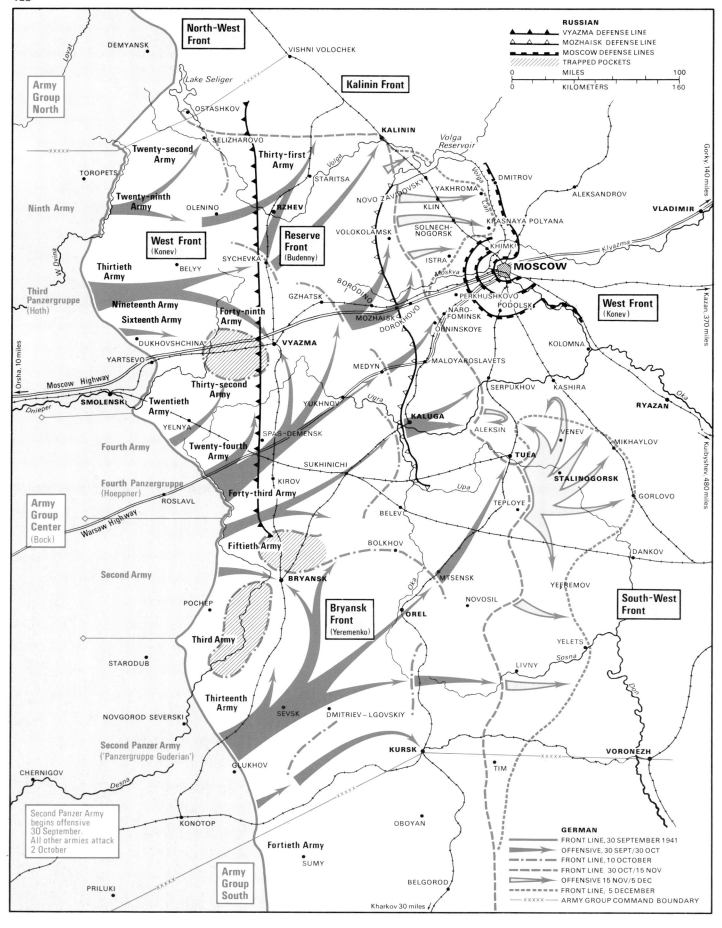

North-West Front

Kalinin Front

RUSSIAN
- VYAZMA DEFENSE LINE
- MOZHAISK DEFENSE LINE
- MOSCOW DEFENSE LINES
- TRAPPED POCKETS

MILES 0 — 100
KILOMETERS 0 — 160

DEMYANSK

Lake Seliger

VISHNI VOLOCHEK

Army Group North

OSTASHKOV

SELIZHAROVO

KALININ

Volga Reservoir

Gorky, 140 miles

TOROPETS

Twenty-second Army

Thirty-first Army

STARITSA

NOVO ZAVIDOVSKY

YAKHROMA

DMITROV

ALEKSANDROV

VLADIMIR

Ninth Army

Twenty-ninth Army

OLENINO

RZHEV

KLIN

SOLNECH-NOGORSK

KRASNAYA POLYANA

Volga

Tsch

West Front (Konev)

Reserve Front (Budenny)

SYCHEVKA

VOLOKOLAMSK

ISTRA

KHIMKI

MOSCOW

Klyazma

Third Panzergruppe (Hoth)

Thirtieth Army

BELYY

BORODINO

Moskva

PERKHUSHKOVO

PODOLSK

West Front (Konev)

Kazan, 370 miles

Nineteenth Army

Sixteenth Army

Forty-ninth Army

GZHATSK

MOZHAISK

DOROHOVO

NARO-FOMINSK

OBNINSKOYE

KOLOMNA

DUKHOVSHCHINA

VYAZMA

MEDYN

MALOYAROSLAVETS

SERPUKHOV

KASHIRA

RYAZAN

Oka

YARTSEVO

Orsha, 10 miles

Moscow Highway

Twentieth Army

YUKHNOV

KALUGA

ALEKSIN

VENEV

MIKHAYLOV

Kuibyshev, 480 miles

SMOLENSK

Dnieper

YELNYA

Thirty-second Army

SPAS-DEMENSK

Ugra

TULA

STALINOGORSK

GORLOVO

Fourth Army

Twenty-fourth Army

SUKHINICHI

Upa

TEPLOYE

Fourth Panzergruppe (Hoeppner)

KIROV

DANKOV

Army Group Center (Bock)

ROSLAVL

Warsaw Highway

Forty-third Army

BELEV

BOLKHOV

YEFREMOV

Second Army

Fiftieth Army

BRYANSK

MTSENSK

NOVOSIL

South-West Front

POCHEP

Bryansk Front (Yeremenko)

OREL

Oka

YELETS

LIVNY

Sosna

Third Army

STARODUB

Thirteenth Army

SEVSK

DMITRIEV-LGOVSKIY

Don

NOVGOROD SEVERSKI

Second Panzer Army ('Panzergruppe Guderian')

GLUKHOV

KURSK

TIM

VORONEZH

CHERNIGOV

Desna

Second Panzer Army begins offensive 30 September. All other armies attack 2 October

KONOTOP

Fortieth Army

OBOYAN

SUMY

Army Group South

BELGOROD

PRILUKI

Kharkov 30 miles

GERMAN
- FRONT LINE, 30 SEPTEMBER 1941
- OFFENSIVE, 30 SEPT/30 OCT
- FRONT LINE, 10 OCTOBER
- FRONT LINE 30 OCT/15 NOV
- OFFENSIVE 15 NOV/5 DEC
- FRONT LINE, 5 DECEMBER
- XXXXX ARMY GROUP COMMAND BOUNDARY

The German Attack on Moscow

Although the Russians had failed to hold Smolensk, the sturdy defense of that city had delayed the German advance on Moscow. Meanwhile, ahead of the German advance, the Russians were evacuating as much as possible of their factory equipment and key workers, intent on relocating them far to the east. The evacuation of railroad equipment meant that the Soviets had more locomotives and freightcars per mile of track, so Hitler's expectation of a transport breakdown was disappointed. The order for the capture of Moscow was issued on 2 October, and specified the encirclement of the city by 51 divisions, including 13 armored divisions. As the Germans closed in on the capital the fighting grew fiercer and,

for both sides, more desperate. The German and Russian high commands both knew that the delay at Smolensk meant that there would be little time to capture the Soviet capital before the onset of winter. In fact, the Germans never succeeded in totally encircling the city, whose lines of communication to the east remained open. This enabled the ministries to be evacuated and, in due course, permitted the arrival by train of fresh divisions from Siberia.

The Germans had virtual command of the air, although this advantage was not properly exploited so far as the ground fighting was concerned. Nevertheless, bombing was intense enough to cause the anniversary of the Russian revolution to be celebrated in an underground station of the Moscow Metro. Russian workers were given a week's training and sent to the front, while Moscow's women dug trenches and helped with supplies. By the end of November German units had reached the western suburbs but

two attempts to take the entire city by assault had failed. The encirclement was still incomplete and, moreoever, just as had happened to Napoleon's army in 1812, there had been an early onset of winter. In 1941, the temperature dropped to 40 degrees below zero as early as the first week of November. The Germans were not provided with winter clothing, nor was their equipment properly prepared. Engines of lorries and tanks froze up, with their cylinders sometimes cracking. Meanwhile the Siberian units had begun to arrive. On 8 December Hitler called off the attack for the duration of the winter. In effect this meant that, despite the shattering of the Red Army, Operation Barbarossa had failed. Neither Moscow nor Leningrad had been captured. Through Archangel, Murmansk, Persia and Vladivostok the USSR was beginning to receive shipments of war material from the west, while her own armaments industry was being re-established far behind the front.

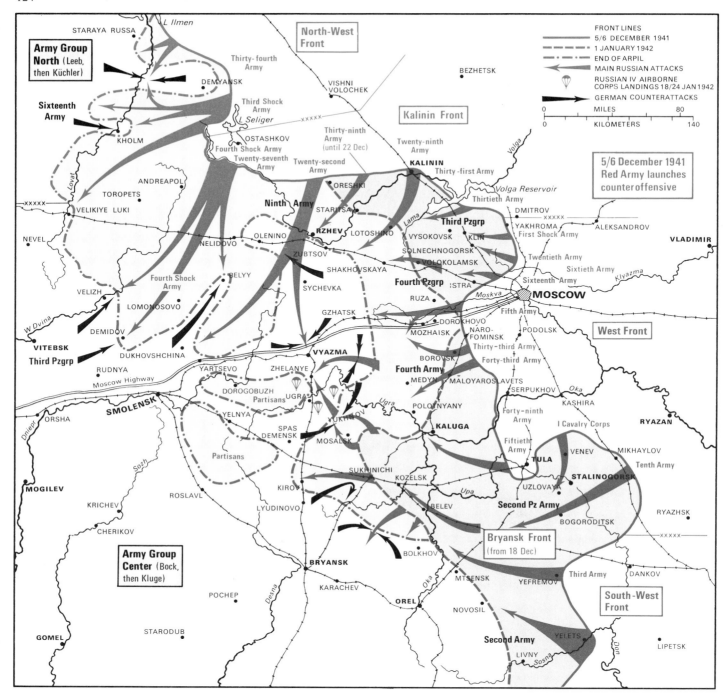

FRONT LINES
5/6 DECEMBER 1941
1 JANUARY 1942
END OF ARPIL
MAIN RUSSIAN ATTACKS
RUSSIAN IV AIRBORNE
CORPS LANDINGS 18/24 JAN 1942
GERMAN COUNTERATTACKS

MILES 0 — 80
KILOMETERS 0 — 140

5/6 December 1941
Red Army launches
counter offensive

The Russian Counterattack, Moscow

On 8 December 1941 Hitler had announced a temporary suspension of operations outside Moscow, but the Soviet High Command soon showed that this was wishful thinking. It was, in fact, on the point of launching a counter-offensive for which it had been accumulating reserves over the previous weeks. Again, the situation of 1812 repeated itself, for the Soviet advance took the form of a mass infiltration which avoided the strongest German points. Passing over fields rather than following the roads, making great use of Cossacks, ski troops and guerilla forces, the Soviets forced the Germans to withdraw from one position after another by threatening them with attacks from the flank or rear. The Germans were handicapped by the effect of low temperatures on their internal-combustion engines, which effectively put the Luftwaffe out of action, and by their difficult supply position, which relied on thinly spread railroad links, hampered by a change of gauge, and the very poor Russian roads.

The Germans were pushed back most in the center. Kalinin and Tula were retaken, and the immediate threat to Moscow removed. The offensive continued to late February, by which time both sides were in need of rest and consolidation. This winter offensive had brought the Russians back as far as Velikiye Luki and Mozhaisk. At the same time, in the north the Germans had given ground around Leningrad, losing Tikhvin and control of Lake Ladoga, across which the Russians built a temporary ice road to the city. In the south the Kerch Isthmus was retaken and the Crimea re-entered, with Feodosia being reoccupied. In these Crimean operations the Red Navy played some role; it had been seriously crippled in the early days of the war and, neither very big nor very effective, its work

The War at Sea

As well as the full-scale carrier battles of the Pacific War and the U-Boat struggle in the Atlantic (which are treated elsewhere) there were many other important and exciting facets of the worldwide naval war.

German U-Boats and surface raiders in fact served in every ocean of the world. The surface raiders, fast, long-range and heavily armed merchant ships, were most active in 1940–41 and during that time they sank more than 600,000 tons of Allied shipping. Major German warships also made a number of commerce-destroying sorties but these were less effective, largely because of restrictive orders from Hitler.

As well as the main transatlantic convoys the Allies had to protect the supplies being sent to northern Russia. If the inhospitable Arctic weather was not enough, these convoys passed close to German air and submarine bases and often came under constant attack. One convoy, PQ.17, was a notable disaster. Equally hard-fought were the battles to send supplies to Malta.

As well as their successively greater losses in the major battles the Japanese Navy found itself at an increasing disadvantage in small scale actions and in the Pacific-wide underwater war. Particularly in the later stages of the New Guinea and Solomons campaigns, the American PT-Boats and other small warships inflicted many losses on the Japanese supply units. There was an even greater imbalance in the effectiveness of the two submarine forces. Both sides succeeded in sinking some major warships but the Japanese had a very poor grasp of the importance of attacking supply and merchant ships. By contrast the Americans achieved a steadily growing degree of success in this field after early equipment problems had been overcome. The Japanese were very slow to institute a convoy system and their escorts' submarine detection equipment and antisubmarine armament were poor. At the outbreak of the war the Japanese merchant fleet had a carrying capacity of about six million tons. At the end of the war, despite the addition of new construction and captures, this had been reduced to just over one million tons. Expressed in other terms, Japan had gone to war largely to win access to the raw material resources of southeast Asia and the East Indies, and although much of this territory was still held by the Japanese in 1945 the resources were useless without the means of transporting them. Even round the Japanese Home Islands sea traffic was reduced to very small coastal vessels by 1945. The US submarine force played a vital part in the final Allied victory.

in the war would be largely confined to cooperation with the Red Army.

Meanwhile, the Germans, still ill-prepared for winter, settled down in their 'hedgehogs,' strongly fortified defensive positions, and awaited the arrival of fresh troops which Hitler had reluctantly decided to dispatch eastward.

When the Soviet offensive began Hitler immediately ordered that there should be no retreat by the German forces. Although the Germans were in fact pushed back in many areas it is now generally agreed by historians that Hitler's policy was correct in this case. After the initial Soviet strength had been expended it was found that the individual German positions could hold out, often with the help of supplies brought in by air, whereas a full scale retreat might well have been completely disastrous. The comparative success of the no retreat policy confirmed Hitler's belief in his own military judgment and his disdain for the advice of his generals.

ARCTIC OCEAN

Scharnhorst sunk,
26 Dec 1943

from
1941

MURMANSK

Arctic Circle

ARCHANGEL

REYKJAVIK

TRONDHEIM?

Supplies to Russia

MOSCOW

Battle of the Atlantic
(Peak 1941-43)

LIVERPOOL

KIEL
WILHELMSHAVEN

QUEBEC
MONTREAL

ST. JOHNS

HALIFAX

LORIENT

Bismarck sunk,
27 May 1941

NEW YORK

1942

GIBRALTAR

MALTA

Supplies
to Russia

AZORES

Mediterranean
partially closed
1940-43

HAIFA

ALEXANDRIA

1943-44

SUEZ

BAN
SHA

ATLANTIC OCEAN

1942

German Mid-Atlantic
refuelling zone

CAPE VERDE
IS

PANAMA

PORT OF SPAIN

DAKAR

Airborne supplies
to Middle East

1942

TAKORADI

LAGOS

Equator

1942

NATAL

ASCENSION I

1943-

RIO DE JANEIRO

1939-40

1939-44

1939-44

LOURENÇO
MARQUES

MONTEVIDEO

Battle of the River Plate,
✕ 13 Dec 1939

CAPETOWN

Graf Spee sunk,
13 Dec 1939

1939-44

ANTARCTIC OCEAN

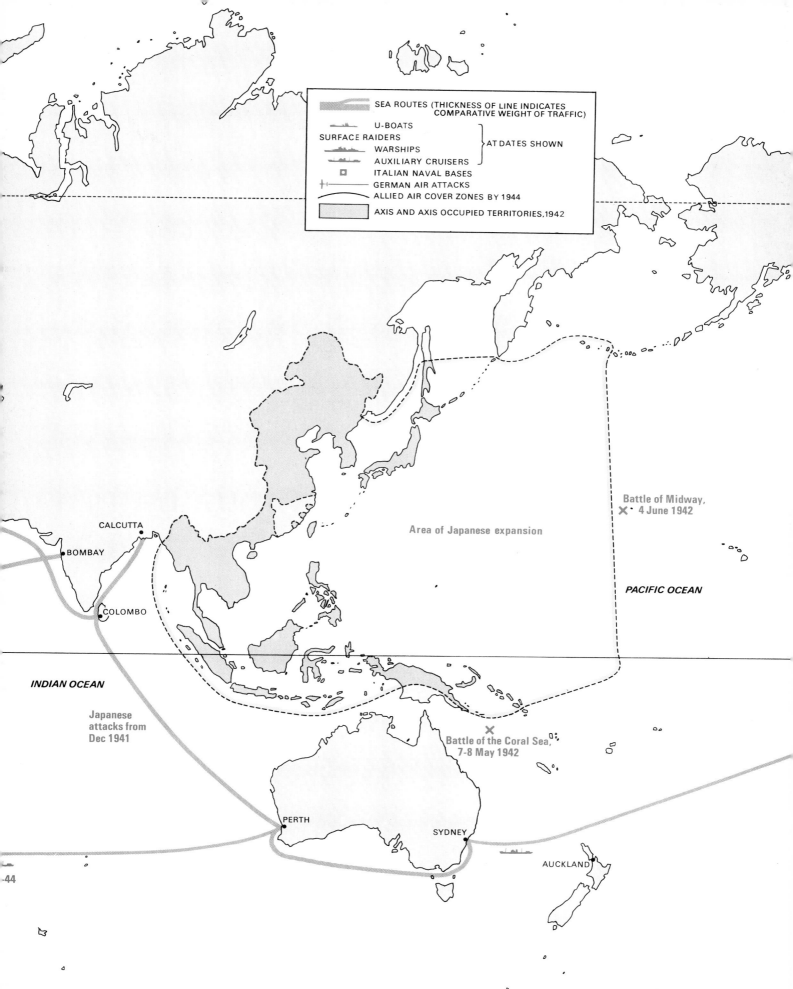

SEA ROUTES (THICKNESS OF LINE INDICATES COMPARATIVE WEIGHT OF TRAFFIC)

U-BOATS

SURFACE RAIDERS

WARSHIPS

AUXILIARY CRUISERS

AT DATES SHOWN

ITALIAN NAVAL BASES

GERMAN AIR ATTACKS

ALLIED AIR COVER ZONES BY 1944

AXIS AND AXIS OCCUPIED TERRITORIES, 1942

Battle of Midway,
4 June 1942

Area of Japanese expansion

PACIFIC OCEAN

CALCUTTA

BOMBAY

COLOMBO

INDIAN OCEAN

Japanese
attacks from
Dec 1941

Battle of the Coral Sea,
7-8 May 1942

PERTH

SYDNEY

AUCKLAND

-44

MERCATOR PROJECTION

The Battle of the Atlantic

Although the German submarine campaign of 1917 had nearly defeated Britain, Hitler's navy was not particularly well prepared to try to improve on this. Submarine building had not been given the highest priority and in the early months of the war Hitler imposed various restrictions on U-Boat operations to try to avoid offending neutral opinion. Drawing on the lessons of 1917 the British immediately introduced a convoy system but escorts could only be provided for part of some voyages and many ships sailed independently. Initially almost all U-Boat successes were from among these 'independents.' Nonetheless, in the first months of war U-Boat successes, although a serious problem, were certainly not out of control.

The events of June 1940 brought about a complete change. British naval responsibilities increased with the Italian entry into the war and the loss of the support of the French fleet, while the German strategic position was transformed by acquisition of bases in western France and Norway for the U-Boats and their supporting long-range reconnaissance aircraft. At this time also the U-Boats had many technical advantages. Their intelligence was good with the German Navy's B Dienst signals service having far more success with the British codes than the British were having with the German Enigma cipher machine. Although the British had Asdic equipment for detecting submerged submarines, radar was still comparatively primitive and escorts did not have sets capable of detecting U-Boats on the surface. A submarine on the surface could only be detected visually and at night a submarine was small and inconspicuous indeed. British patrol aircraft were few in number and, as well as lacking detection equipment, at this stage they were only armed with ineffective antisubmarine bombs. The Battle of the Atlantic became a struggle in all these fields; intelligence, technology, tactics, air support and others, as well as being in the obvious sense an industrial competition with graphs of merchant ship sinkings and cargoes delivered being compared with figures for new construction on both sides and for U-Boats lost. In each of these fields

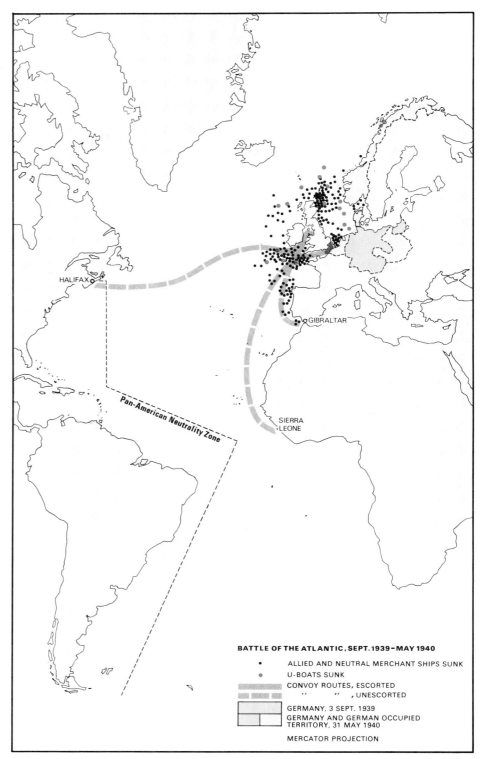

BATTLE OF THE ATLANTIC, SEPT. 1939 – MAY 1940

- ALLIED AND NEUTRAL MERCHANT SHIPS SUNK
- U-BOATS SUNK
- CONVOY ROUTES, ESCORTED
- " " , UNESCORTED
- GERMANY, 3 SEPT. 1939
- GERMANY AND GERMAN OCCUPIED TERRITORY, 31 MAY 1940

MERCATOR PROJECTION

Bottom left: the American destroyer
Reuben James **was the first US Navy ship
to be lost in World War II. She was sunk
by a U-Boat in October 1941 before the
USA joined the war.**
**Below: Admiral Dönitz directed the
German U-Boat offensive against Allied
merchant shipping.**
**Bottom: a tanker blazes after being
torpedoed by a U-Boat.**

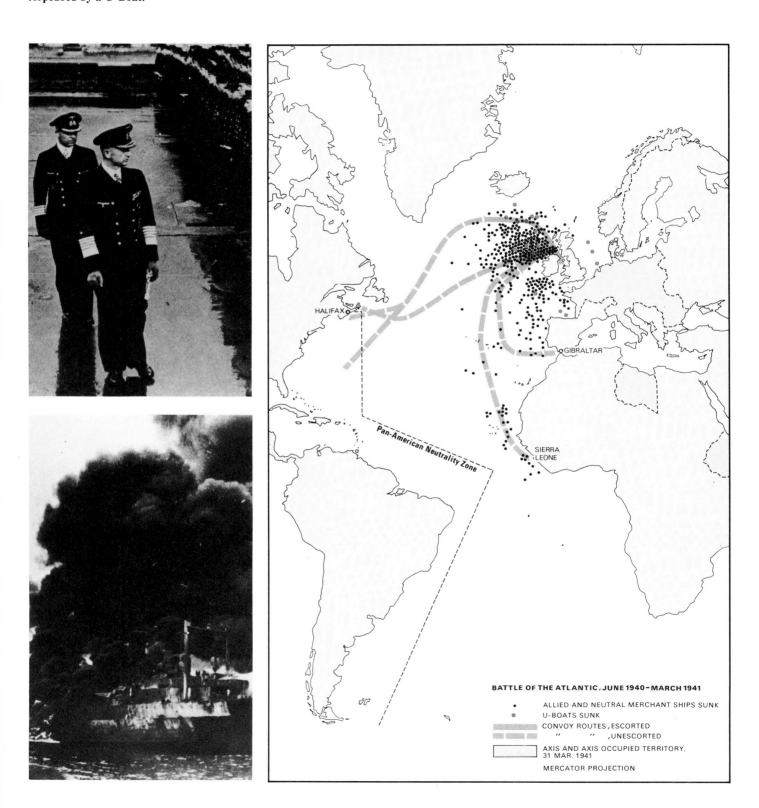

BATTLE OF THE ATLANTIC, JUNE 1940 – MARCH 1941

- •   ALLIED AND NEUTRAL MERCHANT SHIPS SUNK
- •   U-BOATS SUNK

CONVOY ROUTES , ESCORTED

      "   "   , UNESCORTED

AXIS AND AXIS OCCUPIED TERRITORY,
31 MAR. 1941

MERCATOR PROJECTION

HALIFAX

GIBRALTAR

SIERRA
LEONE

Pan-American Neutrality Zone

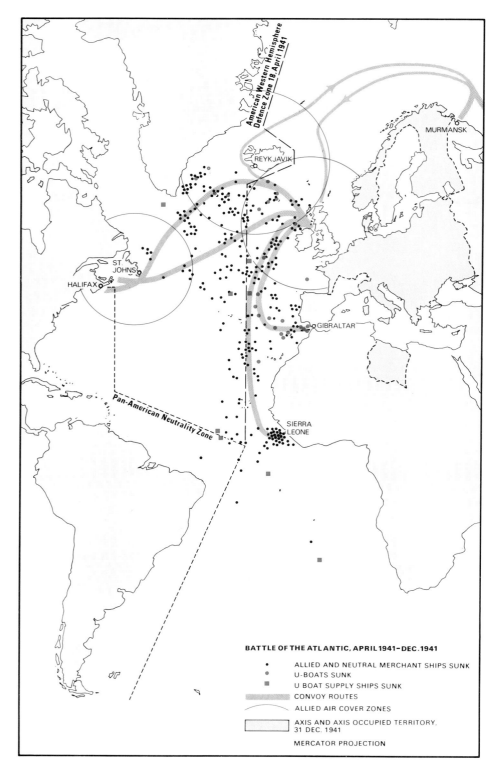

BATTLE OF THE ATLANTIC, APRIL 1941–DEC. 1941

• ALLIED AND NEUTRAL MERCHANT SHIPS SUNK
• U-BOATS SUNK
■ U BOAT SUPPLY SHIPS SUNK
━━ CONVOY ROUTES
━━ ALLIED AIR COVER ZONES
▭ AXIS AND AXIS OCCUPIED TERRITORY, 31 DEC. 1941

MERCATOR PROJECTION

there were gradual developments and sudden breakthroughs.

For the second half of 1940 the U-Boats were on top and the period was known to the German submariners as the 'happy time.' A number of 'ace' commanders each achieved many successes. 'Wolf pack' tactics were developed in which a group of U-Boats made co-ordinated attacks on a convoy in order to swamp the escorts. However, by March 1941 the happy time was definitely over. The German U-Boat strength was virtually at its lowest point, the escort forces were becoming stronger, radar equipment was more widely available and in March three of the highest-scoring U-Boat aces were lost. Also in that month Churchill formed a high-level Battle of the Atlantic Committee (the first use of this title for the campaign) to oversee British efforts in all aspects of the struggle. The careful organization of military, industrial and scientific resources that this encouraged outmatched anything the Germans created and in time contributed greatly to Allied success.

The period from April to December 1941 was one of balance. The strength of the German operational U-Boat fleet was trebled but November 1941 showed the lowest shipping losses of the war to that date. There were various reasons for the

**Left: a US Navy submarine-chaser fires
a depth charge at a suspected U-Boat
contact off the United States Atlantic
coast in 1942.**

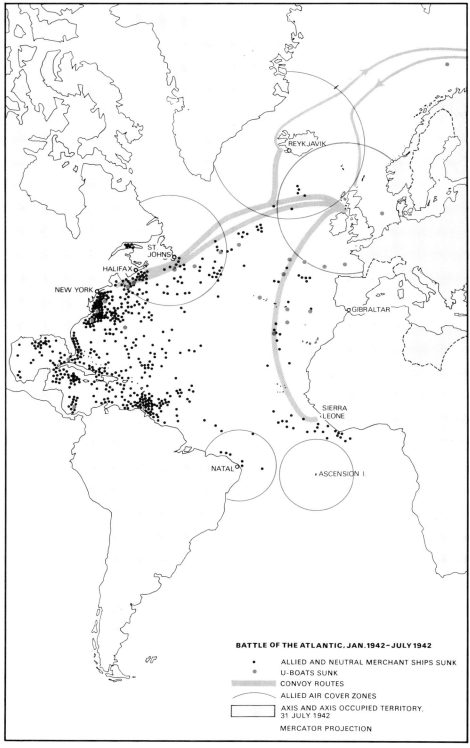

BATTLE OF THE ATLANTIC, JAN. 1942 – JULY 1942

- • ALLIED AND NEUTRAL MERCHANT SHIPS SUNK
- • U-BOATS SUNK
- CONVOY ROUTES
- ALLIED AIR COVER ZONES
- AXIS AND AXIS OCCUPIED TERRITORY, 31 JULY 1942

MERCATOR PROJECTION

better Allied performance. The United States was moving into a more belligerent position both as an industrial supplier and as a military partner providing escorts for convoys in some areas. Following a breakthrough in May 1941 British intelligence was able to read many German signals until changes in February 1942. Convoys were therefore diverted away from U-Boat packs and U-Boats and their supply ships were intercepted and sunk.

The situation was transformed once more with the US entry into the war. U-Boats quickly began operations off the US East Coast and to their delight found virtually peacetime conditions prevailing. Ships sailed unescorted, showed lights at night and even on occasion sent radio signals giving their positions in plain language. The US Navy was naturally distracted by the sudden demands of the Pacific war but the anti-submarine patrols mounted were easily avoided by the U-Boats and were no substitute for even the least effective convoy system. Gradually, however, a convoy system was introduced and in July 1942 was extended south from Florida to cover most of the Caribbean. By the end of July the U-Boats were beginning to resume the struggle for the main North Atlantic convoy routes and their second happy time was over.

Right: Pearl Harbor under attack by warplanes of the Imperial Japanese Navy on 7 December 1941.

Right: Pearl Harbor under attack by warplanes of the Imperial Japanese Navy on 7 December 1941.

Pearl Harbor

At 0755 local time on 7 December 1941 Japanese carrier aircraft attacked the main base of the US Pacific Fleet at Pearl Harbor. They gained complete strategic and tactical surprise. They sank or crippled five of the eight battleships in the port and destroyed 188 aircraft for the loss of 29 of the attacking planes.

The Japanese attack was planned by Admiral Yamamoto and the six aircraft carriers and two battleships of the strike force were led by Admiral Nagumo. The pilots were well trained and their equipment, some of it specially developed, was good. The fine Zero fighter in particular presented the Allies with many unforeseen problems in the months to come. There were, however, two omissions in the Japanese achievement. The US Pacific Fleet aircraft carriers were absent and escaped damage and the massive oil-storage facilities of the base were not struck as Nagumo's staff recommended. These factors combined to provide a solid foundation on which the industrial power of the United States could prepare a comeback. As the far-sighted Admiral Yamamoto had warned the other Japanese leaders,

Japan could expect a few months of success but would then be swamped.

Nonetheless the American authorities had little reason for complacency. US codebreaking services had intercepted a mass of low-level Japanese radio traffic which suggested that an attack, perhaps on Pearl Harbor, was imminent. More importantly, the highest-level Japanese diplomatic cipher had been broken and the final message to the Japanese ambassador in Washington was intercepted. Partly because it was a Sunday, this intercept was passed slowly and there was a delay in sending a warning.

The warning did not reach Pearl Harbor until around midday.

Peacetime customs and inexperience had important detailed effects also. Aircraft on Oahu airfields were parked vulnerably close together; boxes for antiaircraft ammunition were kept locked; large portions of ships' crews were ashore for the day; a submarine sighting by a patrol ship was ignored and a radar warning was disregarded.

The 'day of infamy' (President Roosevelt's description) convinced the American people of the need for war and in the end Yamamoto's prediction was proved correct.

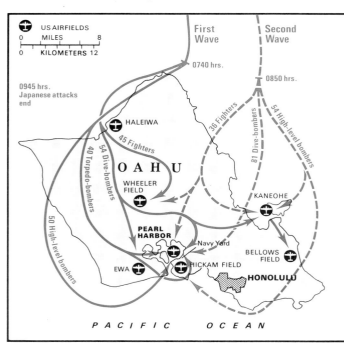

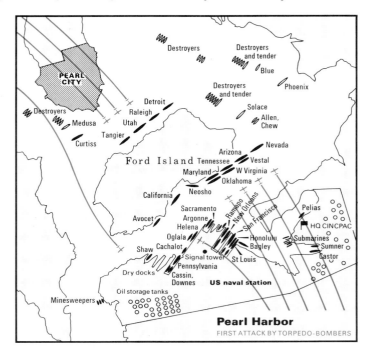

Pearl Harbor
FIRST ATTACK BY TORPEDO-BOMBERS

The Conquest of Malaya

The British withdrawal in Malaya and the fall of Singapore on 15 February 1942 were described by Churchill as the worst disaster in British military history. The British, Australian and Indian forces lost 138,000 men. Many of the prisoners later died of maltreatment or were murdered in the Japanese prison camps. The Japanese lost less than 10,000 casualties. By their own most optimistic assessments the campaign was expected to last 100 days. It took only 70.

The Japanese forces deployed for the attack were three divisions from General Yamashita's Twenty-fifth Army. They were supported by about 200 tanks and 500 aircraft. The Allied infantry force was at least as strong but had virtually no tanks and few antitank weapons. General Percival was in command. The RAF had about 150 aircraft in Malaya, most of them old and inferior types. As well as their crucial advantages in tanks and aircraft the Japanese forces were much better trained and led. By contrast the British military and civilian administration of Malaya was riddled with lethargy and inefficiency. Disruptive peacetime practices of all sorts were maintained up to the start of hostilities and beyond. There was a prevailing attitude of racial contempt for the Japanese who were held to be technologically backward and individually unsuited for military service. Such obtuse racist attitudes were even applied in part to Indian and Malayan soldiers and officers in British service with obvious effects on their morale and fighting efficiency. In a more purely military reckoning the British forces were organized and prepared logistically for a European style of campaign which, in Malayan conditions, made them totally dependent on the few main roads for supplies and tactical movement. The Japanese preferred to travel light, often by bicycle with a ration bag slung over the handlebars, making use of minor roads and tracks and, on the west coast, minor amphibious operations. Little movement was attempted by either side in the true jungle but the Japanese were nonetheless much more flexible and mobile despite, and in part because of, the more lavish scale on which the Allied forces were provided with motor transport. The Jap-

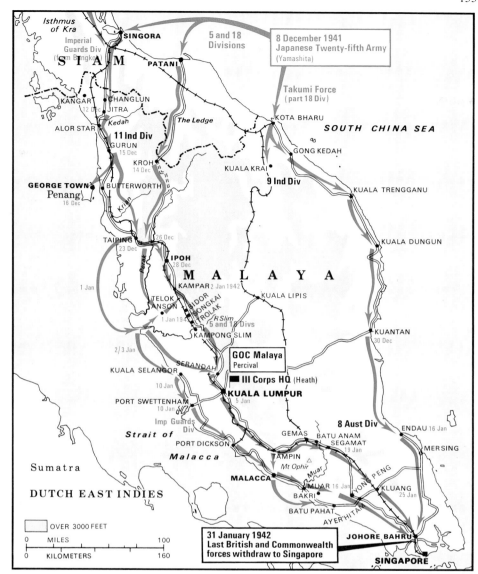

anese tactics were normally based on a combination of two simple techniques. Whenever possible minor roads or paths were used to outflank British forces who were consistently unable to tell whether they were being surrounded by a major force or being bluffed into retreat by a patrol. Alternatively when the Allied units held a strong position the Japanese tanks would break into the position along the main roads and force a retreat. In these ways the Allies were hustled from one defense line to another becoming more disorganized and dispirited as they went.

By the end of January only Singapore remained in British hands. The fleet which the great Singapore naval base had been built to nurture was already gone. The new battleship *Prince of Wales* and the older *Repulse* had been sent to Singapore specifically to deter the Japanese from attacking. They arrived only a few days before the outbreak of war, sailed to attack the Japanese landings on 8 December and were sunk with ease by Japanese aircraft on the 10th, leaving the Allies without a battleship in the Pacific.

The Singapore base did not long survive them. Japanese landings on Singapore Island began on the night of 8/9 February and the British forces surrendered on the 15th. The blow to British and European prestige was felt throughout southeast Asia.

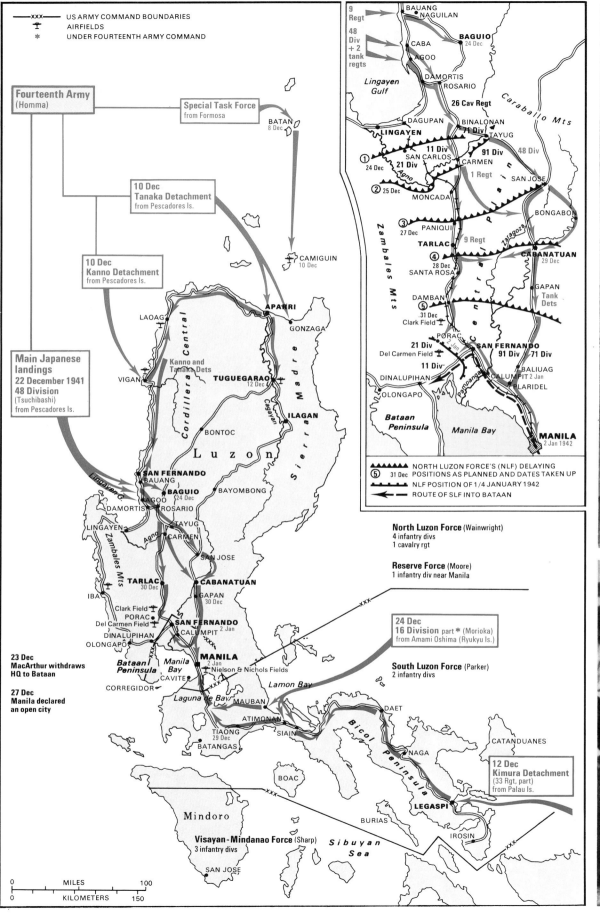

US ARMY COMMAND BOUNDARIES
AIRFIELDS
UNDER FOURTEENTH ARMY COMMAND

Fourteenth Army
(Homma)

Special Task Force
from Formosa

BATAN
8 Dec

10 Dec
Tanaka Detachment
from Pescadores Is.

10 Dec
Kanno Detachment
from Pescadores Is.

CAMIGUIN
10 Dec

**Main Japanese
landings
22 December 1941
48 Division**
(Tsuchibashi)
from Pescadores Is.

LAOAG
VIGAN
Kanno and Tanaka Dets
APARRI
GONZAGA
TUGUEGARAO
12 Dec
ILAGAN
BONTOC
Luzon
BAYOMBONG

Cordillera Central
Sierra Madre
Cagayan

SAN FERNANDO
BAUANG
BAGUIO
24 Dec
AGOO
DAMORTIS
ROSARIO
TAYUG
LINGAYEN
CARMEN
SAN JOSE
Agno
Lingayen G.
Zambales Mts

TARLAC
30 Dec
CABANATUAN
30 Dec
GAPAN
30 Dec
IBA
Clark Field
PORAC
Del Carmen Field
SAN FERNANDO
2 Jan
DINALUPIHAN
CALUMPIT
OLONGAPO

23 Dec
MacArthur withdraws
HQ to Bataan

27 Dec
Manila declared
an open city

Bataan
Peninsula
Manila
Bay
MANILA
2 Jan
Nielson & Nichols Fields
CAVITE
CORREGIDOR
Laguna de Bay
MAUBAN
Lamon Bay
ATIMONAN
TIAONG
29 Dec
SIAIN
BATANGAS
DAET
BOAC
Bicol Peninsula
NAGA
Mindoro
SAN JOSE
CATANDUANES
BURIAS
LEGASPI
IROSIN
Sibuyan
Sea

North Luzon Force (Wainwright)
4 infantry divs
1 cavalry rgt

Reserve Force (Moore)
1 infantry div near Manila

24 Dec
16 Division part * (Morioka)
from Amami Oshima (Ryukyu Is.)

South Luzon Force (Parker)
2 infantry divs

Visayan-Mindanao Force (Sharp)
3 infantry divs

12 Dec
Kimura Detachment
(33 Rgt, part)
from Palau Is.

0   MILES   100
0   KILOMETERS   150

9 Regt
48 Div + 2 tank regts
BAUANG
NAGUILAN
CABA
BAGUIO
24 Dec
AGOO
DAMORTIS
ROSARIO
Lingayen Gulf
Caraballo Mts
26 Cav Regt
DAGUPAN
BINALONAN
LINGAYEN
71 Div
TAYUG
11 Div
SAN CARLOS
91 Div
48 Div
21 Div
CARMEN
1 Regt
SAN JOSE
① 24 Dec
Agno
② 25 Dec
MONCADA
BONGABON
③ 27 Dec
PANIQUI
Zambales Mts
TARLAC
9 Regt
CABANATUAN
29 Dec
④ 28 Dec
SANTA ROSA
Zaragoza
Central
GAPAN
Tank Dets
DAMBAN
⑤ 31 Dec
Clark Field
PORAC
2 Jan
SAN FERNANDO
91 Div
71 Div
21 Div
Del Carmen Field
11 Div
BALIUAG
DINALUPIHAN
CALUMPIT 2 Jan
Pampanga
PLARIDEL
OLONGAPO
Bataan
Peninsula
Manila Bay
MANILA
2 Jan 1942

▲▲▲▲▲ NORTH LUZON FORCE'S (NLF) DELAYING
⑤ 31 Dec POSITIONS AS PLANNED AND DATES TAKEN UP
NLF POSITION OF 1/4 JANUARY 1942
ROUTE OF SLF INTO BATAAN

Left: General Douglas MacArthur commanded in the Philippines until President Roosevelt ordered him to leave. He is seen with General Blamey who led Australian troops in New Guinea under MacArthur's command later in the war.
Bottom: Japanese Marines advance through Caba on Lingayen Gulf in December 1941.

The Fall of the Philippines

As was the case elsewhere in Asia and the Pacific the Allied forces in the Philippines were ill-armed and badly prepared for war. Although the US and Filipino forces had been joined under General MacArthur's command since late July 1941 their training and equipment remained inadequate. MacArthur had about 31,000 regular troops, 19,000 of them American, and something over 100,000 Filipino conscripts to defend the Philippine archipelago. Although the largest force was on Luzon many units were unavoidably dispersed to the other islands of the group. The units on Luzon were divided into the North and South Luzon Forces. The prewar US plan for defending the Philippines was for strong ground and air forces there to hold out until the US Pacific Fleet could bring help. Clearly this would not be forthcoming after the Pearl Harbor attack. Much therefore depended on MacArthur's air strength but at the outbreak of war his air commander General Brereton only had 150 aircraft. By a combination of mismanagement and ill-luck more than half of these were knocked out in Japanese raids on the first day of war. (7 December, Pearl Harbor = 8 December Philippines because of the International Date Line.)

After some early landings to seize airfields for tactical support the main Japanese operation began on 22 December and by 24 December it was clear to MacArthur that he would have to order all his forces to retreat to the Bataan Peninsula. This retreat was successfully accomplished in the subsequent week. The Japanese believed that the campaign was then virtually over and withdrew their best infantry unit, the 48th Division, and a large part of their air support to be used in operations in the East Indies. Attacks by the less experienced Japanese units that remained had some success but by the end of January both they and the defenders were worn out and a long pause ensued. By April, however, the Japanese had built up their forces once more and their renewed attacks compelled an American surrender on the 9th. The final US positions on Corregidor were overrun on 5–6 May. General MacArthur had been evacuated from Bataan in March on orders from President Roosevelt, promising 'I shall return.'

Below: a Japanese column crosses a makeshift footbridge constructed beside the demolished permanent structure south of Moulmein, 1942.

The Dutch East Indies

Owing to their important oil and other resources, the islands of the East Indies were a natural target for the Japanese offensive and once again Japanese air and naval superiority came into its own as the widely spaced garrisons were overwhelmed in turn. The elaborate Japanese plan called for three main lines of attack with comparatively limited ground and air forces being employed in each. The Eastern Force, for example, seized airfields at the northern tip of the Celebes and then used these air bases to cover attacks by the same units on Kendari and Amboina which in turn became bases for the next moves. This leap-frogging technique was repeated in each sector and made efficient and economical use of the forces available and every phase of the operation had powerful air support.

The outnumbered Allied ground and air forces generally fought well but any real check to the Japanese had to come from naval units. Two small actions – off Balikpapan on 24 January and in the Lombok Strait on 19/20 February – failed to achieve any conclusive success. In the larger scale Battle of the Java Sea on 27 February the Allied cruiser and destroyer squadron was decisively beaten and, having been dispersed, was almost wiped out in the next two days. Japanese naval and air supremacy was confirmed on 19 February when carrier aircraft led a devastating raid on Darwin in northern Australia. The Allied forces on Java were the last to succumb on 8 March. A formal surrender was agreed on 12 March 1942.

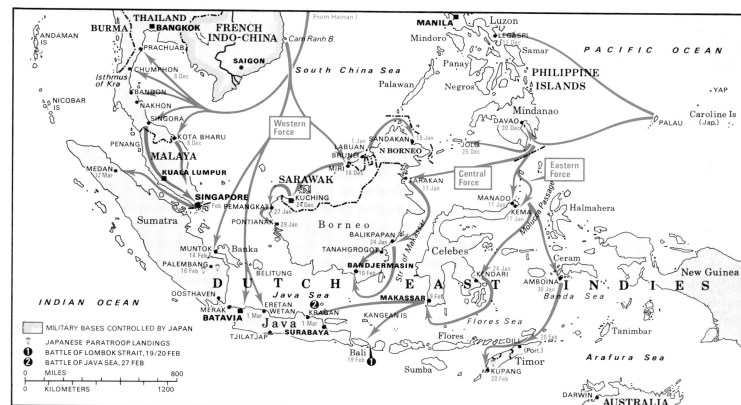

The Japanese Invasion of Burma

With the invasion of Malaya going well the Japanese were ready to extend their offensive into Burma as they had planned. The attack began in mid-January when small units forced the British to abandon their airfields at Victoria Point and Mergui and was extended a few days later when the main body of Fifteenth Army, 33rd and 35th Divisions, moved on Moulmein. The defending forces were also about two divisions strong at this stage but the units had had little collective training and their equipment was poor.

The British plan was simply to defend as stubbornly as possible to prevent the Japanese from reaching Rangoon, the port through which all supplies and reinforcements had to flow. The Allied air forces initially had only one RAF squadron and one squadron of Chennault's American Volunteer Group (The Flying Tigers) to face over 200 Japanese aircraft, but they nonetheless had many successes both in defense of Rangoon and over the front line. On the ground too the battle was fairly well managed for the first three weeks of February, with the Allied forces gradually retreating to the Sittang River. Unfortunately on 23 February the one available bridge over the river was demolished prematurely when most of the 17th Indian Division was still on the wrong side.

After this disaster the pace of the Japanese advance increased and despite the appointment of General Alexander to take command of the British force and the arrival of the veteran British 7th Armoured Brigade, Rangoon quickly fell. The Japanese were now able to draw ground and air reinforcements from Malaya and advance in strength up the great river valleys. Chinese armies (each equivalent in strength to a European division) had by this time arrived to join the Allied forces but the best efforts of their American commander, General Stilwell, could not always make them fight effectively. Both they and the British were soon forced into rapid and continuous retreat. The remnants of the Allied force reached India in mid-May just as the monsoon was beginning to break. They had lost virtually all their heavy equipment.

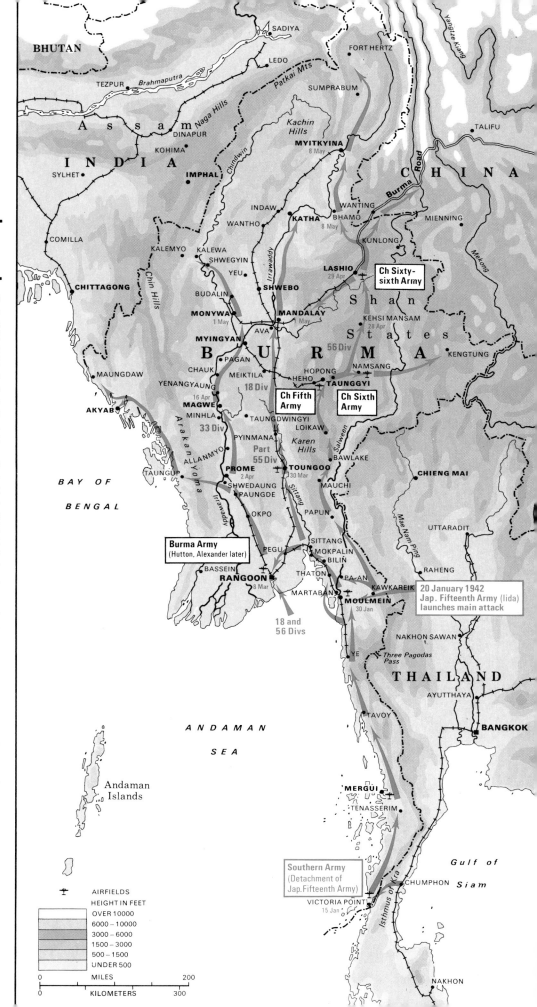

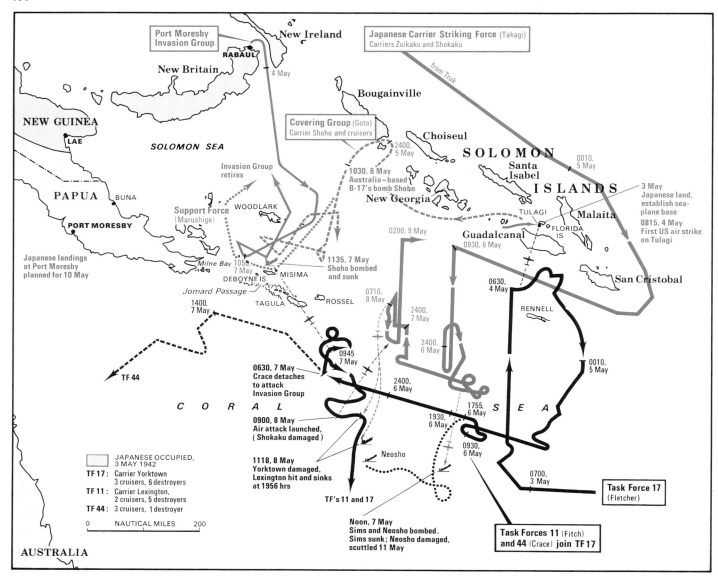

Port Moresby Invasion Group
RABAUL
4 May

Japanese Carrier Striking Force (Takagi)
Carriers Zuikaku and Shokaku
from Truk

New Ireland

New Britain

Bougainville

NEW GUINEA
LAE
SOLOMON SEA

Covering Group (Goto)
Carrier Shoho and cruisers

Choiseul

2400, 5 May

SOLOMON
Santa Isabel

0010, 5 May

ISLANDS

Invasion Group retires

1030, 6 May
Australia–based B-17's bomb Shobo

PAPUA
BUNA

3 May Japanese land, establish seaplane base

New Georgia

WOODLARK

Support Force (Marushige)

0200, 9 May

Guadalcanal
0930, 6 May

TULAGI
FLORIDA IS

Malaita

0815, 4 May First US air strike on Tulagi

PORT MORESBY

Japanese landings at Port Moresby planned for 10 May

Milne Bay 1050, 7 May

1135, 7 May Shoho bombed and sunk

DEBOYNE IS   MISIMA

Jomard Passage

TAGULA   ROSSEL

0710, 8 May

San Cristobal

0630, 4 May

RENNELL

1400, 7 May

0945 7 May

2400, 7 May

2400, 6 May

0010, 5 May

TF 44

0630, 7 May Crace detaches to attack Invasion Group

2400, 6 May

1755, 6 May

C O R A L

0900, 8 May Air attack launched, (Shokaku damaged)

S E A

1930, 6 May

0930, 6 May

JAPANESE OCCUPIED, 3 MAY 1942
TF 17: Carrier Yorktown
3 cruisers, 6 destroyers
TF 11: Carrier Lexington,
2 cruisers, 5 destroyers
TF 44: 3 cruisers, 1 destroyer

1118, 8 May Yorktown damaged, Lexington hit and sinks at 1956 hrs

Neosho

0700, 3 May

Task Force 17 (Fletcher)

0   NAUTICAL MILES   200

TF's 11 and 17

Noon, 7 May Sims and Neosho bombed. Sims sunk; Neosho damaged, scuttled 11 May

Task Forces 11 (Fitch) **and 44** (Crace) **join TF 17**

AUSTRALIA

The Battle of the Coral Sea

Because of the ease with which they had achieved their many successes in the first months of 1942, the Japanese High Command began to consider extending the defensive perimeter which was being set up. This intention was confirmed by the Doolittle Raid on 18 April when bombers launched from an aircraft carrier attacked Tokyo to the shock and dismay of the Japanese leaders. Part of the plan for extending the perimeter was a decision to move into southern Papua by an amphibious attack on Port Moresby. This led to the Battle of the Coral Sea.

The Battle of the Coral Sea holds an important place in naval history as the first naval battle in which the opposing fleets were never in visual contact, leaving the action to be fought entirely by aircraft. Forewarned by codebreaking information the

Americans were able to have two carriers in position to face the Japanese as well as a force of cruisers and destroyers. In addition to the two carriers sent to cover the whole operation the Japanese had a third small carrier in closer support of the invasion group.

The first flurry of action was on 3–4 May when a Japanese seaplane base was established on Tulagi and then attacked the next day by aircraft from the USS *Yorktown*. The Americans then moved south to concentrate their forces and refuel just as the main Japanese operations were getting under way. The action was not renewed until 7 May when Japanese carrier aircraft successfully attacked an American tanker and a destroyer while heavy attacks by land-based aircraft failed to damage any ships of TF.44 which had been unwisely sent to cut off the Japanese Invasion Group. However, American carrier aircraft scored an important success by sinking the *Sholo*. By now the main carrier groups each knew the other's position and a full-scale battle was fought on the 8th. The Japanese lost more aircraft but did

more damage to the American ships especially after errors in damage control contributed to the loss of the *Lexington*. However, with their air strength dissipated the Japanese carriers had to withdraw and the invasion of Port Moresby was cancelled. Thus although the battle was perhaps a draw tactically it was a clear strategic victory for the Americans.

Below left: Yamamoto, Japan's greatest
naval strategist and architect of the Pearl
Harbor attack.
Right: the Japanese heavy cruiser *Mikuma*
abandoned and sinking on 6 June 1942
during the Battle of Midway.

The Battle of Midway

The Japanese High Command decision to extend their defensive perimeter had led firstly to the Battle of the Coral Sea but it was also the motive for the Japanese attack on Midway and the decisive battle which developed there. The Coral Sea battle had important effects on the Midway operation. The two Japanese carriers from the earlier battle were not repaired quickly enough to go to Midway nor were the survivors of their air groups used to bolster the Japanese strength on the other carriers. The Japanese also believed that the *Yorktown* was too seriously damaged to be made ready in time for Midway. In fact she returned to Pearl Harbor with damage that would certainly have taken months to repair in peacetime but she was patched up in 48 hours.

The false assessment of *Yorktown*'s status was only one of a number of intelligence and planning factors that contributed to the Japanese defeat. Admiral Yamamoto believed that, as well as the *Yorktown* being out of action, the other American carriers available, the *Enterprise* and *Hornet*, were likely to be in the South Pacific. Even if this was not the case diversionary attacks on the Aleutians were planned so that the Americans would be distracted from the landings on Midway. Once the capture of the island was complete, the Japanese, warned by their submarine patrols, would destroy the American forces in an all-out battle. Unfortunately for the Japanese the Americans were able to repeat their previous codebreaking successes and thus forewarned they were able to move their carriers into position before the Japanese patrols were established and equally able to disregard the Aleutians attacks so that these became in effect a wasteful dispersal of the Japanese resources (two powerful light carriers and many other ships were employed in the Aleutian operations). The various Midway forces were also widely dispersed leaving further small aircraft and seaplane carriers effectively out of the battle when their scout planes might well have been of decisive help and leaving Nagumo's carriers with only a few ships in company to provide supporting AA fire.

The Japanese were sighted approaching on 3 June and the action began in earnest on

4 June. The Japanese started by virtually wiping out the defending aircraft based on Midway at little cost to themselves. However it was not until the Japanese were ready to recover their aircraft from the first strike that their scouts found the American carriers. The American carrier aircraft were already on their way and made a series of attacks before the Japanese had reorganized to defend properly. Three of the four Japanese carriers were crippled and later sank. The fourth Japanese carrier, the *Hiryu*, fought back causing the *Yorktown* to be abandoned but the *Hiryu* herself was put out of action later in the day. The Japanese leaders made half-hearted attempts on 5

June to close in and fight a gun action with their vastly superior surface forces but the Americans refused to be drawn and the whole operation was abandoned.

Midway was one of the most decisive battles of the war for not only had the Japanese lost four of their best aircraft carriers but with them had gone the cream of their carrier pilots and crews. While they still had a useful supply of aircraft and aircraft carriers the veteran flyers could not be replaced. The next major naval battles in the Pacific, although close fought, would follow the American advance against Guadalcanal. The Japanese had irrevocably lost the initiative.

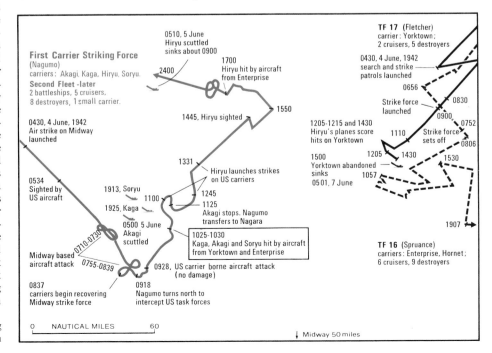

First Carrier Striking Force
(Nagumo)
carriers: Akagi, Kaga, Hiryu, Soryu.
Second Fleet -later
2 battleships, 5 cruisers,
8 destroyers, 1 small carrier.

0430, 4 June, 1942
Air strike on Midway
launched

0534
Sighted by
US aircraft

Midway based
aircraft attack 0710-0730 0755-0839

0837
carriers begin recovering
Midway strike force

0510, 5 June
Hiryu scuttled
sinks about 0900

2400

1700
Hiryu hit by aircraft
from Enterprise

1550

1445, Hiryu sighted

1331

1913, Soryu

1925, Kaga   1100

0500 5 June
Akagi
scuttled

0918
Nagumo turns north to
intercept US task forces

0928, US carrier borne aircraft attack
(no damage)

Hiryu launches strikes
on US carriers

1245

1125
Akagi stops. Nagumo
transfers to Nagara

1025-1030
Kaga, Akagi and Soryu hit by aircraft
from Yorktown and Enterprise

TF 17 (Fletcher)
carrier: Yorktown;
2 cruisers, 5 destroyers

0430, 4 June, 1942
search and strike
patrols launched

0656

Strike force
launched

0830

0900

0752

1110

0806

1205-1215 and 1430
Hiryu's planes score
hits on Yorktown

1500
Yorktown abandoned
sinks
0501, 7 June

1205   1430

1057

1530

1907

TF 16 (Spruance)
carriers: Enterprise, Hornet;
6 cruisers, 9 destroyers

0   NAUTICAL MILES   60

↓ Midway 50 miles

Rommel's Advance into Egypt

Even as he retreated following the prolonged Crusader battles for Tobruk Rommel was looking for an opportunity to riposte. His supply and reinforcement position was improving as Malta came under ever heavier attack and the British communications were naturally being extended by their advance as well as their forces being weakened by withdrawals of troops for the Far East leaving inexperienced units, notably 1st Armoured Division, at the front.

Rommel's German Units (DAK, *Deutsches Afrika Korps*) began probing attacks on 21 January 1942 and in less than three weeks had hustled the British forces back to a line from Gazala to Bir Hacheim, inflicting many casualties. Eighth Army morale was severely damaged in the process, with the lack of trust between infantry and tank units that had become evident during the Crusader battles being further confirmed.

This lack of trust and cooperation became even more obvious when Rommel resumed his offensive on 26 May. Faulty intelligence information and Rommel's bold plan placed the German forces in a very weak position initially but General Ritchie failed to order counterattacks sufficiently promptly to take advantage. When the counterattacks were made they were poorly organized and the numerically-superior British armor was squandered. Rommel's forces then burst forward and stormed into Tobruk on 20 June capturing men and supplies.

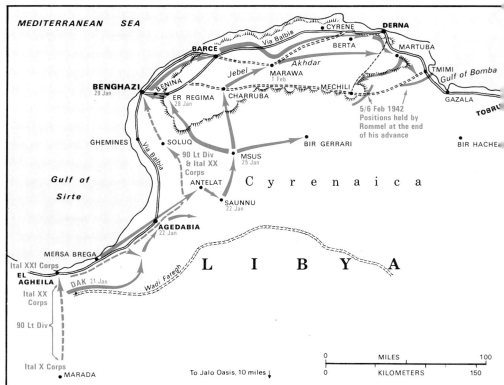

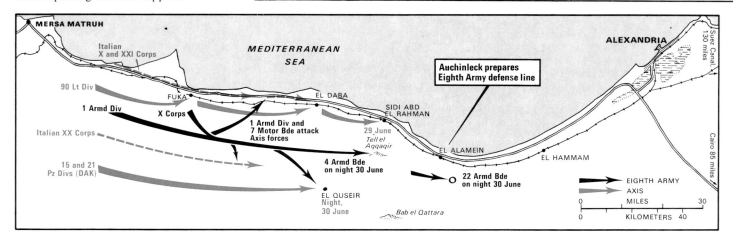

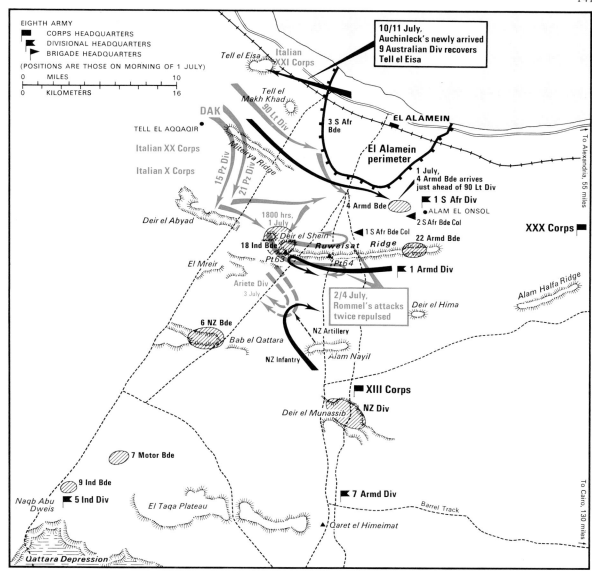

EIGHTH ARMY
■ CORPS HEADQUARTERS
▬ DIVISIONAL HEADQUARTERS
▬ BRIGADE HEADQUARTERS
(POSITIONS ARE THOSE ON MORNING OF 1 JULY)

0   MILES   10
0   KILOMETERS   16

10/11 July,
Auchinleck's newly arrived
9 Australian Div recovers
Tell el Eisa

Italian
XXI Corps

Tell el Eisa

Tell el
Makh Khad

90 Lt Div

DAK

TELL EL AQQAQIR

Italian XX Corps

Italian X Corps

15 Pz Div

21 Pz Div

Miteirya Ridge

Deir el Abyad

1800 hrs,
1 July

Deir el Shein

18 Ind Bde

Ruweisat   Ridge

Pt 63   Pt 64

El Mreir

Ariete Div

3 July

2/4 July,
Rommel's attacks
twice repulsed

Deir el Hima

Alam Halfa Ridge

EL ALAMEIN

El Alamein
perimeter

3 S Afr
Bde

1 July,
4 Armd Bde arrives
just ahead of 90 Lt Div

4 Armd Bde

1 S Afr Div

ALAM EL ONSOL

2 S Afr Bde Col

1 S Afr Bde Col

22 Armd Bde

1 Armd Div

XXX Corps

To Alexandria, 55 miles

6 NZ Bde

Bab el Qattara

NZ Artillery

NZ Infantry

Alam Nayil

XIII Corps

NZ Div

Deir el Munassib

7 Motor Bde

9 Ind Bde

5 Ind Div

Naqb Abu
Dweis

El Taqa Plateau

7 Armd Div

Barrel Track

Qaret el Himeimat

To Cairo, 130 miles

Qattara Depression

At this point the Axis plan was for Rommel to pause while the German and Italian naval and air forces concentrated for an invasion of Malta but, as the hero of the hour, the newly promoted Field Marshal Rommel successfully argued for this plan to be abandoned in favor of an advance to Egypt using the newly captured supplies.

Nonetheless there is no doubt that the British were in considerable disarray and their next attempt to halt Rommel, at Mersa Matruh on 26–27 June, was soon overcome leaving yet more booty to fall into German hands. General Auchinleck, the British Commander in Chief, Middle East, had now taken over tactical command of Eighth Army having sacked General Ritchie, and his firmer control soon became evident. However the retreat had to continue to the next defensible position which was being prepared by Auchinleck's few reserve units in a line south from a small rail station called El Alamein. The move from Mersa Matruh to Alamein was one of the most curious of the war, with advancing Axis columns mixed with retreating British.

The First Battle of Alamein

After the headlong retreat from Mersa Matruh the next defensible position for the Eighth Army was at El Alamein where the gap between the more or less impassable Qattara Depression and the sea was fairly narrow. Although Auchinleck had only a few imperfectly organized reserve units with which to prepare the position in addition to those retreating to it, Rommel's situation was hardly better. He was relying almost entirely on the booty from Tobruk and Mersa Matruh to provide his fuel and other supplies. The recent battles had also reduced his strength severely until he had less than 2000 German infantry and perhaps 65 German tanks. Nonetheless Rommel was confident that if he could maintain his momentum he could bounce the British out of their position and strike for the Nile.

However the initial German and Italian

attacks were fought to a standstill on 2–4 July, a feature of the battle being the improved coordination of Eighth Army's artillery units. Auchinleck was now ready to make some limited counterattacks and chose the Italian *Sabratha* Division at Tell El Eisa as his first victim on 10–11 July. This and other minor operations over the next few days compelled Rommel to spend precious fuel moving his German units to help the Italian formations which were the deliberately-chosen British targets. There were larger Allied efforts in the Ruweisat Ridge area on 14 and 21–22 July and, although the British armor lost heavily because of poor cooperation with its supporting infantry and poor tactics, Rommel's forces too were worn out.

Although General Auchinleck's refusal to continue these attacks completed Churchill's disillusion with his leadership and lost him his command, many commentators now regard this series of actions, together known as the First Battle of El Alamein, as marking the real turning point in North Africa rather than the famous Second Battle.

The German Advance to Stalingrad

In early April Hitler issued his instructions for the 1942 offensive. This time the central sector was to remain fairly quiet, while in the north the capture of Leningrad was envisioned. However, the main effort was to be in the south. Here the Red Army was to be engaged and beaten on the River Don, which would permit an advance to the prized Caucasian oilfields and the capture or neutralization of Stalingrad which, apart from being 'Stalin's City,' was an important rail and river center, and also the site of tank and armament factories. In preparation for this campaign General Manstein expelled the Red Army from the Kerch Peninsula and captured the Crimea, including the naval base of Sevastopol.

The main offensive by Army Group South was delayed for four weeks by a big Soviet attack at Kharkov, so it did not begin until the end of June. But it made good progress and reached the Don in mid-July. Here it was held by a Soviet counteroffensive at Voronezh, but in the south Rostov was again captured by the Germans. At this point

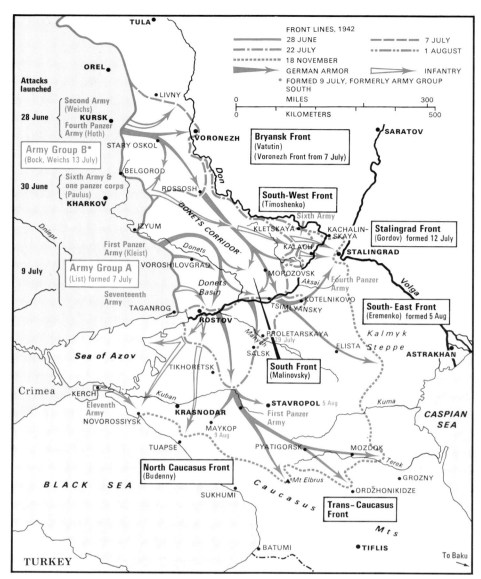

Below left: a Soviet gun crew firing in Stalingrad's factory district during the bitter fighting in 1942.
Below: Soviet Illyushin IL-2s were very successful ground-attack aircraft, but suffered heavy losses.

Hitler appears to have changed the emphasis of his attack; Stalingrad was to be the main target, although the Caucasian oilfields were to remain a priority. His staff officers realized that, with the Red Army still not decisively beaten, this division of effort was strategically risky, but they were over-ruled and some were dismissed by Hitler.

In the Caucasus the German Army Group A did make a rapid advance, capturing Novorossiysk. Paradoxically, shortly after occupying the outlying Maykop oilfield, the German advance ran out of fuel. The main Caucasian oilfields remained out of reach; the allocation of 300,000 troops to the capture of Stalingrad meant that the Caucasus thrust had not achieved its main object.

The German attack on Stalingrad was a simple frontal assault. To have encircled the city would have entailed crossing the Volga, which the Germans felt unable to undertake with the resources available. The Russians deliberately kept as few men as possible in the city itself, relying on high morale and determination to ensure that the Germans would need to fight bitterly for every street and building. This in fact is what happened. Soviet soldiers, joined by armed civilians, withdrew only inch by inch as shells and bombs destroyed the city about their ears. More and more German units were drawn into the brutal struggle while the Soviet commanders were able to husband their forces and prepare for a counteroffensive.

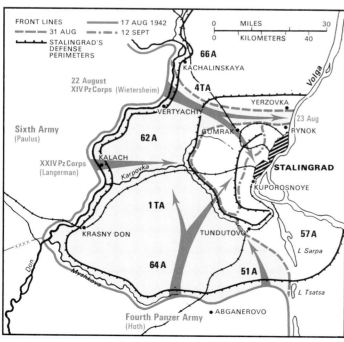

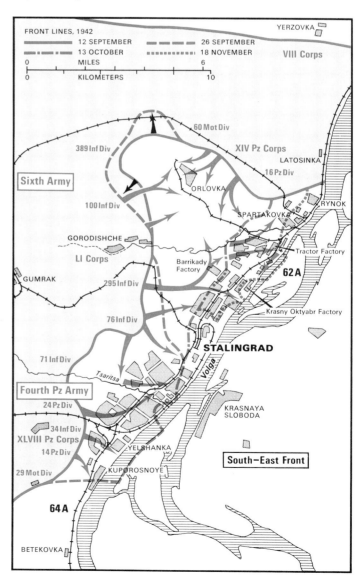

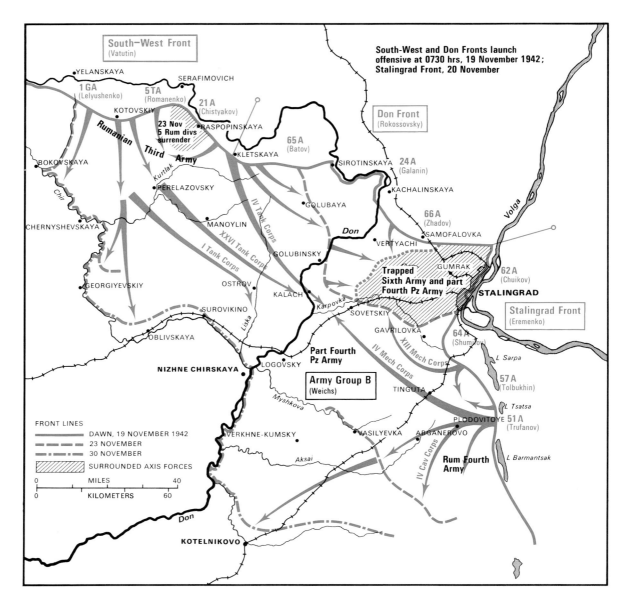

South-West Front
(Vatutin)

South-West and Don Fronts launch
offensive at 0730 hrs, 19 November 1942;
Stalingrad Front, 20 November

YELANSKAYA
1 GA
(Lelyushenko)
5 TA
(Romanenko)
SERAFIMOVICH
21 A
(Chistyakov)
KOTOVSKIY
23 Nov
5 Rum divs
surrender
RASPOPINSKAYA
65 A
(Batov)
KLETSKAYA
Don Front
(Rokossovsky)
BOKOVSKAYA
Rumanian
Third
Army
KURTLAK
PERELAZOVSKY
GOLUBAYA
SIROTINSKAYA
24 A
(Galanin)
KACHALINSKAYA
CHERNYSHEVSKAYA
MANOYLIN
XXVI Tank Corps
IV Tank Corps
Don
66 A
(Zhadov)
SAMOFALOVKA
Volga
I Tank Corps
GOLUBINSKY
VERTYACHI
GEORGIYEVSKIY
OSTROV
KALACH
Karpovka
Trapped
Sixth Army and part
Fourth Pz Army
GUMRAK
62 A
(Chiukov)
STALINGRAD
SUROVIKINO
Liska
SOVETSKIY
Stalingrad Front
(Eremenko)
OBLIVSKAYA
GAVRILOVKA
64 A
(Shumilov)
L Sarpa
Part Fourth
Pz Army
LOGOVSKY
Myshkova
Army Group B
(Weichs)
XIII Mech Corps
IV Mech Corps
TINGUTA
57 A
(Tolbukhin)
L Tsatsa
NIZHNE CHIRSKAYA
VERKHNE-KUMSKY
VASILYEVKA
PLODOVITOYE
ABGANEROVO
51 A
(Trufanov)
Aksai
IV Cav Corps
Rum Fourth
Army
L Barmantsak
Don
KOTELNIKOVO

FRONT LINES
———— DAWN, 19 NOVEMBER 1942
– – – 23 NOVEMBER
–·–·– 30 NOVEMBER
///// SURROUNDED AXIS FORCES
0   MILES   40
0   KILOMETERS   60

The Stalingrad Counteroffensive

While Soviet resistance inside Stalingrad prevented the Germans capturing that city in its entirety, the Soviet High Command was assembling forces north of the Don for a counteroffensive. The general situation was that the German general, Paulus, had about 300,000 men concentrated to the west of Stalingrad. His northwest flank was protected by Italian and Rumanian troops while on his southern flank he had more Rumanian units.

The Soviet offensive began on 19 November 1942. It consisted of some diversionary action on the central, Moscow, front with the aim of attracting German reinforcements which otherwise might be sent to Stalingrad, and the main thrust, which was to relieve Stalingrad. General Zhukov, disposing of the whole Soviet

operational reserve, had three army groups ['fronts'] which were to attack from the north, south, and northwest, initially concentrating their blows on the Italians and Rumanians, whose morale was lower than the Germans'. In fact the Italian and Rumanian positions in the northwest soon crumbled, enabling the Soviet troops to penetrate into the German rear and then link up with the Stalingrad Front advancing westward from its concentration area in the south. Paulus was now surrounded but Hitler, assured by Göring that an airlift could keep the encircled troops supplied, insisted that the siege of Stalingrad should continue. In mid-December General Manstein led an attack which broke through the Russian lines, by then far to the west, in an attempt to relieve Paulus, but the Soviet high command, diverting troops from the battle with Paulus, blocked this move. With Hitler's agreement Paulus made no attempt to break out and join Manstein. The Red Army could then turn back to the steady destruction of Paulus's Sixth Army. On 2 February

1943 the German forces at Stalingrad surrendered, after being reduced to little more than a headquarters and isolated detachments. Although the Germans had been defeated earlier by the British at El Alamein, this was the first really major defeat suffered by the German Army and had an enormous psychological effect. Hitler had shown incompetent generalship; his refusal to allow Paulus to withdraw from Stalingrad while there was still time was directly responsible for this catastrophic defeat. Many thousands of the German troops taken prisoner died in Russian camps. Many were held for several years after the end of the war.

Bottom: Russian troops overrun a forward German airfield on the outskirts of Stalingrad. The loss of such airfields made it even more difficult for Göring to keep his promise to supply the surrounded army.

The Battle of Alam Halfa

Despite the defensive success of the First Battle of El Alamein, Churchill arrived in the Middle East early in August 1942 determined to make changes. After some deliberation General Alexander was chosen to replace Auchinleck as Commander in Chief and Montgomery arrived to take over at Eighth Army. It was clear that Rommel was going to attack again soon in an effort to reach the Nile before the British forces were fully rebuilt after the disasters of the summer. While historians generally compliment Montgomery on his conduct of the Battle of Alam Halfa which resulted, most believe that it was fought along lines already laid down by Auchinleck. However, some authorities suggest that Montgomery's determined and vigorous leadership was needed to transform a previously half-hearted plan.

Broadly speaking the defense plan was to hold the northern half of the line very strongly while guarding against a 'right hook' outflanking maneuver by fortifying the Alam Halfa Ridge and deploying strong armored forces in the southern area. Such an outflanking move was exactly Rommel's aim but a combination of unexpectedly strong British forward defenses, harrassing air attacks and fuel shortages forced him to turn north earlier than planned. Although some British tank units suffered heavily, the German attacks on Alam Halfa Ridge foundered on an improved British antitank defense system. On 2 September Rommel ordered a retreat. By 6 September the Axis forces were back where they started and settling down to meet a British attack.

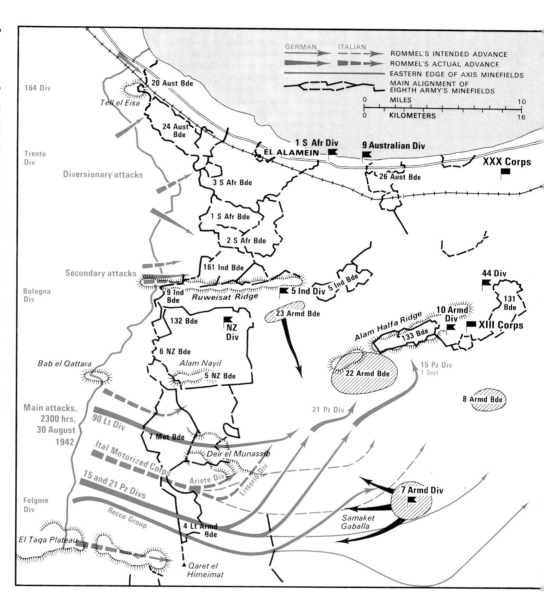

Advance in the Caucasus

Even before Paulus surrendered at Stalingrad the Soviet High Command was able to divert part of its southern, Stalingrad Front to the southwest toward Rostov, the aim being to cut off the German Army Group A in the Caucasus. The Soviet advance was so rapid that Rostov was indeed threatened by the beginning of January. At the same time, the Russian Trans-Caucasus Front, which hitherto had been merely holding back the Germans on the line of the Terek River, launched a counteroffensive. Threatened from both north and south, Kleist, the commander of Army Group A, decided that an immediate withdrawal was the only guarantee of survival. But he was too late to escape through Rostov. Only one of his armies, the motorized First Panzer Army, achieved this. The remainder of Kleist's troops took refuge in the Taman Peninsula.

Here they were beset by both Soviet fronts and driven into a small defended area around Novorossiysk. Rostov fell in mid-February.

By this time, although the Russian tactics of mass assault continued to cause them casualties several times higher than those suffered by the Germans, and although the losses of the first months of the war had not been replaced, the Red Army had become a formidable fighting force. One reason for this was the psychological effect of the Stalingrad battle which removed the last trace of defeatism from the Russian ranks. Another was that the ineffective Party generals like Voroshilov and Budyenny had been removed to positions where they could do less harm to the military effort.

Right: Manstein headed the German Army Group Don during the Kharkov battles. He had devised the plan for the attack on France in 1940 and is regarded as one of the most able generals of the war.

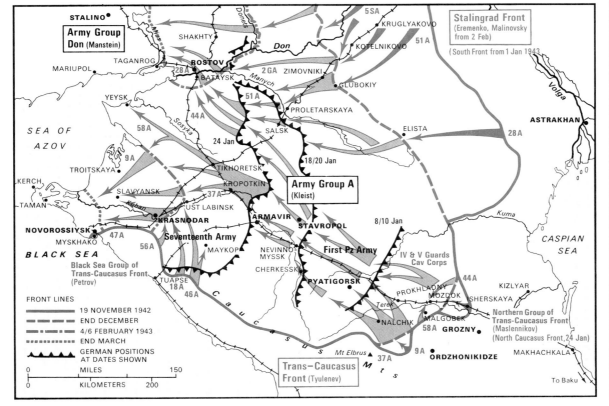

Bottom: Russian soldiers in the northern Caucasus during the battle for Yuzel settlement. The soldier on the left is armed with an obsolescent antitank rifle.

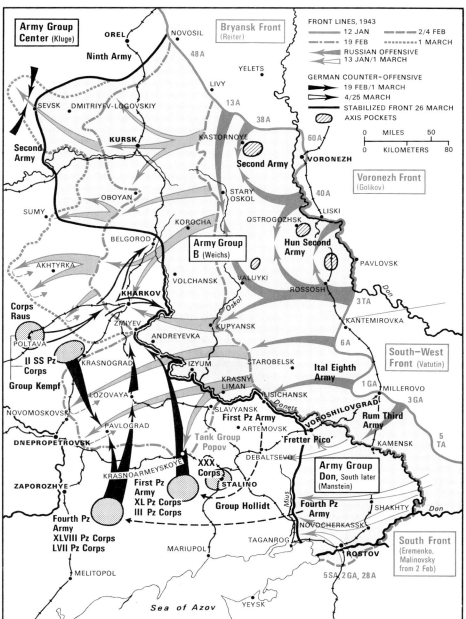

The Advance to Kharkhov and the German Counterattack

Before the defeats of World War I the Russian Army had been popularly known as the 'Russian Steamroller.' By 1943 it was evident to the Germans that this description was still applicable. The USSR had lost millions of men and enormous expanses of its most productive territory, yet more and more well-equipped divisions were entering service. Even while they were squeezing the last remnants of Paulus's army in Stalingrad, the Russians were undertaking offensives not only in the Caucasus, but also in the Ukraine, with Kharkov as its main objective.

The Soviet High Command devoted four fronts to this attack, including the new

South Front comprising divisions released from Stalingrad. The northern prong of the attack made dramatic advances, surrounding much of the German Second Army and putting the rest to flight. In the center, Kharkov was captured early in February, while in the south the Russian advance went equally well at first, although in its onward rush it created vulnerable salients Manstein, commanding Army Group Don, exploited the opportunity to attack the strong but over-extended Southwest Front. He assembled a reconstituted army of 24 divisions, of which 12 were armored, around Dnepropetrovsk and moved north to engage the Russians south of Kharkov, pushing them back over the River Donets and, on 2 March, recapturing Kharkov. After this effort the exhaustion of both sides, and the onset of the thaw, brought the winter campaign of 1942–43 to a halt. Despite

Manstein's technically brilliant attacks the manpower losses of the winter campaign had been disastrous for the Germans.

El Alamein

Following their defeat in the Battle of Alam Halfa and bearing in mind their continuing fuel supply problems which that battle highlighted, the German leaders prepared to conduct the next battle in the North African theater from strong defense lines rather than rely on the mobility which had been the Afrika Korps' trade mark in the past. Although the forward defenses were mainly manned by Italian troops, German units were intermingled with them to provide extra strength and reliability. The fuel shortage meant that the armored reserve had to be split up to ensure that at least part of it would have enough fuel to reach any threatened sector. For the month before the battle Rommel was in Germany on sick leave and General Stumme commanded in his place. Rommel returned to Africa on 25 October after the battle was under way.

Throughout his earlier career General Montgomery had shown himself to be deeply concerned with improving the morale and training of the troops, and planning the battle meticulously before beginning to fight. This concern was nowhere more evident than in the preparation for Alamein. Many of the faults which had affected Eighth Army in the past were ironed out and confidence was high. The plan, as shown below, was for infantry units of XXX Corps to win corridors through the Axis minefields through which the armor of X Corps would pass unhindered, ready to meet and destroy the German tanks in open ground.

Despite the careful preparations on which Montgomery insisted, the actual events were only broadly similar to this plan. The powerful preparatory artillery barrage helped the infantry attacks to make a good start

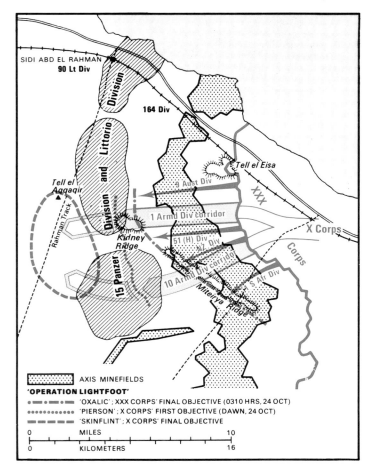

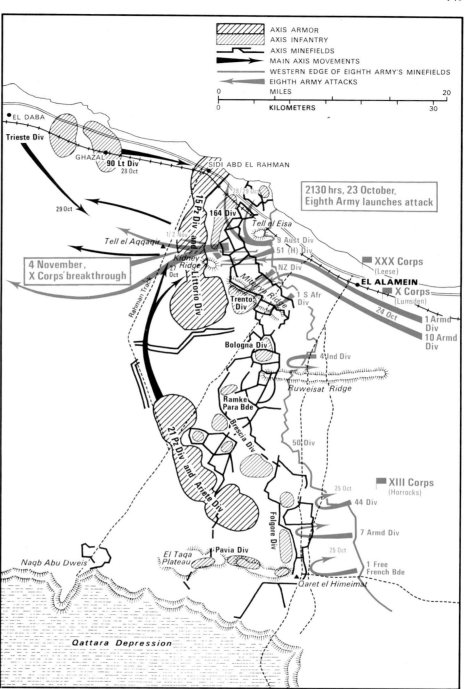

but it proved impossible to move the tanks forward in the way envisioned. The German defense was not helped by General Stumme's death from a heart attack on the afternoon of the 24th as heavy fighting continued. The German 21st Panzer Division was kept out of the main battle for the first days by diversionary efforts by XIII Corps. Although attempts to push the main British armored force forward continued, by the 26th it was clear that it had becomed down and Montgomery largely halted his forces for regrouping. The chief events of the following five days were unsuccessful German counterattacks throughout the main sector and a powerful northward advance by 9th Australian Division which drew in the German reserves. Montgomery's revised breakthrough plan, Operation Supercharge, was put into action on the night of 1/2 November. Although Rommel's forces fought well, by the end of the 2nd he was left with only 35 tanks. He signalled to Hitler that he must retreat. Hitler immediately forbade this but by 4 November further German and Italian losses made the retreat inevitable. Although the Battle of El Alamein was undoubtedly a decisive success for the Allies, Montgomery was unable to follow up his victory quickly enough and the remainder of Rommel's forces was able to make good its retreat.

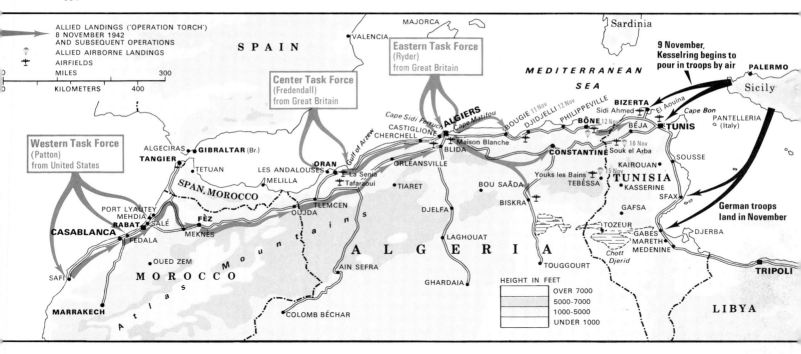

Operation Torch

On 8 November 1942 as Rommel's forces were retreating from Egypt, American and British troops began a series of landings in French North Africa. The codename for the landings was Operation Torch. Although the operation gave US ground forces their first large-scale opportunity to fight in the European war, the plan had been strongly opposed by the US Chiefs of Staff who saw it as a diversion from their preferred strategy of preparing exclusively for a direct invasion of western Europe. This

opposition had been overruled by President Roosevelt because he believed that if the US delayed becoming involved in Europe then pressure would grow in US political circles for the abandonment of the policy of putting the defeat of Germany first.

In preparation for the landings there had been secret talks with various local French leaders (the USA had maintained diplomatic links with Vichy France) in an effort to ensure that the landings would not be resisted by the strong Vichy forces in North Africa. The Americans had taken the lead in this as much Anglo-French hostility remained as a legacy of events of 1940. For this reason also the American presence in the

initial phases of the operation was deliberately increased and publicly exaggerated when in fact the British contribution, particularly in warships and transport shipping, was rather larger. Nonetheless Torch was certainly the first truly combined Allied operation of the war. Whatever his other shortcomings as a general, the Commander in Chief, General Eisenhower, from the outset demonstrated the ability to create a genuinely integrated and efficient staff.

The map shows the three main landing areas and the early advances. Although there was sporadic resistance from the Vichy forces in most areas the landings generally went well with less than 2000

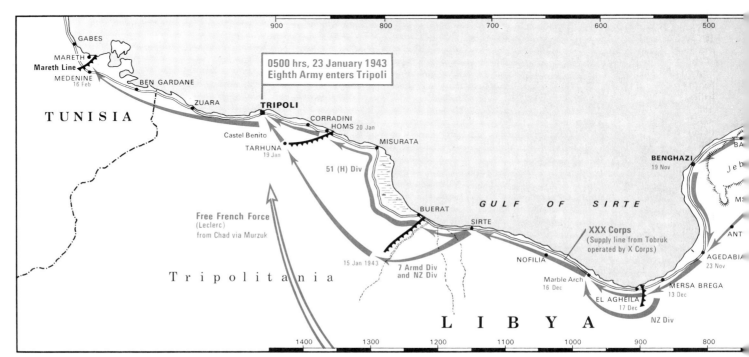

casualties all told. Admiral Darlan, one of the principal leaders of the Vichy government happened to be in Algiers on private business and was captured and persuaded to use his considerable influence in the Allied cause.

Despite the comparative success of the initial landings there were obviously logistic difficulties involved in pushing any large force quickly forward the 400 miles to Tunis. In retrospect it would probably have been better, as some of the planners of the operation had urged, for the initial landings to have been extended as far east as Bône. In the event the Germans reacted with very great speed and on instructions from Hitler and the Commander in Chief, Mediterranean, Field Marshal Kesselring, they poured in troops and aircraft. The Vichy forces in Tunisia made little attempt to resist this move and in a series of battles in late November and December the Germans were able to halt the Allied advance.

El Alamein to Tripoli

Montgomery is often criticized for the slow pace of Eighth Army's pursuit of Rommel's broken forces at the end of the Battle of El Alamein. A number of factors contributed to this slowness. Heavy rain made some areas impassible and there were massive traffic holdups in the corridors through the Alamein minefield belts. Both the pursuing units and their supplies were delayed as a result. Nonetheless Agedabia was reached before there had to be a major halt to allow the supplies to catch up. The advance was resumed on 12 December and the El Aghelia position was quickly outflanked. The German rear guard skilfully delayed the advance to Sirte and Buerat but once these positions were turned Eighth Army quickly pushed forward to Tripoli.

The Germans had done what they could to wreck the port installations at Tripoli and although it was partly in use by the end of January Eighth Army's supply difficulties remained acute. Small British units entered Tunisia on 4 February and had pushed forward to Medenine by the end of the month. Montgomery was still worried, rightly, about his supplies and only advanced as far as this in an attempt to distract the Germans from their Kasserine attack. As a result his forward units were only just reinforced in time to beat off a German attack on 6 March. The advance was resumed two weeks later by which time Tripoli was in fairly full use.

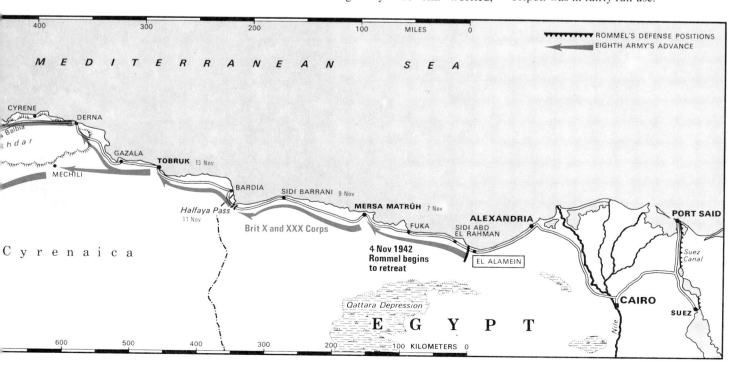

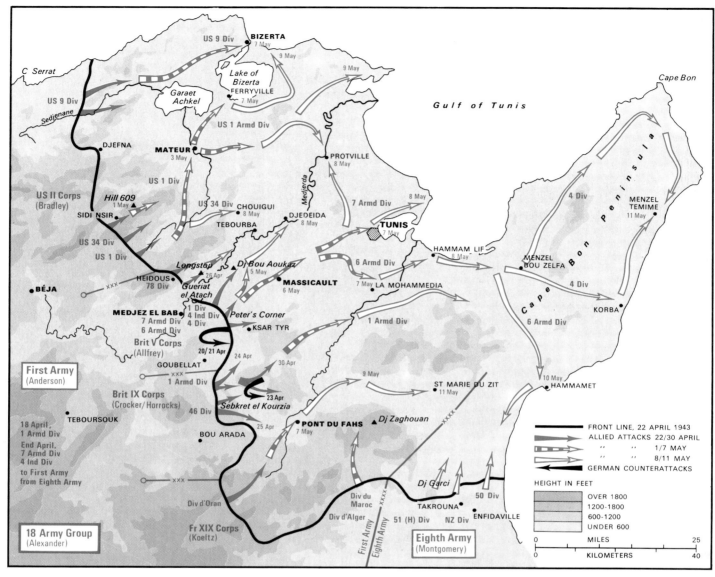

Map legend:

FRONT LINE, 22 APRIL 1943
ALLIED ATTACKS 22/30 APRIL
"   "   1/7 MAY
"   "   8/11 MAY
GERMAN COUNTERATTACKS

HEIGHT IN FEET

OVER 1800
1200-1800
600-1200
UNDER 600

MILES 0 — 25
KILOMETERS 0 — 40

Tunisia

Although the German and Italian forces had fought a brave series of delaying actions during their retreat into Tunisia, particularly on the Mareth Line and at Wadi Akarit, by April 1943 Eighth Army had pushed well forward. Similarly, although the Allied units from the Torch landings had suffered heavily in mid-February when the Germans attacked at Kasserine, this setback had been overcome and the Axis forces driven back. By 14 April the Germans and Italians had taken up the positions shown on the map defending the last line of hills before the plain around Tunis and Bizerta.

Allied attacks on this line began on 22 April especially in the sectors between Hill 609 and Peter's Corner. Although some progress was made by American forces at Hill 609 and in the nearby Mousetrap Valley and by the British at Longstop Hill and toward Djebel Bou Aoukaz, no decisive gains were made at first. General Alexander decided to switch experienced British units from Eighth Army to V Corps and with their help renewed British and US attacks from 5 May soon broke through. The German and Italian resistance collapsed and by 12 May Marshal Messe and General von Arnim had surrendered along with 250,000 troops.

Rommel had left Africa on 9 March and had urged that the German and Italian forces be evacuated. Hitler refused to countenance this and there can be little doubt that, despite the delaying actions they fought, the forces lost in Africa would have served the Axis better in defending Sicily and Italy against the seaborne assaults that would be the British and Americans' next move. The early stages of the battle for Tunisia also contributed to another German disaster by occupying large numbers of transport aircraft at a time when Göring was failing to fulfill his promise to supply Stalingrad by air.

Right: Italian troops on a desert reconnaissance mission.

The Battle of Kursk

For the summer of 1943 the German High Command planned no big offensive in Russia. It needed time to re-equip and, moreover, expected that its resources would be needed in other theaters. Nevertheless, to regain a psychological advantage, and to throw the expected Soviet offensive off balance, it was decided to stage a large but essentially limited attack toward Kursk. Here the Russians had ended the 1942–43 winter campaign holding a large salient which seemed very vulnerable to the kind of pincer movement which had won so many German successes in 1941.

Through various espionage channels, the Soviets were well informed of the German intentions, although they were probably not prepared for the repeated postponement of the operation; some German commanders were having second thoughts and were not in a hurry to get into position. All this enabled the Soviets to construct three lines of defense around the salient, each line consisting of elaborate trenches and antitank positions with appropriate artillery cover. The Germans began their advance on 5 July, in the belief that they were making a surprise

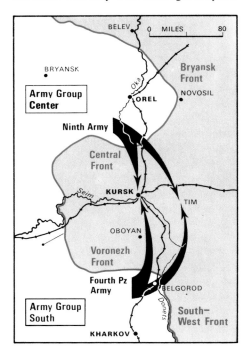

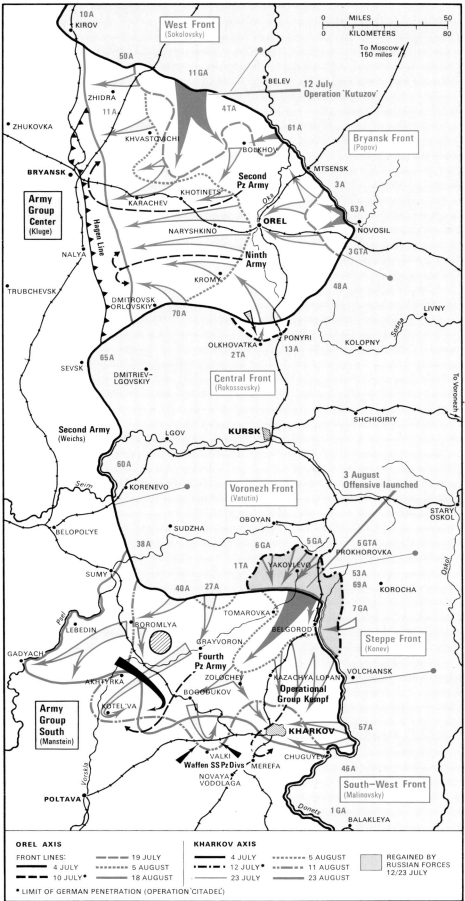

Below: a disabled Elefant tank destroyer pictured on the battlefield at Kursk. Following their unpromising debut at Kursk most of the surviving Elefants were redeployed to Italy.

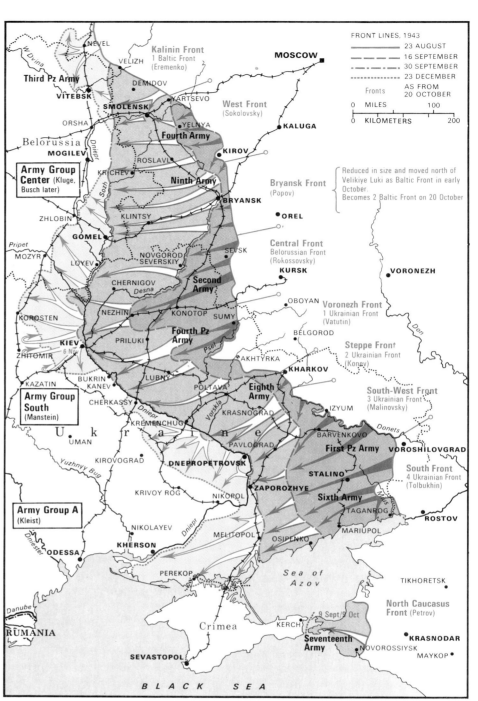

attack, but immediately encountered resistance far stiffer than they had expected. Moreover, the Soviets were technically better-off than they had been earlier in the war. Their T.34 tank was robust and reliable and available in large numbers, whereas the new types of German tank were not quite out of their teething troubles and, moreover, were entrusted to crews which had not had sufficient time to become familiar with them. Even more ominously, the Soviets could now secure, at least locally, command of the air over the battlefield. Their aircraft and their aircrews were not yet up to the German standard, but they now appeared in overwhelming numbers.

Thus the northern arm of the German pincer made only small penetrations into the Soviet salient, and at a very high cost. The southern arm, led by Manstein, fared somewhat better. His Fourth Panzer Army overcame the Russian Sixth Army but was then confronted with fresh Soviet tank units brought forward from reserve. Near Prokhorovka converging tank armies began what is regarded as the biggest tank battle of all time. It started on 12 July, and by the end of the next day the Germans seemed to be winning it, although both sides had already lost hundreds of tanks. However, at this point the German effort slackened, although the battle continued for five days longer. A Soviet offensive north of the salient toward Bryansk had altered the situation, and moreover the western Allies were landing in Sicily. Many of the German tanks were dispatched straight to Italy as soon as they were extricated from the Kursk battlefield. With this abandonment of the German offensive the Russians were free to begin their own advance all along the front south of Moscow.

The Dniepr and Smolensk Battles

In little more than a month after Hitler's abandonment of the Kursk battle, the Soviet front line had been pushed far to the west by a general offensive. The German local commanders were handicapped by the transfer of some of their best units to the Italian front, and in the circumstances their withdrawal was conducted very creditably, never degenerating into a rout and making the best possible use of the geo-graphical situation. Nevertheless, the Soviets soon captured the two base areas used by the Germans for their pincer movement on Kursk, Orel and its salient in the north, and Kharkov and its salient in the south. In the south, too, Stalino and Taganrog soon fell to the Russians, and Smolensk in the north, all by the autumn. Then, at the beginning of October, three fronts commanded by generals Rokossovsky, Vatutin and Konev forced crossings of the River Dniepr, on which the Germans had been expecting to form their defense line for the winter. Having established their bridgeheads, Soviet troops poured across. Dnepropetrovsk and Melitopol were captured, while Manstein

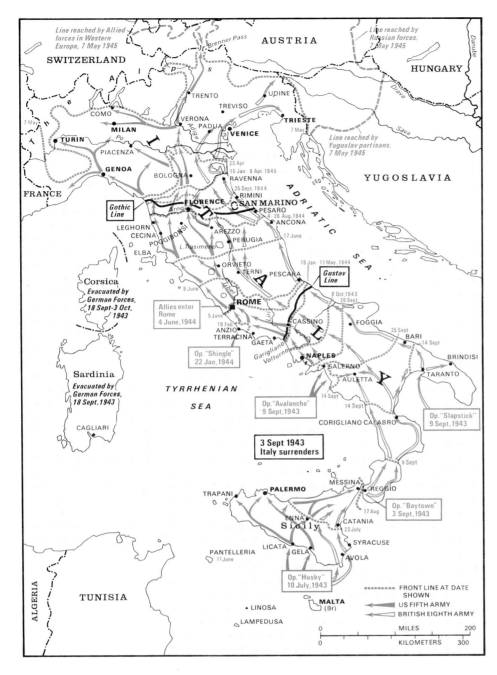

Map labels:

Line reached by Allied forces in Western Europe, 7 May 1945

Line reached by Russian forces, 7 May 1945

SWITZERLAND — AUSTRIA — HUNGARY

Brenner Pass

TRENTO — TREVISO — UDINE

COMO — VERONA — PADUA — TRIESTE — *7 May*

7 May — MILAN — VENICE

TURIN — PIACENZA — *Line reached by Yugoslav partisans, 7 May 1945*

GENOA — BOLOGNA — 23 Apr — YUGOSLAVIA

FRANCE — 15 Jan - 8 Apr. 1945 — RAVENNA

25 Sept. 1944 — RIMINI — SAN MARINO

Gothic Line — FLORENCE — PESARO — 4 - 26 Aug. 1944 — ANCONA

LEGHORN — CECINA — AREZZO — PERUGIA — 17 June

POGGIBONSI — *L. Trasimeno*

ELBA — ORVIETO — TERNI — PESCARA — 15 Jan - 11 May, 1944

Gustav Line

Corsica — *Evacuated by German Forces, 18 Sept - 3 Oct, 1943* — 9 June — ROME — 8 Oct. 1943 — 28 Sept.

Allies enter Rome 4 June, 1944 — 5 June — CASSINO — FOGGIA

19 Feb — ANZIO — TERRACINA — 25 Sept — BARI — 14 Sept

GAETA — Gariglianо — BRINDISI

Op. "Shingle" 22 Jan, 1944 — Volturno — NAPLES — SALERNO — TARANTO

Sardinia — *Evacuated by German Forces, 18 Sept, 1943*

TYRRHENIAN SEA — AULETTA

Op. "Avalanche" 9 Sept, 1943 — 14 Sept

CAGLIARI — 14 Sept — **Op. "Slapstick" 9 Sept, 1943**

CORIGLIANO CALABRO

3 Sept 1943 Italy surrenders — 5 Sept

MESSINA — REGGIO

TRAPANI — PALERMO — 17 Aug — **Op. "Baytown" 3 Sept, 1943**

ENNA — CATANIA — 23 July

Sicily — LICATA — GELA — SYRACUSE

PANTELLERIA — 11 June — AVOLA

Op. "Husky" 10 July, 1943

ALGERIA — TUNISIA

FRONT LINE AT DATE SHOWN
US FIFTH ARMY
BRITISH EIGHTH ARMY

MALTA (Br) — LINOSA — LAMPEDUSA

MILES 0 — 200
KILOMETERS 0 — 300

ADRIATIC SEA

The Italian Campaign

By the time the Allied campaign in North Africa was coming to an end it was clear to the Allied leaders that there was no prospect of building up their forces in Britain sufficiently to allow the invasion of northwest Europe to take place in 1943. It had been agreed at the Casablanca conference in January that Sicily should be captured once the campaign in Africa was complete because this would largely free the Mediterranean sea lanes but this comparatively limited objective did not seem to be making full use of the very large Allied forces already in the theater or the massive base organization that had been built up there. The British were strongly in favor of moving on to attack mainland Italy and the Americans too came round to this opinion when Mussolini's government fell in July. Throughout the campaign in Italy the British remained far more ready to press for reinforcements to be sent and an aggressive policy to be followed. The American views prevailed, however, and thus in late 1943 experienced units and commanders were withdrawn to go to England to prepare for D-Day. Again in the summer of 1944, after Rome had been taken, a large proportion of the Allied force was withdrawn to take part in the invasion of southern France.

The campaign in Italy saw some of the fiercest battles of the war. The initial seaborne landings at Salerno and the Anzio attempt to outflank the German Gustav Line were both very vigorously opposed by the Germans because of Hitler's hope that this would deter the Allies from such operations in northwest Europe. Once ashore the Allied forces found themselves facing successive river crossings which were usually overlooked by rugged and dominating hills carefully fortified by the Germans. The most famous of these positions was that at Monte Cassino which defied repeated Allied attacks in the early months of 1944. Even when the Germans were retreating between defense lines demolitions, rear guard actions, booby traps and miserable weather often combined to reduce Allied progress on the few good roads. Only when the Allied attacks were resumed in April 1945, after a long pause, did the German resistance collapse. The German forces in Italy surrendered on 2 May 1945.

tried to find forces for a counterattack to secure a position which he could hold for the winter in the bend of the Dniepr. But his attack, although pressed vigorously, was overwhelmed by the Soviet numerical advantage and he was forced back. Further north Rokossovsky, after crossing the Dniepr, took Kiev and pushed farther in order to cut the vital railroad running north to south from Mogilev to Kazatin. But at Zhitomir his troops were confronted by yet another force assembled by Manstein, and their occupation of that town was very short.

Right: a Russian tankman points to the damage he has inflicted on a Tiger tank.

The Defeat of the U-Boats

By the summer of 1942 the Allies had instituted a comprehensive convoy system off the US East Coast and throughout the Caribbean. The U-Boats' second 'happy time' was therefore at an end. Although the focus of the struggle then began to return to the main North Atlantic convoy routes, several more distant areas still provided important successes for the U-Boats. The convoy system off the American coast was not fully extended south from the Caribbean area to Trinidad until October 1942 and many important oil tankers and other vessels were lost there. The U-Boats also found victims off the Brazilian coast but a particularly audacious run of attacks in August helped bring Brazil into the war, opening new bases to the Allies. A further fruitful area for the U-Boats at this time was off the Cape of Good Hope.

There were several important developments in the Allied effort in the second half of 1942 also. The most important of a number of organizational changes was the the establishment, in September, of the first Support Groups. These were specially trained groups of escort vessels which were to be sent to help hard-pressed convoys or to some other area where there were known to be U-Boats. The support groups were then to stay and hunt the U-Boats to destruction without being distracted by an escort's normal duties. Ideally a group would include a small aircraft carrier, an escort carrier, as well as the surface forces. A further boost to the Allies was a cryptographic breakthrough in December 1942. From then until the end of the war, despite major changes in the German code system introduced in March 1943, the Allied intelligence was normally very accurate and up to date while the equivalent German efforts were frustrated by changes made in June 1943.

Despite the increasing Allied resources the final months of 1942 and the early part of 1943 were the most difficult times of the battle for the Allies. Allied commitments were increased by the Torch invasion of North Africa in November and the newly-formed support groups had to be diverted there. Although a considerable U-Boat force

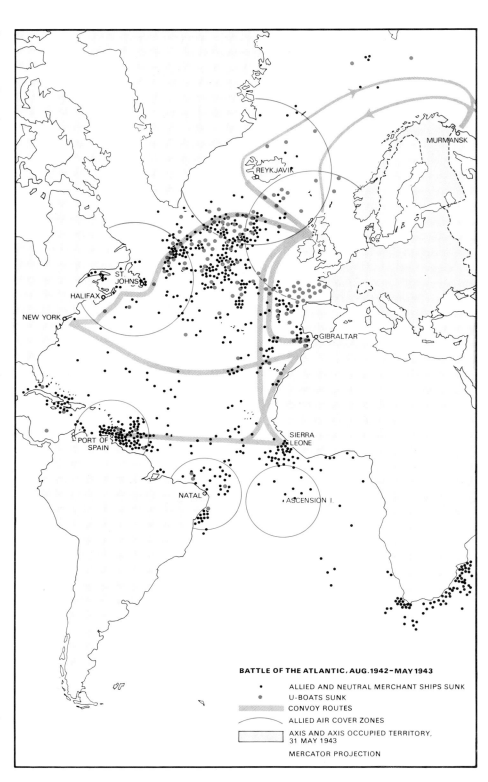

BATTLE OF THE ATLANTIC, AUG. 1942 – MAY 1943

- • ALLIED AND NEUTRAL MERCHANT SHIPS SUNK
- • U-BOATS SUNK
- CONVOY ROUTES
- ALLIED AIR COVER ZONES
- AXIS AND AXIS OCCUPIED TERRITORY, 31 MAY 1943

MERCATOR PROJECTION

was sent to North Africa also, for little gain, the North Atlantic escort forces remained weakened until March 1943. Losses in these months were very heavy.

The climax of the Battle of the Atlantic came in March 1943. Seventy-three ships were sunk from the North Atlantic convoys out of a total loss of 120 ships of 693,000 tons and for a time it seemed that the Germans were winning the battle. However, as suddenly as the crisis had arisen it was over. The shipping losses in April were much more moderate and in May 41 U-Boats were destroyed while 50 ships were lost to submarine attack. Such losses were insupportable and on 22 May the U-Boats were ordered to withdraw from the North Atlantic. The reasons for this sudden reversal cannot be exactly stated. The United States' industrial effort was beginning to come on stream, particularly in the provision of escort carriers, the support groups returned to the fray in late March and they and the other escorts were more highly trained and experienced while on the technical side improved radar and long-range scout planes helped capitalize on intelligence and radio direction finding information.

As the final map illustrates, the U-Boat offensive continued up to the end of the war but it was never again a serious threat. There was a brief attempt to renew the convoy battles in September-October 1943 after the introduction of new equipment but Allied countermeasures were ready and 25 submarines were lost and only nine merchantmen sunk in this period, although at the time the Germans believed that they had done better. In March 1944 the superiority of the escort forces was recognized when Donitz ordered the U-Boats to disperse from their hunting groups and work singly. In the final months of the war the U-Boats mostly operated in the area close to the British Isles Despite some technical advances they achieved little although there were still some 150 boats operational early in 1945. The Allied victory was won essentially by the co-ordination of all aspects of their effort and it is symbolic that, although German submarine research led the world, bad industrial and scientific management meant that only a handful of the most advanced U-Boats were in service when the Third Reich was finally overrun.

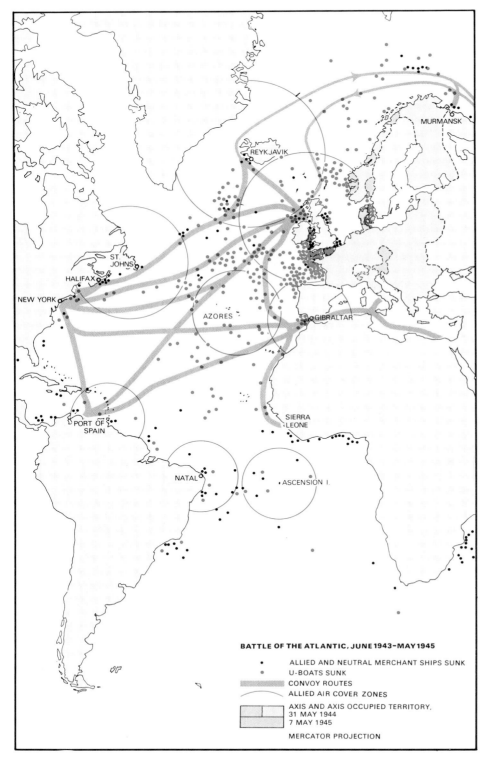

BATTLE OF THE ATLANTIC, JUNE 1943-MAY 1945

- ● ALLIED AND NEUTRAL MERCHANT SHIPS SUNK
- ● U-BOATS SUNK
- CONVOY ROUTES
- ALLIED AIR COVER ZONES
- AXIS AND AXIS OCCUPIED TERRITORY, 31 MAY 1944 / 7 MAY 1945

MERCATOR PROJECTION

The Solomons Campaign

Although the Japanese plans to take full control of the Solomons and New Guinea had received a major setback in the Battle of the Coral Sea in May 1942, they made a further attempt to reach Port Moresby by an overland advance from Buna in July–September 1942. This was halted by the defending Australian formations. Australian and American forces had already begun to strike back by building and holding an airstrip at Milne Bay and despite the worst imaginable ground and weather conditions they then succeeded in advancing over the Owen Stanley Range to take Buna and Sanananda. (The later stages of the New Guinea campaign are covered separately.)

The advance in the Solomons, of course, began with the long drawn struggle for Guadalcanal. Once this initial base had been taken the operations took on the soon-to-be-familiar island hopping pattern. Naval and air superiority kept the Japanese guessing about the point of attack and once ashore the Construction Battalions or Seabees quickly built or repaired airstrips for local defense and as a base to provide cover for

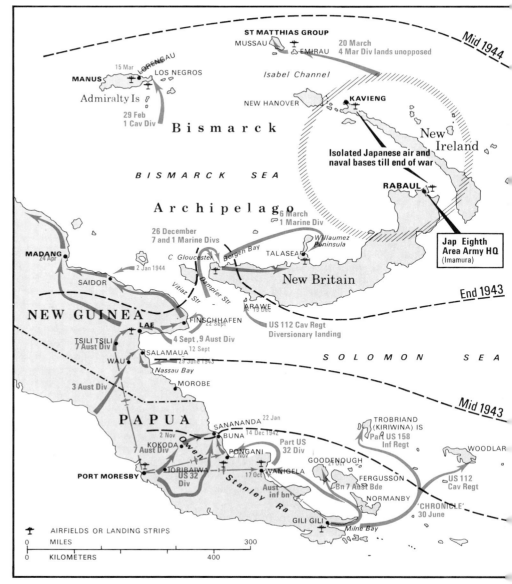

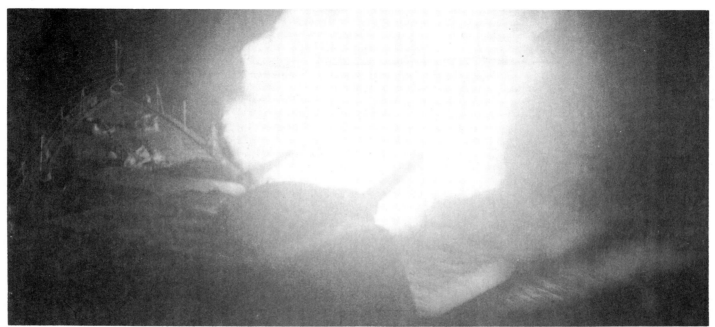

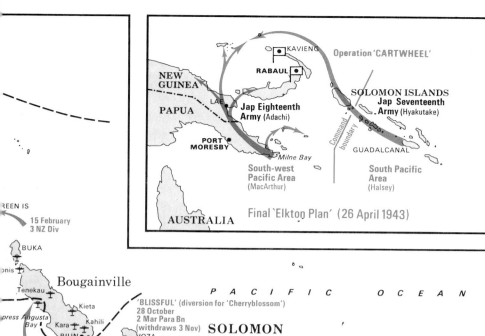

Final `Elkton Plan´ (26 April 1943)

Operation 'CARTWHEEL'

KAVIENG

RABAUL

NEW GUINEA

PAPUA

LAE

Jap Eighteenth Army (Adachi)

PORT MORESBY

Milne Bay

SOLOMON ISLANDS

Jap Seventeenth Army (Hyakutake)

GUADALCANAL

South-west Pacific Area (MacArthur)

South Pacific Area (Halsey)

AUSTRALIA

REEN IS

15 February 3 NZ Div

BUKA

onis

Bougainville

Tenekau

Kieta

press Augusta Bay

Kara

Kahili

RYBLOSSOM' ember ine Div

BIUN

SHORTLAND IS

FAURO

TREASURY IS

VELLA LAVELLA

'GOODTIME' 27 October 8 NZ Bde Group

'BLISSFUL' (diversion for 'Cherryblossom') 28 October 2 Mar Para Bn (withdraws 3 Nov)

VOZA

SAGIGAI

Choiseul

The Slot

KOLOMBANGARA

4 July

15 Aug

13 Aug

MUNDA

RENDOVA

SOLOMON ISLANDS

P A C I F I C   O C E A N

Santa Isabel

New Georgia

(New Georgia Sound)

VANGUNI

'TOENAILS' 30 June US 43 Inf Div

RUSSELL IS

BANIKA

PAVUVU

'CLEANSLATE' 21 February 1943 US assault bns

FLORIDA IS

Malaita

Henderson Field

Guadalcanal 7 Aug 1942/7 Feb 1943

San Cristobal

nd 1942

the next step. The technique is perhaps best shown in the landings on Bougainville. This island was defended by about 60,000 Japanese but only a few hundred of these were near Empress Augusta Bay and it was over four months before the Japanese could mount a full-scale attack against the beach-head, by then well defended.

When the plans for the Solomons were first made it seemed clear that it would be necessary to take both the main Japanese bases at Rabaul and Kavieng but in August 1943 it was agreed by bypass Rabaul and in March 1944 it was decided to leave Kavieng also. By that time the harbors and airfields at both bases were largely out of action. Landings in eastern New Britain and the Admiralty and St Matthias groups completed a very economical and effective campaign. The various isolated Japanese garrisons remained in being to the end of the war but could achieve little.

Below left: destroyer guns blaze during a confused night action which took place off Cape Esperance.
Below: an Aichi D3A is shot down directly over the carrier *Enterprise* in the Battle of the Eastern Solomons.

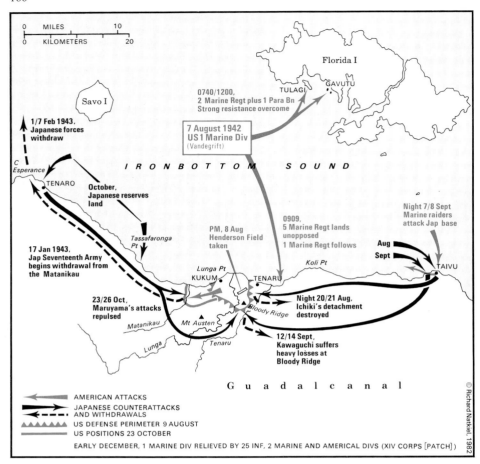

0 MILES 10
0 KILOMETERS 20

Savo I

Florida I

TULAGI
GAVUTU

1/7 Feb 1943,
Japanese forces
withdraw

0740/1200,
2 Marine Regt plus 1 Para Bn
Strong resistance overcome

C
Esperance

7 August 1942
US 1 Marine Div
(Vandegrift)

I R O N B O T T O M   S O U N D

TENARO

October,
Japanese reserves
land

Night 7/8 Sept
Marine raiders
attack Jap base

Tassafaronga
Pt

0909,
5 Marine Regt lands
unopposed
1 Marine Regt follows

PM, 8 Aug
Henderson Field
taken

Aug
Sept

17 Jan 1943,
Jap Seventeenth Army
begins withdrawal from
the Matanikau

Koli Pt

TAIVU

Lunga Pt
KUKUM

TENARU

23/26 Oct,
Maruyama's attacks
repulsed

Night 20/21 Aug,
Ichiki's detachment
destroyed

Bloody Ridge

Matanikau

Mt Austen

12/14 Sept,
Kawaguchi suffers
heavy losses at
Bloody Ridge

Lunga

Tenaru

G u a d a l c a n a l

© Richard Natkiel, 1982

AMERICAN ATTACKS
JAPANESE COUNTERATTACKS
AND WITHDRAWALS
US DEFENSE PERIMETER 9 AUGUST
US POSITIONS 23 OCTOBER

EARLY DECEMBER, 1 MARINE DIV RELIEVED BY 25 INF, 2 MARINE AND AMERICAL DIVS (XIV CORPS [PATCH])

Below: a US Marine stares at a picture of the girl he left behind from his foxhole on Guadalcanal. Note the hand grenades in the foreground.
Bottom: tents constructed on a framework of small logs on the New Guinea mainland.

The Struggle for Guadalcanal

The land and sea battles of the Guadalcanal campaign were the first major steps in the Allied counteroffensive against Japan. Since the American mobilization was only just getting under way and the Japanese were still near the peak of their strength, the forces were finely balanced and the battles were fiercely contested indeed.

The American landings were hurriedly improvised in response to news that the Japanese were beginning to build an airfield on the island. There were, therefore, no formations available for some time to reinforce the assault units from 1st Marine Division. The Japanese Navy made use of its superior torpedo equipment and night fighting training to assert control of the waters round the island at night, winning a number of engagements. They made use of this superiority to land successively stronger forces on the island. The airfield, soon renamed Henderson Field, was quickly put into use by the Marines and planes based there helped give the Americans control of the sea lanes by day. There were two carrier battles, the Battle of the Eastern Solomons in August and the Battle of Santa Cruz in October, in which the Japanese attempted

to dispute this air superiority and cover their supply operations but both of these were indecisive although losses on both sides were heavy.

On land the Japanese mounted three major attacks. The attacks in August and September were not made in sufficient strength because the Japanese had under-estimated the size of the American force. Both efforts were defeated after a fierce struggle. By the time the Japanese had again built up their forces the Americans were very well prepared and the badly co-ordinated assaults were thrown back.

By this time also the US Navy had improved its night fighting skills and was making better use of radar. The Japanese night supply operations, known as the Tokyo Express, remained a problem but once the exhausted Marines were relieved in December the battle could only go one way. At the end of the year the Japanese High Command decided to withdraw and this was successfully achieved in February. Naval losses in the campaign were about equal but the Japanese lost far more men on land.

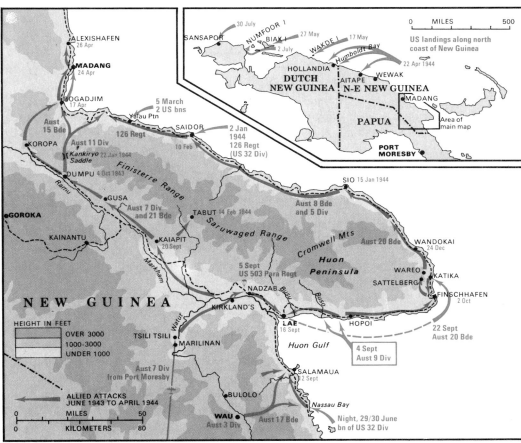

New Guinea

The Allied campaign in New Guinea was one of the most imaginative and tactically sophisticated of the war. The Allied air forces played a very prominent role in this victory, driving off or sinking Japanese supply ships, transporting large quantities of supplies and dropping paratroop units as well as striking at Japanese ground positions. One little known but vital part of the Allied effort in these and the Solomons battles was the information provided by the Australian coast-watchers, who gave vital warning of many Japanese moves.

The Allied forces, and indeed the Japanese, faced many difficulties nonetheless. The problems of bad weather and tropical disease were acute and difficulties with rugged terrain were compounded by lack of accurate maps and, for landing operations, poor information about tides and reefs. During the Hollandia operation, for example, some units were sent ashore on to totally unsuitable beaches.

The campaign can conveniently be divided into two main phases after the Japanese had been thrown out of Buna at the end of 1942. The first phase, the capture of Lae and the Markham Valley, was made easier by the Japanese forces being cleverly drawn forward by earlier attacks on Salamaua. These successes were followed up by other smaller operations all round the Huon Peninsula. The second major stage brought landings at Hollandia and Aitape. These cut off perhaps 200,000 Japanese troops and civilian workers who were mostly around Wewak. The final landings on Biak and Numfoor and at Sansapor, were designed to take airfields to support Marianas and Philippine operations.

The Ukraine

Although counterattacks west of Kiev had brought the Germans some breathing space, their forces in the southern Ukraine at the end of 1943 were very vulnerable, particularly in the salient around Krivoy Rog and Nikopol which Hitler insisted was to be held because of the mineral resources situated there. The renewed Soviet offensive began on Christmas Eve with attacks by Vatutin's First Ukraine Front which soon reached into former Polish territory as well as striking to the southwest. The next stage was a limited advance by Konev's troops toward Kirovgrad and this was quickly followed by the elimination of the Nikopol salient and the encirclement of important German formations in a pocket around Korsun. German counterattacks enabled about half the surrounded force to break out.

Despite the difficult conditions imposed by the spring thaw, the Soviet momentum was maintained and on 4 March First and Second Ukraine Fronts led new attacks. Again considerable German forces were threatened with encirclement and some units retreated at a speed which almost approached a rout. Later in March First Ukraine Front moved south, crossed the Dniestr and captured Chernovtsy, thereby severing the last rail link between the Germans in Poland and those in the southern USSR. Farther south Malinovsky's troops captured Odessa in April with hardly a fight, while Tolbukhin took Perekop and cleared the Germans out of the Crimea.

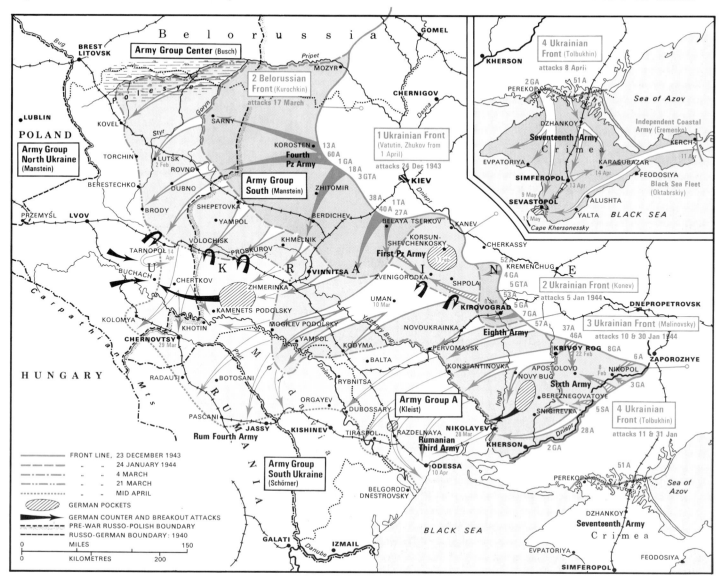

The Advance into Poland

Intentionally, the Soviet summer offensive of 1944 started just after the western Allies had landed in Normandy. An early success was in the north, where the Russians broke through the Finns' defenses and forced Finland out of the war. Then, at the end of June, a main offensive opened in the central sector, with four fronts advancing with the aim of encircling the German army groups in the Minsk-Vitebsk-Rogachev triangle. Soviet air superiority, and the activities of guerrillas against German supply routes, eased the Red Army's task, although the crossing of the River Berezina was a costly success. Minsk was captured on 3 July and so rapid was the German retreat that Bialystok and Brest Litovsk were taken later the same month. These two towns controlled the approach to Warsaw, and although German counterattacks delayed Rokossovsky's drive against the Polish capital, by 15 August his advanced troops were in the eastern suburbs.

The Soviet approach to Warsaw coincided with a long-planned rising in the capital by the Polish Home Army, a generally anti-communist resistance group owing its allegiance to the exiled Polish government in London. That government wished Warsaw to be liberated by Poles rather than by the Red Army, not only for sentimental reasons but because it would put the Polish government into a stronger bargaining position later. But, contrary to the expectations of the Home Army, Rokossovsky advanced no further; it was not until the following year that the Russians entered Warsaw, and long before then the Germans had ruthlessly destroyed the Home Army and much of Warsaw as well. Subsequently this tragedy was attributed to Soviet malignance, but the Soviet explanation that a consolidation was needed, before embarking on the river crossing needed to enter Warsaw proper, does have some plausibility.

Right: T-34 tanks moving up for the attack on the Third Belorussian Front in 1944.

The Baltic States

By 1944 the Red Army was not only better led than in 1941, but better equipped. Shipments from the western allies had comparatively little effect in the field of weapons, but were quite decisive in transport and other supplies. Not only was the Red Army soldier in 1944 learning to like Spam, but he was travelling on, or at least supplied by, American-built trucks and transport aircraft, the latter very often running on aviation fuel brought to Russia by sea or through Iran. The pace of the Soviet advance in 1944 and 1945 could therefore be fast, depending more on the intensity of German resistance than on problems of supply and communication. This was important not only for the drive through Poland to Berlin, but also for the campaigns in the Balkans and the Baltic States.

The fronts of Eremenko and Maslenikov entered the latter in the summer of 1944. In Estonia, Narva was captured first, while in neighboring Latvia a deep penetration was made. Meanwhile Govorov's Leningrad Front advanced along the coast and captured Tallinn. In October Riga was assaulted and captured by Bagramyan's First Baltic Front, which went on to cut off no fewer than 20 German divisions in Courland. The latter, supplied sporadically by sea, held out right until the end of the war. However, the fall of Riga really marked the end of the war as far as the Baltic states were concerned. Their inhabitants had not welcomed incorporation into the USSR in 1940, and many of them braved the perils of evacuation with the German troops rather than stay behind as citizens of the USSR.

Right: the KV-1 tank was the principal Soviet heavy tank in the first years of the war. It originally carried a 76mm gun as shown here but later versions had a more powerful 85mm weapon. It was superseded by the JS-series of tanks.

Fragment labels on the map:

First Pz and Hun First Armies form Armeegruppe Heinrici
Eighth Army and Rum Fourth Army form Armeegruppe Wöhler
Sixth Army and Rum Third Army form Armeegruppe Dumitrescu

Ⓐ 6TA, 27 A, 52 A, 53 A, 7 GA and Cav Mech Group Gorshkov
Ⓑ 37 A, 46 A, 57 A and Cav Mech Group Pliev

4 Ukrainian Front (Petrov)
2 Ukrainian Front (Malinovsky)
3 Ukrainian Front (Tolbukhin)

Army Group South Ukraine (Friessner)
Army Group F (Weichs)
Army Group E (Löhr)

Second Pz Army
Tito's partisans
Albanian partisans

23 August 1944 Rumania surrenders. Declares war on Germany, 25 August

4 September 1944 Bulgaria declares end to state of war with Allies. Declares war on Germany 8 December

FRONT LINES
20 AUGUST 1944
29 AUGUST
24 SEPTEMBER
12 OCTOBER
31 JANUARY 1945

RUMANIAN AND BULGARIAN ATTACKS
AXIS COUNTERATTACKS
WITHDRAWAL OF ARMY GROUPS 'E' AND 'F'
GERMAN POCKETS

INTERNATIONAL BOUNDARIES: 1944
PRE-WAR RUSSO-POLISH BOUNDARY
RUSSO-GERMAN BOUNDARY: 1940

LAND OVER 1600 FEET

MILES 300
KILOMETERS 500

The Soviet Offensive in the Balkans

Shortly after Finland had withdrawn from the war, Rumania also surrendered. Tolbukhin's Third and Malinovsky's Second Ukrainian Fronts had used bridgeheads on the western side of the River Dniestr to start an advance on 20 August which made rapid progress because the Rumanian soldiers, who had never been enthusiastic fighters, were willing by this stage of the war to surrender or desert as opportunity offered. When the Soviets occupied Iasy the King of Rumania dismissed his pro-German government and initiated negotiations. The Germans in Rumania fought on, but the German Sixth Army was encircled and destroyed near Kishinev. Bucharest was captured by the end of August and this helped to persuade another of Hitler's allies, Bulgaria, to surrender also, on 26 August. Three weeks later Soviet troops entered Sofia, the Bulgarian capital. After these successes the Second Ukrainian Front turned to occupy Transylvania, reaching Arad in September, while Tolbukhin moved north from Bulgaria toward Belgrade, making contact with Tito's Yugoslav partisans in October. Meanwhile, Malinovsky entered Hungary and by mid-November was in sight of Budapest. By the end of March 1945 Hungary was largely cleared of German resistance and the Red Army entered Austria. An energetic counteroffensive around Lake Balaton had been initially successful, but foundered for lack of fuel and in April the Red Army entered Bratislava and Vienna. The Ukrainian fronts ended the war by overrunning Czechoslovakia and linking up with US forces advancing from the west. The last German forces in this area surrendered on 11 May 1945.

D-Day

The Allied invasion of France on 6 June 1944 was the largest combined land, sea and air operation ever undertaken in war. The planning process and the forces involved were on the largest and most elaborate scale. The Supreme Commander for Operation Overlord was General Eisenhower and he had nearly 3,000,000 men under his control. A massive quantity of equipment, much of it specially designed, had also been assembled. One of the most important aspects of the Allied plan was the preparation of parts for two artificial ports (Mulberry Harbors) which were to be towed across the Channel and sunk or anchored off the Omaha and Gold beaches to enable heavy supplies to be landed easily before a major port had been taken.

Although they had a crushing superiority in fighting aircraft and warships, because of shortages of paratroop-carrying aircraft and naval landing craft and the natural advantages of the defense, the Allied plan relied heavily on elaborate deception schemes and preparatory air attacks to prevent the Germans overwhelming the comparatively limited ground forces deployed initially. The main deception plan was to suggest – by way of reports from double agents, false radio traffic and other means – that a notional First US Army Group was being assembled in southeast England under the command of General Patton ready to invade across the narrowest part of the Channel. The many preparatory air attacks for the real operation were designed mainly to isolate the Normandy area from the rest of France but these were only a proportion of the attacks made and thus the true purpose was concealed and the deception reinforced.

The deception plan contributed greatly to uncertainties in the German command. The German Commander in Chief, West, Field Marshal von Rundstedt believed that beach defenses should come second to the assembly of a strong central reserve to throw the Allied forces back into the sea once they had clearly shown where their main attack was going to be. Rommel, who now commanded the German armies in northern France and the Low Countries, believed that Allied air power would prevent Rundstedt's reserve coming into action

and that the Allies must instead be defeated on the beaches before they could develop their full strength. Hitler insisted on a compromise between these schemes, neither allowing Rommel to strengthen the forces defending the beaches as much as would have been possible, while hamstringing the action of the reserve forces by insisting that they remain under his personal control. On 6 June this arrangement meant among other things that a counterattack by the powerful 21st Panzer Division from the Caen area was delayed for several hours until its effects could only be limited.

As the map shows, the Allies planned landings on five beach areas with paratroop units being dropped on either flank. There was hard fighting on each of the three beaches chosen for the British and Canadian forces but with the aid of specially designed armored vehicles the defenses were overcome and fairly good progress inland was made. The easiest progress of all was in the American area at Utah beach where navigational errors concentrated the landings in sectors that happened to be lightly defended. The other American beach, Omaha, offered a complete contrast. The German defenses were strong and there were important errors in the planning and execution of the attack. As a result, casualties were high but a solid footing had been taken by the end of the day. Many of the airborne troops on either flank were not dropped in the correct areas but nevertheless they achieved most of their objectives in a series of small, hard-fought actions.

By the end of 6 June the Allies had almost 150,000 men ashore and although the first day's objectives had not been reached a strong lodgment had been made. Rommel's plan to win on the beaches had failed and now it was a question of whether the Allied air forces could slow the assembly of German reserves to below the rate at which the Allied armies could be landed and supplied.

Above right: landing craft arrive at Omaha Beach, where German defenses were well-prepared and casualties high.
Right: A scene on Omaha Beach shortly after the first landings.

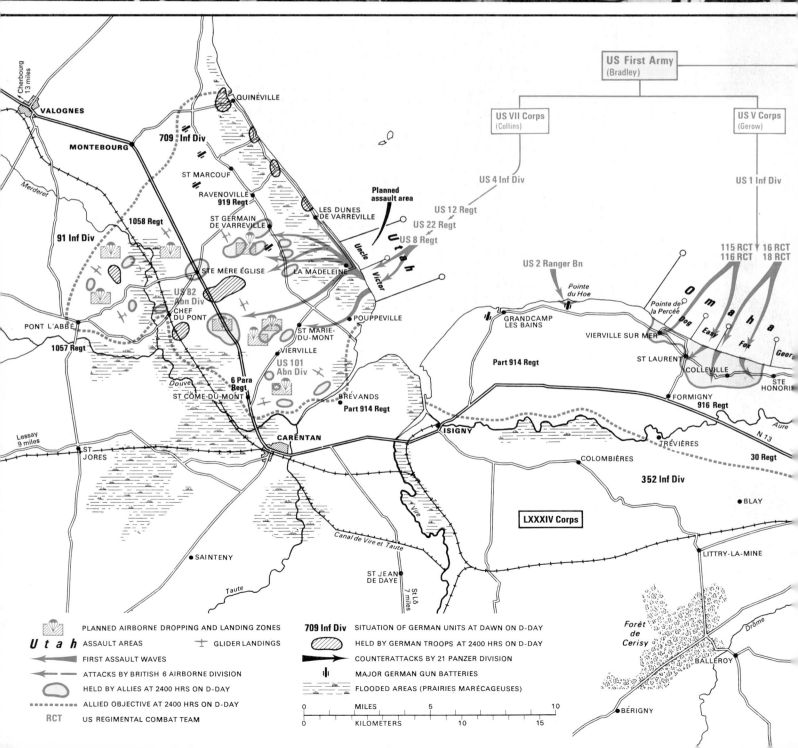

US First Army
(Bradley)

US VII Corps
(Collins)

US V Corps
(Gerow)

US 4 Inf Div

US 1 Inf Div

US 12 Regt

US 22 Regt

US 8 Regt

115 RCT   16 RCT
116 RCT   18 RCT

Cherbourg
13 miles

VALOGNES

QUINÉVILLE

MONTEBOURG

709 Inf Div

Merderet

ST MARCOUF

RAVENOVILLE
919 Regt

LES DUNES
DE VARREVILLE

1058 Regt

ST GERMAIN
DE VARREVILLE

Planned
assault area

91 Inf Div

STE MÈRE ÉGLISE

LA MADELEINE

Uncle

Utah

US 2 Ranger Bn

Pointe
du Hoe

Pointe de
la Percéé

Omaha

PONT L'ABBÉ

US 82
Abn Div

CHEF
DU PONT

Victor

POUPPEVILLE

GRANDCAMP
LES BAINS

Dog

Easy

Fox

Geor

1057 Regt

Douve

ST MARIE-
DU-MONT

VIERVILLE

US 101
Abn Div

VIERVILLE SUR MER

ST LAURENT

Colleville

STE HONORI

6 Para
Regt

ST CÔME-DU-MONT

BRÉVANDS

Part 914 Regt

FORMIGNY
916 Regt

Part 914 Regt

Lessay
9 miles

ST
JORES

CARENTAN

ISIGNY

COLOMBIÈRES

TRÉVIÈRES

Aure

N 13

30 Regt

Vire

352 Inf Div

BLAY

Canal de Vire et Taute

LXXXIV Corps

SAINTENY

Taute

ST JEAN
DE DAYE

St Lô
7 miles

LITTRY-LA-MINE

Forêt
de
Cerisy

Drôme

BALLEROY

BÉRIGNY

PLANNED AIRBORNE DROPPING AND LANDING ZONES

709 Inf Div   SITUATION OF GERMAN UNITS AT DAWN ON D-DAY

Utah   ASSAULT AREAS   ✈ GLIDER LANDINGS

HELD BY GERMAN TROOPS AT 2400 HRS ON D-DAY

FIRST ASSAULT WAVES

COUNTERATTACKS BY 21 PANZER DIVISION

ATTACKS BY BRITISH 6 AIRBORNE DIVISION

MAJOR GERMAN GUN BATTERIES

HELD BY ALLIES AT 2400 HRS ON D-DAY

FLOODED AREAS (PRAIRIES MARÉCAGEUSES)

ALLIED OBJECTIVE AT 2400 HRS ON D-DAY

RCT   US REGIMENTAL COMBAT TEAM

0   MILES   5   10

0   KILOMETERS   10   15

Left: the Allied invasion chiefs at a press conference in Allied Command Headquarters: left to right; Bradley, Ramsay, Tedder, Eisenhower, Mongomery, Leigh-Mallory and Bedell-Smith.
Right: after the D-Day landings, Allied troops pressed inland. A command tank leads a unit of British-manned Sherman tanks.

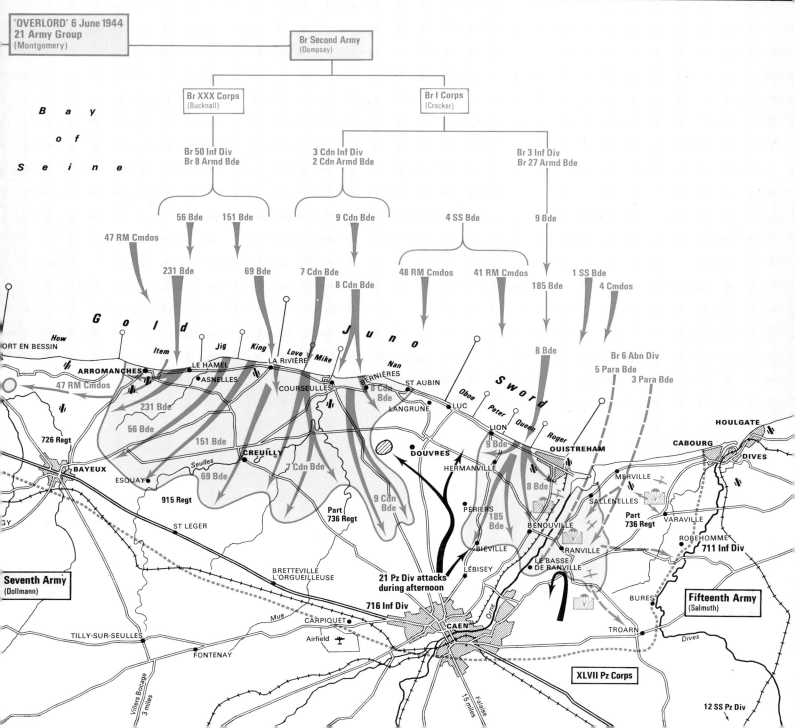

Invading Southern France

The Allied plans for landings in the south of France were a cause of much debate and disagreement between the British and American leaders. The Americans, of course, laid overwhelming emphasis on invading northern France and defeating the German forces there. They were somewhat reluctant participants in the Italian campaign, seeing it in a diversionary role rather than as having important strategic objectives in its own right. They believed that landings in southern France would contribute considerably to the initial success of D-Day by drawing off German forces and, by opening the port of Marseilles, would be valuable in the long term. Many of the forces involved were to be drawn from the armies fighting in Italy. The British would have preferred either to maintain them in Italy or to use them to lead a major landing in the Adriatic or even farther east. The Americans refused to countenance this scheme, with support from Stalin who was only too pleased for the western Allies to keep away from the Balkans.

The plan for the landings was originally made under the code name 'Dragoon' but because of fears that this had become known to the Germans 'Anvil' was substituted at a late stage. The original scheme was for the main D-Day invasion and Anvil to be simultaneous but shortages of landing craft dictated a postponement. To opponents of the operation this delay made it seem even more unnecessary. When the landings were made on 15 August resistance was light with only 183 Allied casualties on the first day. Churchill was aboard one of the supporting ships and, from the account in his memoirs, seems to have been bored by the lack of action. General Wiese's German Nineteenth Army had only eight poorly trained and equipped divisions with which to guard the whole of south and southeast France and not surprisingly he was soon compelled to retreat. The Allied force was quickly expanded to become Seventh US and First French Armies and as 6 Army Group took post on the right of the Allied line advancing into Germany.

Below: paratroops drop from C-47 transport aircraft to attack behind enemy lines during the invasion of Southern France in August 1944.

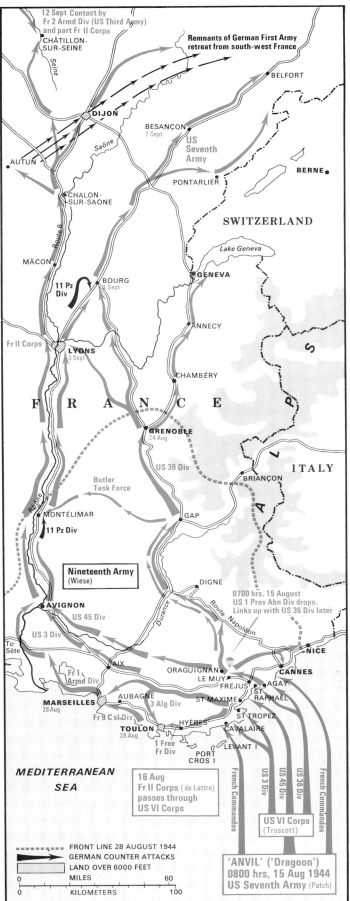

12 Sept Contact by Fr 2 Armd Div (US Third Army) and part Fr II Corps

CHÂTILLON-SUR-SEINE

Remnants of German First Army retreat from south-west France

Seine

BELFORT

DIJON

BESANÇON
7 Sept

US Seventh Army

AUTUN

Saône

PONTARLIER

BERNE

CHALON-SUR-SAONE

SWITZERLAND

Route 6

MÂCON

Lake Geneva

GENEVA

11 Pz Div

BOURG
2 Sept

ANNECY

Fr II Corps

LYONS
3 Sept

CHAMBÉRY

F   R   A   N   C   E

GRENOBLE
24 Aug

A   L   P   S

ITALY

US 36 Div

BRIANÇON

Butler Task Force

Rhône

MONTÉLIMAR

GAP

11 Pz Div

Nineteenth Army
(Wiese)

DIGNE

0700 hrs, 15 August
US 1 Prov Abn Div drops.
Links up with US 36 Div later

Durance

Route Napoléon

AVIGNON

US 45 Div

US 3 Div

To Sète

NICE

AIX

ORAGUIGNAN

CANNES

Fr 1 Armd Div

LE MUY

FRÉJUS

AGAY

ST RAPHAEL

MARSEILLES
28 Aug

AUBAGNE

3 Alg Div

ST MAXIME

Fr 9 Col Div

ST TROPEZ

TOULON
28 Aug

HYÈRES

CAVALAIRE

1 Free Fr Div

LEVANT I

PORT CROS I

MEDITERRANEAN SEA

16 Aug
Fr II Corps (de Lattre) passes through US VI Corps

French Commandos

US 3 Div

US 45 Div

US 36 Div

French Commandos

US VI Corps
(Truscott)

- - - - - FRONT LINE 28 AUGUST 1944
▶ GERMAN COUNTER ATTACKS
▭ LAND OVER 6000 FEET

0 ———— MILES ———— 60
0 ———— KILOMETERS ———— 100

'ANVIL' ('Dragoon')
0800 hrs, 15 Aug 1944
US Seventh Army (Patch)

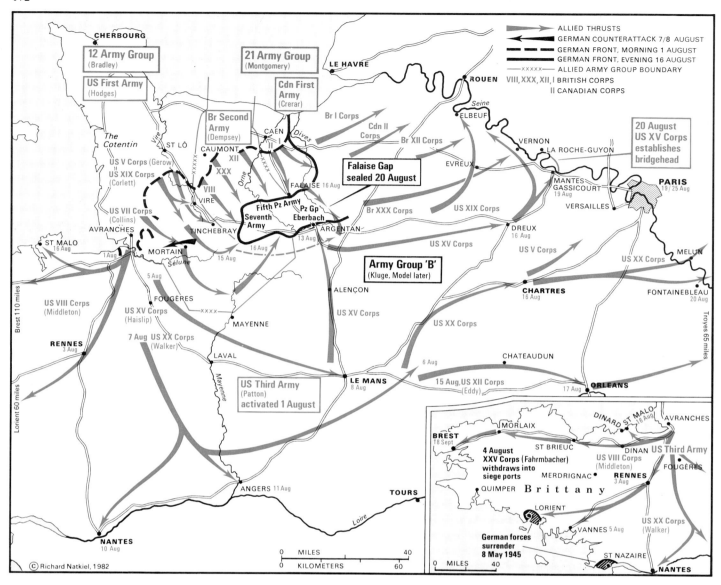

Map legend:

- ALLIED THRUSTS
- GERMAN COUNTERATTACK 7/8 AUGUST
- GERMAN FRONT, MORNING 1 AUGUST
- GERMAN FRONT, EVENING 16 AUGUST
- XXXXX ALLIED ARMY GROUP BOUNDARY
- VIII, XXX, XII, I BRITISH CORPS
- II CANADIAN CORPS

CHERBOURG

12 Army Group (Bradley)

US First Army (Hodges)

21 Army Group (Montgomery)

LE HAVRE

Cdn First Army (Crerar)

ROUEN

Seine

ELBEUF

Br I Corps

Cdn II Corps

Br XII Corps

VERNON

LA ROCHE-GUYON

20 August US XV Corps establishes bridgehead

Br Second Army (Dempsey)

The Cotentin

ST LÔ

CAEN

Dives

EVREUX

MANTES GASSICOURT 19 Aug

PARIS 19/25 Aug

CAUMONT

XII

VERSAILLES

US V Corps (Gerow)

US XIX Corps (Corlett)

XXX

Orne

FALAISE 16 Aug

Falaise Gap sealed 20 August

Br XXX Corps

US XIX Corps

DREUX 16 Aug

VIII

VIRE

Fifth Pz Army Seventh Army

Pz Gp Eberbach

US XV Corps

US V Corps

US XX Corps

MELUN

US VII Corps (Collins)

TINCHEBRAY

ARGENTAN 13 Aug

FONTAINEBLEAU 20 Aug

AVRANCHES

ST MALO 16 Aug

MORTAIN

16 Aug

Army Group 'B' (Kluge, Model later)

1 Aug

Sélune

15 Aug

ALENÇON

CHARTRES 16 Aug

Brest 110 miles

US VIII Corps (Middleton)

5 Aug

FOUGÈRES

US XV Corps (Haislip)

MAYENNE

US XV Corps

US XX Corps

Troyes 65 miles

RENNES 3 Aug

7 Aug US XX Corps (Walker)

LAVAL

Mayenne

US Third Army (Patton) activated 1 August

LE MANS 8 Aug

6 Aug

CHATEAUDUN

Lorient 60 miles

15 Aug, US XII Corps (Eddy)

ORLEANS

17 Aug

ANGERS 11 Aug

TOURS

Loire

NANTES 10 Aug

© Richard Natkiel, 1982

MILES 40

KILOMETERS 60

Inset map (Brittany):

DINARD ST MALO 16 Aug

AVRANCHES

MORLAIX

BREST 18 Sept

ST BRIEUC

DINAN

US Third Army

4 August XXV Corps (Fahrmbacher) withdraws into siege ports

US VIII Corps (Middleton)

MERDRIGNAC

FOUGÈRES

QUIMPER

Brittany

RENNES 3 Aug

LORIENT

VANNES 5 Aug

US XX Corps (Walker)

German forces surrender 8 May 1945

ST NAZAIRE

NANTES

MILES 40

Allied Breakout from Normandy

Throughout June and July 1944 the Allies gradually extended their initial beachheads inland into Normandy. General Montgomery remained in control of the ground forces and the campaign was fought along the lines which he had first laid down. The plan was for British and Canadian pressure on the Allied left to draw in the strongest German forces and allow American units on the right to advance more rapidly. Montgomery was not well liked by some of the American leaders and did little to improve his position by poor handling of the press but nonetheless his blueprint for the campaign was largely adhered to and brought success.

By the end of July the breakout had begun and newly arrived forces of Patton's Third Army began moving from Avranches into Brittany and east into central France. The other Allied armies also pressed forward. Hitler's response was to order immediate counterattacks from around Mortain to cut off Patton's advances but these were quickly checked by Allied ground and air forces. The German forces involved now found themselves trapped in an exposed salient west of Falaise and Argentan and many were killed or captured in the subsequent Allied attempts to seal off the pocket. The German position was not helped by Hitler's continued insistence on no retreat and his distrust of his generals. Field Marshal von Kluge had replaced both Rundstedt and Rommel early in July and was himself dismissed on 17 August.

While the heavy fighting around the Falaise Gap was coming to an end all the Allied armies joined Third Army in the rapid advance to the Seine. Although some historians believe that the Falaise operations were badly mismanaged by the Allies there is no doubt that the German forces defending Normandy had largely been written off as military formations. Resistance forces began the fight to free Paris on 19 August

and on 20 August the first Allied bridgehead over the Seine was established. The Allies had made far less progress in the June and July battles than their planners had expected but the rapid advances in early August more than restored the original schedule.

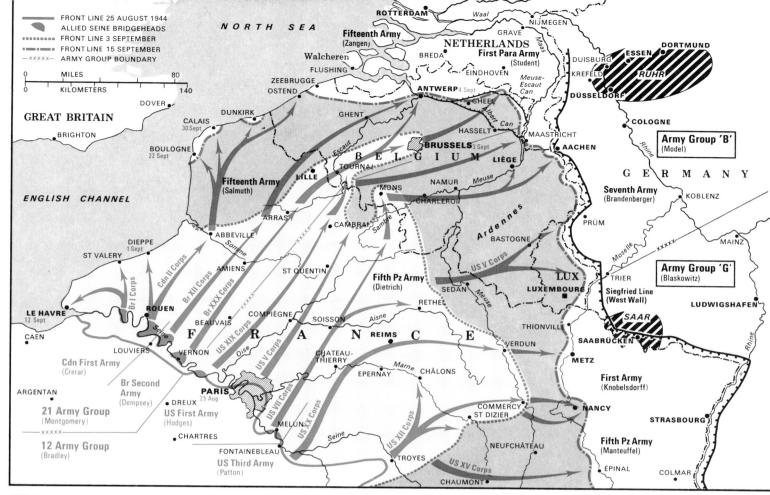

Advance to Antwerp

As the Allied forces extended their advance north and east of the Seine in late August 1944 their generals were arguing fiercely about the strategy to be adopted. The Allied armies were still almost entirely dependent on supplies landed over the Normandy beaches which were a growing distance behind the front. These supplies were not sufficient to keep every unit advancing at full pace and at full strength. Various generals, of whom Montgomery was the most prominent, proposed that advantage should be taken of the German disorganiza-

tion and a proportion of the Allied force given overriding priority in an attempt to support a narrow-front advance into Germany to end the war in 1944. This plan was rejected by General Eisenhower, the Supreme Commander, who took over direct control of the Allied ground forces early in September. Although Eisenhower gave some priority to the British forces for the advance into Belgium and the Arnhem operation that followed, he insisted on a broad front policy in which all the Allied armies would have an equal share of the supplies and the glory attending an advance. There was little possibility of quick success by this method but far less risk of a defeat. Although the narrow-front advance had obvious at-

tractions it is by no means clear that it would have been logistically possible even if the German resistance could have been overcome. There can be no doubt that Eisenhower would have faced considerable political difficulties if he had tried to halt the advance of Patton's Third Army for example while allowing the British forces to continue their attacks.

The key to solving the whole problem was to alleviate the supply situation. The Canadian First Army managed to take several of the French Channel ports in September but these were too small to be of more than limited help. The more important port of Antwerp was seized virtually intact on 4 September but despite the relationship of the vehement strategic debate to the supply problem the importance of Antwerp was not appreciated at first and a series of minor errors and delays allowed the Germans to consolidate their hold on the seaward approaches to the port.

Left: Corporal Franczalsi hands out the mail to troops recently landed in France. Letters from home played a vital part in maintaining morale.

The Advance to the Rhine

The Allied advance in August and early September 1944 had been rapid and successful and in an ambitious effort to retain this momentum General Montgomery devised and had accepted a plan for paratroop landings to seize a series of important river and canal crossings which might otherwise provide serious checks to the advance. A further attraction of the scheme was that the route through Arnhem led into Germany round the north end of the supposedly formidable West Wall defenses. The whole operation had to be planned in a great hurry to fit in with the rapidly developing Allied advance. Although the two US airborne divisions achieved their objectives with the help of the advancing British XXX Corps, shortcomings in the preparation became more apparent with the third part of the operation. It was accepted that the British airborne division dropped at Arnhem would have a difficult task and so it was decided to drop it some way from its objectives to allow for some organization before the attack should go in. The consequent loss of surprise gave the German forces, which were in any case far stronger than Allied intelligence believed, time to recover and the paratroops were not able to reach their objectives in any strength. German resistance to the advance of XXX Corps also increased and after a bitter fight the operation was abandoned. Most of the British paratroops were taken prisoner.

Even as the Arnhem operation was coming to an end British and Canadian troops were beginning a long struggle to clear the Germans away from the Schelde Estuary and open the port of Antwerp. Arguably this operation should have been given higher priority and more of Montgomery's attention than the paratroop plan. The Allies were only able to begin minesweeping to open Antwerp on 4 November after elaborate amphibious attacks and much

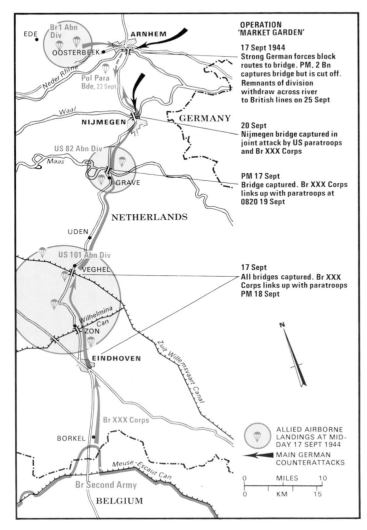

hard fighting in difficult conditions. The first cargoes were landed on 28 November and from then on the supply position for all the Allied armies improved dramatically.

Throughout this period the US forces were gradually pushing forward in a number of sectors but the German resistance was becoming better organized and their defense system more formidable. The battles fought by US First Army around Aachen and Patton's Third Army around Metz were particularly fierce. Hopes of finishing the war in 1944, however, had been abandoned.

Above: paratroops being dropped during the Arnhem operation.
Left: British paratroops move cautiously through a ruined building on the outskirts of Arnhem.

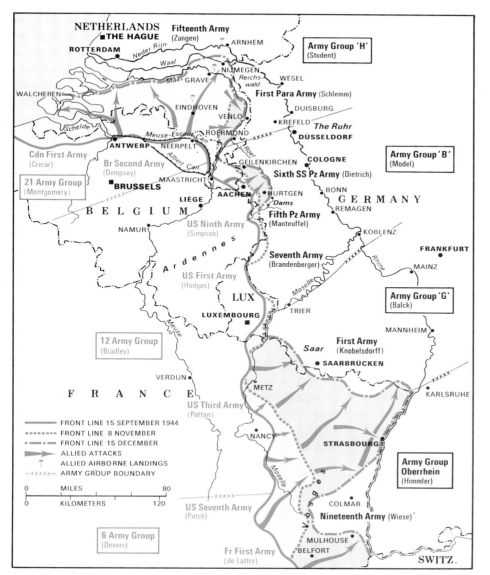

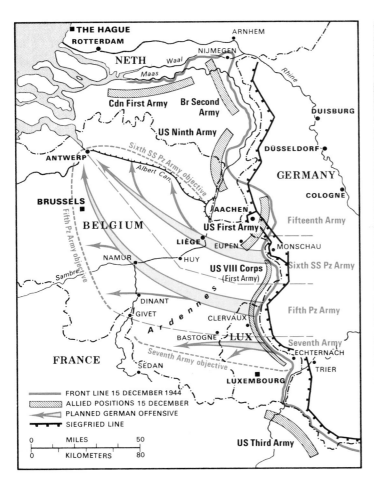

Planning Germany's Last Offensive

By September 1944 the Western Front had begun to settle down after the fluid operations that followed the Allied breakout from Normandy and although heavy Allied attacks continued in many sectors the German line had been shortened and their forces recovered some strength. The position on the Eastern Front was broadly similar. Hitler and his staff, therefore, began planning for a major counteroffensive using the reserves which this respite would enable them to build. Hitler believed that there was little real cooperation between the British and Americans, that both countries were weary of war and that, at heart, they were

hostile to Soviet communism. Accordingly he decided to attack in the west, convinced that a major success would at worst make Britain sue for peace and America devote her resources to the Pacific while at best there would be changes in the British and American leadership and both countries would join him in the crusade to save European civilization from the Bolsheviks.

The area chosen for the attack was the Ardennes region, where the decisive advance had been made in 1940. The grand aim was to recapture Antwerp, the Allies' most valuable port, and cut the Allied armies in two. Most of the planning was done by Hitler's immediate advisers and when Rundstedt, the Commander in Chief West, and Model, commander of Army Group B were told of the plan, both argued that it was impossibly over-ambitious. They were over-ruled and the preparations continued.

The Battle of the Bulge

When the German Ardennes offensive began on 16 December 1944 complete tactical and strategic surprise was achieved and the 24 German divisions in the attack were soon making gains at the expense of the six defending divisions of US V and VIII Corps. The Germans employed 10 armored divisions in the advance while most of their infantry was from newly-formed *Volksgrenadier* units. The German preparations had been conducted in extreme secrecy. The assembly of forces had been successfully concealed from Allied reconnaissance while radio traffic had been kept to a minimum, orders being distributed by land line or

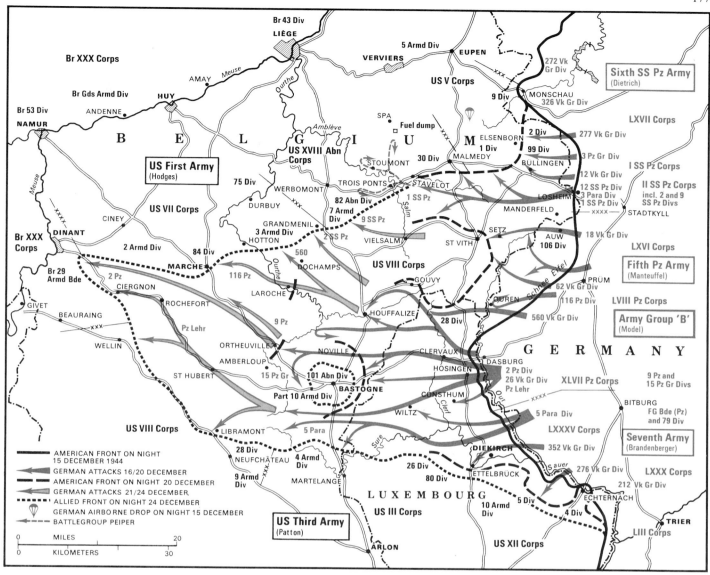

messenger. Although some information had reached the Allies they had become so accustomed to having clear and comprehensive proof of German intentions from their codebreaking services that the scattered hints were ignored.

Several other factors contributed to the initial German success. The overwhelming Allied air support was largely grounded for the first few days of the battle because of bad weather. Special German units, composed of English-speaking troops wearing American uniforms, were sent through the front line on sabotage missions. Although their physical achievements were slight they did succeed in causing considerable confusion. The defending American troops were also an unfortunate mixture of inexperienced newcomers and tired veterans.

The Allied response to the German attack was, however, immediate. Patton's Third Army quickly pulled forces from its front line and rushed them north while the US 82nd and 101st Airborne Divisions were the first of many units to arrive from the main

Allied reserve. On 19 December Eisenhower revised the Allied command arrangements giving Montgomery control of the British and American units north of the Bulge and Bradley charge of the forces to the south. Despite Montgomery's unpopularity with many of the American generals this was an efficient and sensible arrangement.

The Ardennes terrain is dominated by steep wooded hillsides and this places great emphasis on road movement. The decisive points in the battle were, therefore, the junctions at St Vith and Bastogne. Bastogne was successfully defended in an epic struggle by 101st Airborne and 10th Armored Divisions under the command of General McAuliffe. St Vith held out until 22 December by which time so much delay had been inflicted on the advance that all the German commanders wanted the offensive to be abandoned. Hitler insisted that the attacks be continued but by Christmas Eve they had been halted for good. Bastogne was relieved on 26 December as Allied counterattacks got under way. There was hard fighting

throughout January but by the end of the month all the German gains had been retaken. The overall result was a delay of a few weeks in the Allied operations but Germany's last reserve had been dissipated.

Warsaw to the Oder

Having reached the eastern suburbs of Warsaw in the summer of 1944, the Red Army waited until January 1945 before renewing its advance in this sector. The reason for this was partly because the main effort was being made in the Balkans and the Baltic states, partly because the Red Army needed to regroup and re-equip before starting on the final advance to Berlin.

The offensive toward Berlin began on 12 January. While an intense artillery bombardment prevented any German blow from the bridgehead south of Warsaw,

Zhukov advanced past Warsaw, then turned north and threatened the capital from the west, forcing the Germans to evacuate. On 17 January the Russians entered Warsaw and two days later were in Kutno. Konev, meantime, had been advancing through southern Poland and took Krakow on 19 January. In East Prussia, where German forces would have been in a position to threaten the rear of the Russian advance, Rokossovsky crossed the Vistula, passed the site of the Battle of Tannenberg, and reached the Baltic near Elbing. This cut off the Germans in East Prussia, who could be dealt with by Chernyakhovsky's forces, which had broken through the Masurian Lakes defense line farther north.

Only the River Oder now stood between the Red Army and Berlin. In the south, Konev encircled Breslau but postponed its capture while he pushed on to cross the Oder and to halt on the border with Saxony. Zhukov pursued a similar tactic, surrounding Poznan, reaching the Oder, and then occupying East Pomerania to secure his rear. By this time, having captured Danzig, Rokossovsky's troops could join Zhukov's. In preparation for the final stage of the war, Zhukov then forced a crossing of the Oder, establishing two bridgeheads to the north and south of Kustrin. Finally, bringing this phase to a satisfying conclusion, Königsberg surrendered to the Red Army on 9 April, ending German rule in East Prussia.

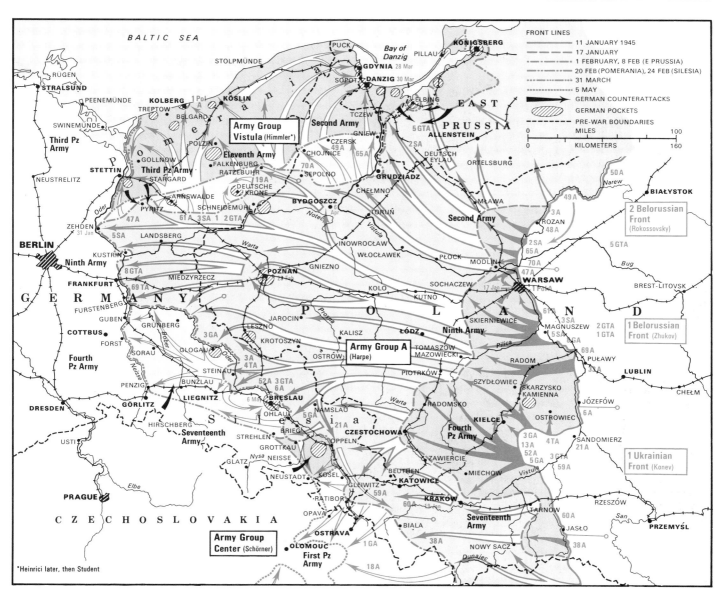

Below: US troops and equipment pour across the Remagen Bridge over the Rhine and into the heartland of Germany.

Across the Rhine

By the end of January 1945 the Battle of the Bulge was over and the German forces were on the defensive all along the Western Front.

The Allies were ready to resume their advance to the Rhine. The Allied plan was to begin their major efforts in the north in early February where British and Canadian forces were to advance through the difficult and heavily defended Reichswald terrain. In the next phase, from about the middle of the month, US Ninth and First Armies joined in. Initially there was fierce German resistance along the Roer especially at Düren and Jülich. The German defense was strengthened by use of floodwater from the Schwammenauel Dam. By this time Third Army was also advancing all along its front.

By early March the Allied forces had reached the Rhine almost everywhere north of Cologne when the US 9th Armored Division unexpectedly captured the Ludendorff railroad bridge at Remagen before it could be destroyed by the retreating Germans. Although the bridge collapsed on 17 March as a result of German air attacks and wear and tear from heavy use First Army was able to seize and consolidate a useful bridgehead on the right bank.

While this was going on Patton's Third Army and units of Sixth Army Group were rushing forward to the Rhine everywhere between Koblenz and Mannheim and less obviously 21 Army Group, including Ninth US Army, was regrouping for a carefully prepared crossing of the river. They were forestalled, however, by Patton's Third Army which sent units across at Nierstein in a rapidly improvised operation on 22 March. The British and Canadian crossing, Operation Plunder, got under way successfully on 23 March with the Ninth Army joining in on the 24th. Units of Third Army began crossing the Rhine south of Koblenz on the 25th and Seventh Army took its first bridgehead near Worms on the 26th. Resistance on the German side was collapsing accompanied by increasingly strident orders from Hitler for the institution of a scorched earth policy.

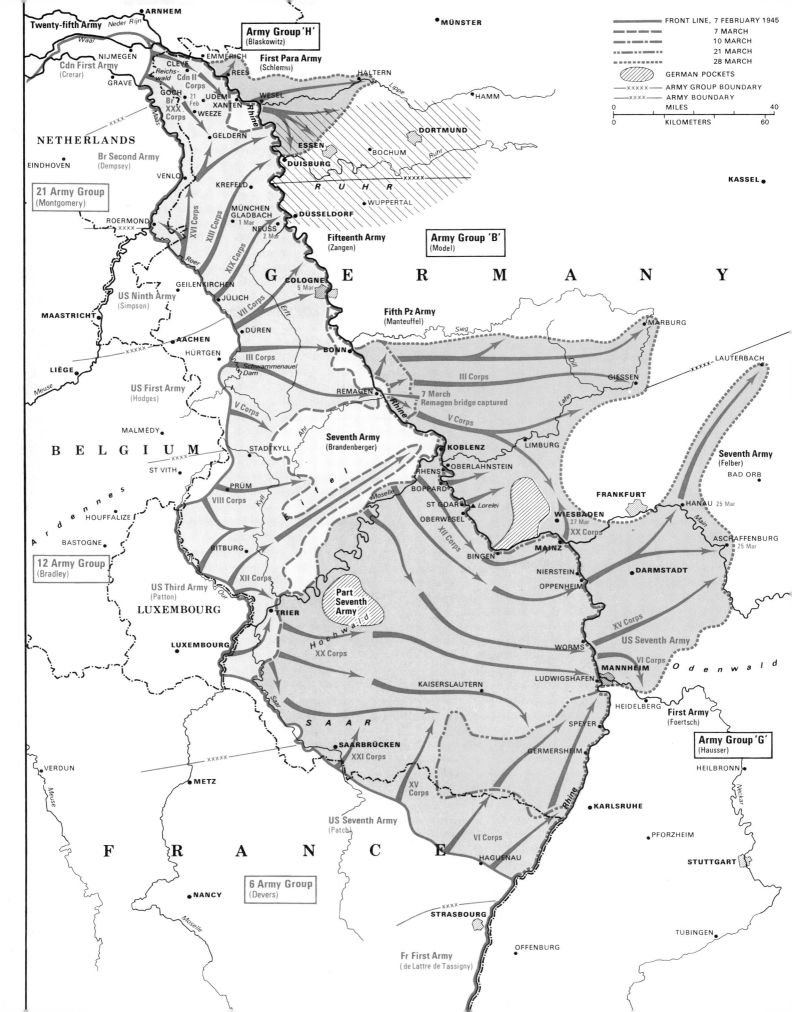

ARNHEM

Twenty-fifth Army
Neder Rijn

MÜNSTER

FRONT LINE, 7 FEBRUARY 1945
7 MARCH
10 MARCH
21 MARCH
28 MARCH
GERMAN POCKETS
ARMY GROUP BOUNDARY
ARMY BOUNDARY

MILES
0   40
KILOMETERS
0   60

Waal

NIJMEGEN

EMMERICH

REES

HALTERN

Army Group 'H'
(Blaskowitz)

First Para Army
(Schlemm)

Cdn First Army
(Crerar)

GRAVE

CLEVE
Reichs-
wald

Cdn II
Corps

Lippe

HAMM

GOCH
Br
XXX
Corps

21
Feb

UDEM
XANTEN

WESEL

Rhine

WEEZE

GELDERN

DORTMUND

NETHERLANDS

ESSEN

DUISBURG

BOCHUM

KASSEL

EINDHOVEN

Br Second Army
(Dempsey)

VENLO

KREFELD

R U H R

Ruhr

ROERMOND

21 Army Group
(Montgomery)

MÜNCHEN
GLADBACH
1 Mar

NEUSS
2 Mar

DÜSSELDORF

WUPPERTAL

XVI Corps

XIII Corps

Fifteenth Army
(Zangen)

Army Group 'B'
(Model)

Roer

XIX Corps

G   E   R   M   A   N   Y

GEILEN
KIRCHEN

COLOGNE
5 Mar

MAASTRICHT

US Ninth Army
(Simpson)

JÜLICH

Fifth Pz Army
(Manteuffel)

MARBURG

VII Corps

Erft

III Corps

Sieg

Dill

AACHEN

DÜREN

BONN

GIESSEN

LAUTERBACH

HÜRTGEN

III Corps
Schwammenauel
Dam

REMAGEN

7 March
Remagen bridge captured

Lahn

LIÈGE

Meuse

US First Army
(Hodges)

V Corps

Rhine

V Corps

LIMBURG

MALMÉDY

Ahr

Seventh Army
(Brandenberger)

KOBLENZ

Seventh Army
(Felber)

STADTKYLL

RHENS

OBERLAHNSTEIN

BAD ORB

B   E   L   G   I   U   M

ST VITH

PRÜM

Kyll

E i f e l

BOPPARD

Moselle

ST GOAR

FRANKFURT

HANAU   25 Mar

Ardennes

VIII Corps

OBERWESEL

Lorelei

WIESBADEN
27 Mar

XX Corps

ASCHAFFENBURG
25 Mar

HOUFFALIZE

XII Corps

MAINZ

BASTOGNE

BITBURG

BINGEN

NIERSTEIN

DARMSTADT

12 Army Group
(Bradley)

US Third Army
(Patton)

Our

XII Corps

Part
Seventh
Army

OPPENHEIM

LUXEMBOURG

TRIER

H o c h w a l d

XV Corps

XX Corps

WORMS

US Seventh Army

LUXEMBOURG

Saar

KAISERSLAUTERN

LUDWIGSHAFEN

VI Corps

O d e n w a l d

MANNHEIM

S   A   A   R

HEIDELBERG

First Army
(Foertsch)

VERDUN

SAARBRÜCKEN

XXI Corps

SPEYER

Army Group 'G'
(Hausser)

METZ

GERMERSHEIM

HEILBRONN

Meuse

XV Corps

Rhine

KARLSRUHE

US Seventh Army
(Patch)

PFORZHEIM

F   R   A   N   C   E

HAGUENAU

STUTTGART

NANCY

6 Army Group
(Devers)

Moselle

Neckar

TÜBINGEN

STRASBOURG

Fr First Army
(de Lattre de Tassigny)

OFFENBURG

Below: at the end of the war millions of Germans fled from the east as the Russian war machine advanced.

The Western Advance to the Elbe

By the end of March 1945 the western Allies had established substantial bridgeheads over the Rhine both north and south of the Ruhr industrial area. Although it had previously been his intention to aim his main effort farther north, General Eisenhower, the Supreme Commander, now became concerned by reports that the Germans were fortifying an 'Alpine Redoubt' in the south and were intending to make a last stand there. Eisenhower accordingly decided to switch his main attacks farther south to capitalize on the unexpected ease with which First and Third Armies had crossed the

Rhine and forestall retreat by the Germans into such a redoubt. Eisenhower signalled this decision directly to the Soviet High Command. Many of the British leaders felt that this decision was a mistake and that Eisenhower was exceeding his authority by communicating directly with the Soviets without permission from his superiors in Washington and London.

The Allied advance, however, continued as Eisenhower ordered. Although there were occasional stubborn pockets of German resistance most German formations were extremely short of fuel and ammunition and were only too glad to surrender to the western Allies rather than the Russians after a token fight. The Alpine Redoubt proved to be little more than one of Hitler's fantasies. In retrospect, therefore, Eisenhower's decision to concentrate on the

military objective of defeating the German Army seems to have been unnecessarily cautious and many would now argue that, although the various Allied occupation zones had already been agreed, it might well have profited the west to advance over the Elbe and farther into Czechoslovakia as would certainly have been possible.

The surrender of the German forces facing the British and Americans was agreed on 4 and 5 May and the formal German surrender was signed on the 7th. Fighting continued for a few days longer in Czechoslovakia. The Allied advances freed many thousands of concentration camp inmates and other victims of the Nazi regime. Although much was already known about Nazi crimes, film and pictures from the camps finally demonstrated the scale and enormity of these to the world.

D E N M A R K

BALTIC SEA

NORTH SEA

FLENSBURG

KIEL

Kiel Canal

ROSTOCK

RÜGEN

7 May

LÜBECK

WISMAR

SCHWERIN

STETTIN

HAMBURG
3 May

NEUSTRELITZ

STARGARD

WILHELMSHAVEN

BREMERHAVEN

18 Apr

Elbe

DANNENBERG

DÖMITZ

WITTENBERG

EMDEN

BREMEN
26 Apr

Lüneberg

ÜLZEN

Oder

KUSTRIN

GRONINGEN

OLDENBURG

Belsen

Heath

TANGERMÜNDE

BERLIN

AMSTERDAM

Army Group 'H'
(Blaskowitz)

OSNABRÜCK

4 Apr

Weser

HANNOVER
10 Apr

US Ninth Army

POTSDAM

FRANKFURT

NETHERLANDS

Twenty-fifth Army

ARNHEM

MÜNSTER

First Para Army

MINDEN

G   E

HAMELN

BRUNSWICK

MAGDEBURG

Twelfth Army

BARBY

ROSSLAU

R   M   A   N   Y

Teutoburger Wald

PADERBORN

Eleventh Army

BLANKENBURG

DESSAU
24 Apr

COTTBUS

Neisse

Cdn First Army
(Crerar)

WESEL

HAMM

LIPPSTADT

Harz Mts
Brocken Pk

US First Army

GÖTTINGEN

Leine

Saale

HALLE

GÖRLITZ

Br Second Army
(Dempsey)

ESSEN

DORTMUND

KASSEL

NORDHAUSEN

MERSEBURG

LEIPZIG

US Ninth Army
(Simpson)

DUISBURG

BOCHUM

Ruhr

WUPPERTAL

4
Apr

Sauerland

WEISSENFELS

COLDITZ

Elbe

DRESDEN

21 Army Group
(Montgomery)

DÜSSELDORF

Fifteenth Army

Army Group 'B'
(Model)

BUCHENWALD

ERFURT

WEIMAR

ZEITZ

CHEMNITZ

COLOGNE

Fifth Pz Army

GOTHA

JENA

OHRDRUF

US Third Army

USTÍ

LIEGE

BONN

Sieg

Dill

MARBURG

Thüringian Forest

Erzgebirge

BELGIUM

REMAGEN

Rhine

Lahn

GIESSEN

Seventh Army

FULDA 2 Apr

KARLOVY VARY

KOBLENZ

US First Army
(Hodges)

BAD ORB

HAMMELBURG

PRAGUE

12 Army Group
(Bradley)

WIESBADEN

FRANKFURT

HANAU

Spessart Mts

SCHWEINFURT

HOF

CZECHOSLOVAKIA

LUX

Main

MAINZ

ASCHAFFEN-
BURG

WÜRZBURG

BAMBERG

Odenwald

Bohemian Jura

PILSEN

LUXEMBOURG

TRIER

Moselle

OPPENHEIM

US Third Army
(Patton)

Seventh Army

BAYREUTH

WORMS

US Seventh Army
(Patch)

KITZINGEN 5 Apr

4 Apr

NÜREMBERG
20
Apr

Franconian Jura

FÜRTH

18 Apr

Bohemian Forest

CESKE
BUDEJOVICE

7 May

6 Army Group
(Devers)

MANNHEIM

Army Group 'G'
(Hausser)

ANSBACH

Danube

LINZ
5 May

SAARBRÜCKEN

First Army

HEILBRONN

REGENSBURG 26 Apr

THIONVILLE

KARLSRUHE

4 Apr

Löwenstein Hills

US Seventh
Army

LANDAU

PASSAU

US Third Army

Fr First Army
(de Lattre de Tassigny)

PFORZHEIM

8 Apr

STUTTGART

INGOLSTADT

Isar

LANDSHUT
30 Apr

NANCY

ESSLINGEN

KIRCHHEIM

Franconian Highlands

DONAUWÖRTH

First Army

STRASBOURG

TÜBINGEN

DILLINGEN

LANDSHUT
30 Apr

BRAUNAU

FRANCE

Schwarzwald

Nineteenth
Army

Swabian Highlands

ULM
23 Apr

AUGSBURG

Dachau

MUNICH
30 Apr

ROSENHEIM

SALZBURG
4 May

COLMAR

SIGMARINGEN

EHINGEN

LANDSBERG

US Seventh Army

Inn

FREIBURG

MEMMINGEN

OBERAMMERGAU
FÜSSEN

GARMISCH-
PARTENKIRCHEN

KUFSTEIN

BERCHTESGADEN
4 May

Eggs

BASLE

Fr First Army

*Lake
Constance*

BREGENZ

*Oberjoch
Pass*

*Fern
Pass*

KITZBÜHEL

SWITZERLAND

*Aalberg
Pass*

IMST

INNSBRUCK

A U S T R I A

T y r o l

LANDECK

Alps

TAMSWEG

*Brenner
Pass*

4 May

Resia Pass

KLAGENFURT

BOLZANO

I T A L Y

YUGOSLAVIA

US Fifth Army

OCCUPIED BY ALLIED FORCES, 28 MARCH 1945

BRITISH ATTACKS

US ATTACKS

FRENCH ATTACKS

GERMAN POCKETS

OCCUPIED BY RUSSIAN FORCES, 16 APRIL

CONCENTRATION CAMPS

MILES   120

0

KILOMETERS   200

0

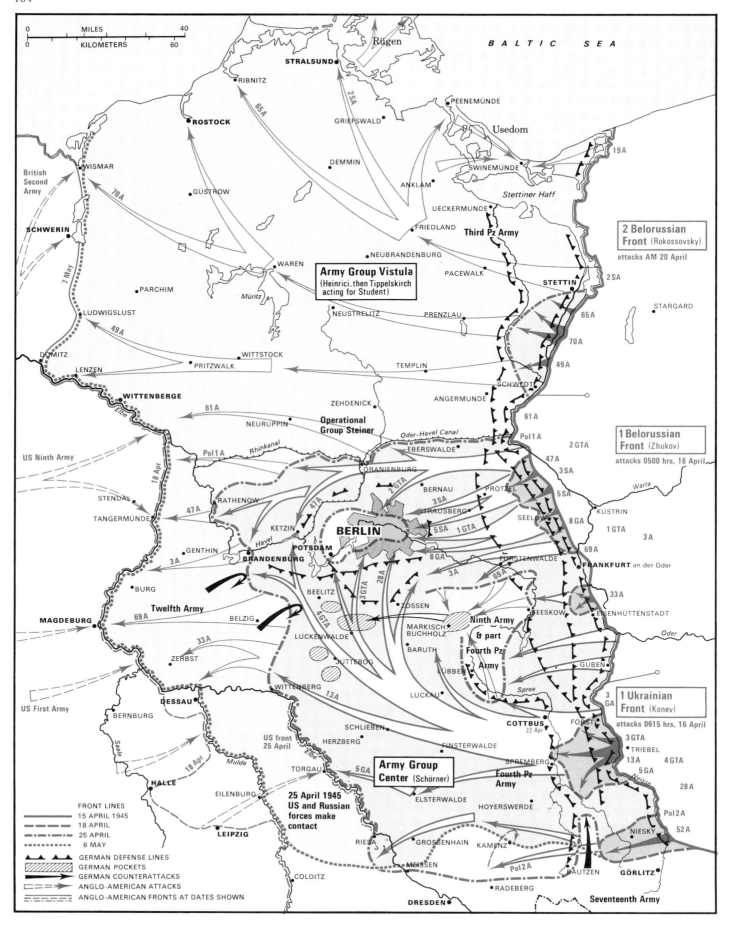

MILES 0 40
KILOMETERS 0 60

BALTIC SEA

Rügen
STRALSUND
RIBNITZ
PEENEMÜNDE
ROSTOCK
GRIEFSWALD
Usedom
DEMMIN
SWINEMÜNDE
19A
ANKLAM
Stettiner Haff
British
Second
Army
WISMAR
Third Pz Army
UECKERMUNDE
2 Belorussian
Front (Rokossovsky)
attacks AM 20 April
SCHWERIN
FRIEDLAND
STETTIN
65A
2SA
GÜSTROW
NEUBRANDENBURG
70A
STARGARD
7 May
Army Group Vistula
(Heinrici, then Tippelskirch
acting for Student)
PACEWALK
65A
PARCHIM
WAREN
Müritz
NEUSTRELITZ
PRENZLAU
70A
LUDWIGSLUST
49A
49A
DÖMITZ
WITTSTOCK
SCHWEDT
LENZEN
PRITZWALK
TEMPLIN
ANGERMÜNDE
WITTENBERGE
Elbe
ZEHDENICK
61A
61A
NEURUPPIN
Operational
Group Steiner
Oder-Havel Canal
Pol 1A
2 GTA
61A
Rhinkanal
EBERSWALDE
1 Belorussian
Front (Zhukov)
attacks 0500 hrs, 16 April
US Ninth Army
Pol 1A
ORANIENBURG
47A
3SA
Warta
18 Apr
2 GTA
BERNAU
PROTZEL
5SA
STENDAL
RATHENOW
47A
STRAUSBERG
8GA
KUSTRIN
TANGERMÜNDE
47A
KETZIN
BERLIN
5SA 1GTA
SEELOW
1 GTA
3A
Havel
POTSDAM
8 GA
69A
GENTHIN
BRANDENBURG
FÜRSTENWALDE
FRANKFURT an der Oder
3A
BURG
3A
28A
69A
BEELITZ
3GTA
33A
Twelfth Army
ZOSSEN
BEESKOW
EISENHÜTTENSTADT
MAGDEBURG
69A
BELZIG
4GTA
MARKISCH-
BUCHHOLZ
Ninth Army
& part
Fourth Pz
Army
Oder
33A
LUCKENWALDE
BARUTH
GUBEN
ZERBST
JÜTTEBOG
LÜBBEN
US First Army
WITTENBERG
13A
LUCKAU
Spree
1 Ukrainian
Front (Konev)
attacks 0615 hrs, 16 April
DESSAU
BERNBURG
Saale
US front
25 April
SCHLIEBEN
3
GA
COTTBUS
22 Apr
FORST
3GTA
HERZBERG
FINSTERWALDE
TRIEBEL
18 Apr
Mulde
Army Group
Center (Schörner)
Fourth Pz
Army
SPREMBERG
13A
4GTA
HALLE
TORGAU
5A
Elbe
Neisse
5GA
EILENBURG
25 April 1945
US and Russian
forces make
contact
ELSTERWERDA
HOYERSWERDE
28A
LEIPZIG
RIESA
GROSSENHAIN
KAMENZ
NIESKY
Pol 2A
52A
COLDITZ
MEISSEN
Pol 2A
BAUTZEN
GÖRLITZ
RADEBERG
DRESDEN
Seventeenth Army

FRONT LINES
15 APRIL 1945
18 APRIL
25 APRIL
6 MAY
GERMAN DEFENSE LINES
GERMAN POCKETS
GERMAN COUNTERATTACKS
ANGLO-AMERICAN ATTACKS
ANGLO-AMERICAN FRONTS AT DATES SHOWN

Bottom: Soviet tanks advance down a
street in Berlin during the closing weeks of
the war in Europe.

The Fall of Berlin

The Red Army's final advance began on 16
April 1945. From his two bridgeheads at
Kustrin, Zhukov's troops broke through
the German defenses and advanced toward
Berlin. His ultimate objective was the River
Elbe, beyond Berlin, which was the pre-
viously-agreed line where the Anglo-American and Russian occupation zones should
meet. South of Zhukov, Konev used bridgeheads on the west bank of the Neisse to start
an advance whose left flank was to take
Dresden while its right turned north to help
surround Berlin. It was Konev's men who,
having bypassed Dresden, were the first
Russian soldiers to link up with the Americans advancing from the west; this happened
at Torgau, on the Elbe, on 25 April.

On 22 April, Zhukov's First Belorussian
Front reached the autobahn ringing Berlin,
and moved along it to Spandau. With
Konev's troops, this effected the complete
encirclement of the German capital. Inside
Berlin were Hitler and his closest associates,
about two million civilians, and 30,000
defenders. On the outskirts, however, were
up to one million German troops destined
for a last-ditch defense of the city. By this

time the bottom of the German manpower
barrel had been scraped, and many of these
troops were only half-trained, or of doubtful
health, or well below military age. Nevertheless, in the circumstances of a backs-to-
the-wall struggle they could be expected to
take a heavy toll of the attackers. The latter,
with their supporting units, numbered about
two and one-half million men, well-trained,
well-equipped, experienced, and having the
advantage of Soviet command of the air.

In the final assault, Zhukov's Front
attacked from the north and Konev's First
Ukrainian Front from the south. After two
days of fierce fighting Zhukov's tanks
reached the northern outskirts on 28 April,
by which time Konev's infantry and tanks
had fought their way as far as the Tiergarten,
which lay close to the center of Berlin. The
two Russian fronts were thus only a mile
apart, but it took another four days of
house-to-house fighting, a Stalingrad in
reverse, before they linked up. By this time
Hitler, whose bunker lay between these two
Russian pincers, had killed himself. The
senior surviving German officer, General
Krebs, went to negotiate with the Russians
and was confronted with a demand for un-
conditional surrender. By 2 May the red
flag was flying from the chancellery and
fighting had ceased.

Battle of the Philippine Sea

After the capture of Kwajalein and Eni-
wetok in the Marshall Islands the next
targets for the US offensive were Saipan,
Tinian and Guam in the Marianas. The
main US carrier forces began preparatory
attacks for the landings on 11 June 1944 and
Admiral Toyoda, the Commander in Chief
of the Japanese Combined Fleet, prepared
for a full-scale battle. The Japanese naval
forces came under the direct command of
Admiral Ozawa and included five fleet
carriers, two light and two seaplane carriers
as well as five battleships and numerous
supporting vessels. Altogether these ships
carried about 470 aircraft and there were
about 100 more on Guam which survived
the preliminary American attacks to take
part in the battle. The Americans had about
950 aircraft on their seven fleet and eight
light carriers as well as superior numbers in
other classes of ship. Most of the US ships
were from Admiral Mitscher's TF.58 but
Admiral Spruance, the overall commander
of the Marianas invasion, was also present.
The US forces were well warned of the

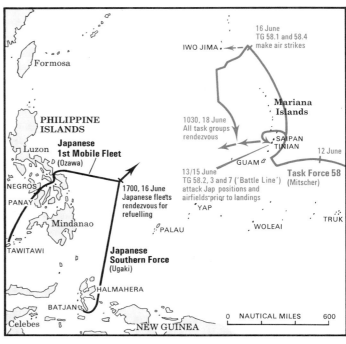

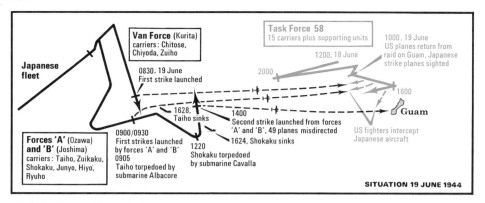

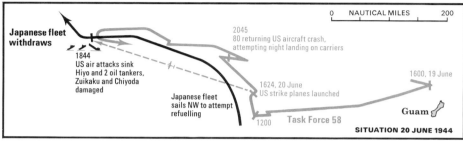

The Battles for Leyte

After considerable discussion the Allied High Command decided that, on completion of the Marianas battles and the campaign in New Guinea, the American forces should next begin the reconquest of the Philippines with landings on Leyte Island. General MacArthur's forces from the Southwest Pacific command area combined with Admiral Nimitz's for this operation.

Japanese approach through submarine sightings and a further disadvantage for Ozawa was that the Marianas commanders had failed to inform him how badly hit their air forces had been by the early US attacks. Practically the sole Japanese advantage was that their aircraft generally had a longer range and so they could expect to get in their strikes first.

This in fact they did on 19 June, the first day of the battle. The Americans were content to defend and did so so successfully that their pilots and gunners dubbed the battle the 'Great Marianas Turkey Shoot.' The Americans lost 29 planes and the Japanese about 300 including a number destroyed over Guam. Only one bomb hit an American ship. Two Japanese carriers were sunk by American submarines. On the 20th the Americans pursued and managed to sink a third carrier but lost a number of aircraft.

The Battle of the Philippine Sea dealt a further serious blow to Japanese naval power. Far more than the ships lost, the trained carrier pilots and their aircraft could not be replaced and in the next major naval encounter, the Battle of Leyte Gulf, the Japanese carriers could only find token air groups to embark.

With the US naval forces dominant the ground battles for the Marianas Islands could only go one way despite the ferocious Japanese resistance. There were landings on Saipan on 15 June even before the Philippine Sea Battle, on Guam on 21 July and on Tinian on 24 July. The largest Japanese garrison, 27,000 men, was on Saipan but the last effective resistance there was wiped out on 9 July and the battles for Tinian (garrison 6000) and Guam (10,000) were both concluded by mid-August. Almost all the Japanese defenders on all three islands were killed while the Americans lost over 5000 dead and 20,000 wounded.

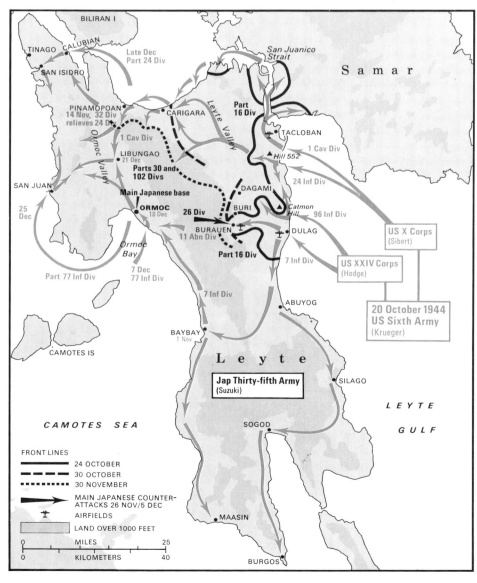

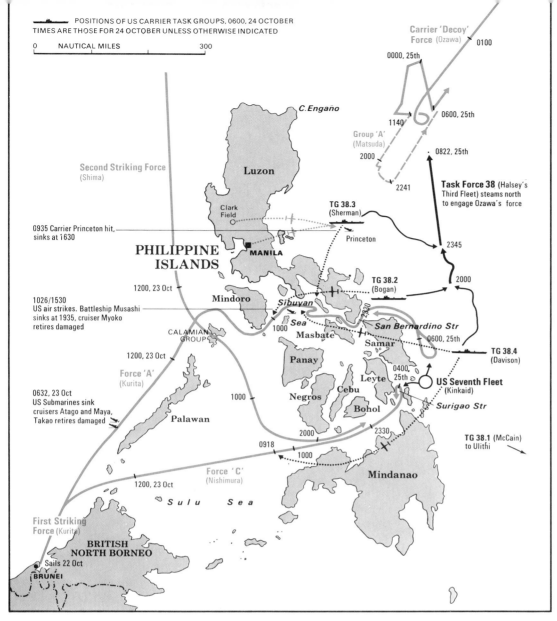

POSITIONS OF US CARRIER TASK GROUPS, 0600, 24 OCTOBER
TIMES ARE THOSE FOR 24 OCTOBER UNLESS OTHERWISE INDICATED

0   NAUTICAL MILES   300

Carrier 'Decoy' Force (Ozawa)   0100

0000, 25th

Group 'A' (Matsuda)

1140   0600, 25th

0822, 25th

2000

2241

Task Force 38 (Halsey's Third Fleet) steams north to engage Ozawa's force

2345

2000

Second Striking Force (Shima)

C. Engano

Luzon

Clark Field

TG 38.3 (Sherman)

0935 Carrier Princeton hit, sinks at 1630

Princeton

PHILIPPINE ISLANDS

MANILA

TG 38.2 (Bogan)

1200, 23 Oct

Mindoro

Sibuyan

2330

San Bernardino Str

0600, 25th

TG 38.4 (Davison)

1026/1530 US air strikes. Battleship Musashi sinks at 1935, cruiser Myoko retires damaged

Sea

1000

Masbate

Samar

CALAMIAN GROUP

0400, 25th

Leyte

US Seventh Fleet (Kinkaid)

1200, 23 Oct

Panay

Force 'A' (Kurita)

Cebu

1000

Negros

Bohol

Surigao Str

0632, 23 Oct US Submarines sink cruisers Atago and Maya, Takao retires damaged

Palawan

2000

2330

TG 38.1 (McCain) to Ulithi

0918

1000

Force 'C' (Nishimura)

Mindanao

1200, 23 Oct

S u l u   S e a

First Striking Force (Kurita)

BRITISH NORTH BORNEO

Sails 22 Oct

BRUNEI

On land the familiar story of overwhelming American forces gradually wearing down a totally determined defense was repeated. General Krueger's Sixth Army could call on up to 200,000 troops of whom some 130,000 landed on the first day. Initially the Japanese had just over 20,000 men on Leyte and although substantial reinforcements were brought in, these usually took heavy casualties in transit from US air attacks. The Japanese 26th Division, for example, arrived practically bereft of rations and artillery. Although mopping up extended well into 1945 there were few important engagements after Christmas 1944. Japanese casualties have been estimated variously from 50–80,000. The Americans lost 3600 dead.

At sea the Japanese again tried to turn the tide of the war by bringing on a major fleet action. The three-part battle that resulted is known as the Battle of Leyte Gulf. The Japanese naval air arm had lost so many planes and pilots earlier in the war that the remaining aircraft carriers had very few aircraft to embark. It was decided, therefore,

to use the carriers as a decoy while the substantial battleship and cruiser force did the real damage. The strongest squadron, Force A, was to reach the American invasion area via the San Bernardino Strait while two smaller forces advanced by the Surigao Strait.

Force A was detected en route by American submarines and heavily attacked by them and aircraft summed from the main US carrier formation, TF.38. These attacks made Force A turn away. Mistaking this temporary move for a permanent withdrawal, the American carriers then sped north to catch Ozawa's decoy force. Since Force C had also been detected the bombardment support ships of Seventh Fleet were moved to block its approach, in the belief that the San Bernardino Strait was still guarded by TF.38. Nishimura's ships were almost all destroyed in a night battle and Shima turned back after also suffering some losses. The American carriers sank many of Ozawa's ships including the last veteran of Pearl Harbor, the *Zuikaku*. However, Kurita had reversed course and on the morning of

25 October his battleships and cruisers came into gun range of some of the vulnerable and practically unsupported escort carriers of Seventh Fleet. If the Japanese ships had been well and resolutely commanded they might even have penetrated into the American transport fleet and caused untold destruction. Instead they withdrew tamely after only limited success. The Battle of Leyte Gulf was the last important effort of the Japanes Navy.

The task of the Allied naval forces was made more hazardous by the beginning of preplanned suicide attacks by Japanese aircraft. The first ship hit by a Kamikaze attack, on 21 October, was the cruiser *Australia*, one of several Australian ships serving with the American forces.

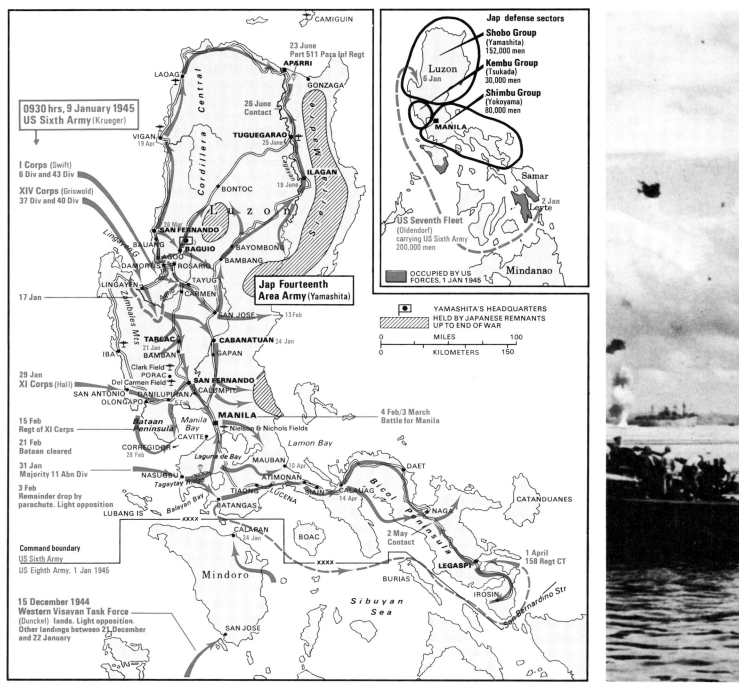

The following labels appear on the map:

CAMIGUIN

23 June
Part 511 Para Inf Regt
APARRI
LAOAG
GONZAGA
26 June
Contact
VIGAN
19 Apr
TUGUEGARAO
25 June

**0930 hrs, 9 January 1945
US Sixth Army** (Krueger)

Cordillera Central

ILAGAN
19 June

I Corps (Swift)
6 Div and 43 Div

XIV Corps (Griswold)
37 Div and 40 Div

BONTOC
Luzon
Sierra Madre

26 Mar
SAN FERNANDO
BAUANG
BAGUIO
AGOO
DAMORTIS
ROSARIO
BAYOMBONG
BAMBANG
LINGAYEN
17 Jan
TAYUG
CARMEN

**Jap Fourteenth
Area Army** (Yamashita)

SAN JOSE
13 Feb

TARLAC
21 Jan
BAMBAN
IBA
Clark Field
PORAC
Del Carmen Field
CABANATUAN 24 Jan
GAPAN
SAN FERNANDO
CALUMPIT

**29 Jan
XI Corps** (Hall)
SAN ANTONIO
OLONGAPO
DANILUPIHAN
5 Feb

MANILA
4 Feb/3 March
Battle for Manila
Nielson & Nichols Fields

**15 Feb
Regt of XI Corps**
**Bataan
Peninsula**
Manila
Bay
CAVITE
Lamon Bay

**21 Feb
Bataan cleared**
CORREGIDOR
28 Feb

**31 Jan
Majority 11 Abn Div**
Laguna de Bay
MAUBAN
10 Apr
DAET

NASUGBU
Tagaytay Ridge
ATIMONAN
LUCENA
Bicol Peninsula

**3 Feb
Remainder drop by
parachute. Light opposition**
TIAONG
SIAIN
CALAUAG
14 Apr
CATANDUANES

LUBANG IS
Balayan Bay
BATANGAS
XXXX

Command boundary
US Sixth Army
US Eighth Army, 1 Jan 1945
CALAPAN
24 Jan
BOAC
NAGA
2 May
Contact
1 April
158 Regt CT
LEGASPI

Mindoro
XXXX
BURIAS
IROSIN
San Bernardino Str

**15 December 1944
Western Visayan Task Force**
(Dunckel) lands. Light opposition.
Other landings between 21 December
and 22 January
SAN JOSE
Sibuyan
Sea

Inset map labels:

Jap defense sectors
Shobo Group
(Yamashita)
152,000 men
Kembu Group
(Tsukada)
30,000 men
Shimbu Group
(Yokoyama)
80,000 men
Luzon
6 Jan
MANILA
Samar
2 Jan
Leyte

US Seventh Fleet
(Oldendorf)
carrying US Sixth Army
200,000 men
Mindanao

OCCUPIED BY US
FORCES, 1 JAN 1945

YAMASHITA'S HEADQUARTERS
HELD BY JAPANESE REMNANTS
UP TO END OF WAR

0   MILES   100
0   KILOMETERS   150

The Capture of Luzon

The Japanese commander responsible for the whole Philippines group, General Yamashita, had been ordered, against his better judgment, to do his utmost to hold Leyte in face of the American attacks. Thus when the Americans quickly moved to invade Luzon as the fighting on Leyte died down, the Japanese forces, though numerically strong, were neither well armed nor well prepared. Kamikaze attacks against the landing fleet were fairly successful in their way for the first few days of the operation but after this almost all the Japanese aircraft were with-drawn from the Philippines to Formosa or had been destroyed.

After his losses on Leyte Yamashita did not believe that he could repel an American landing and accordingly the beach defenses were only lightly held. Instead Yamashita planned to make his stand in the inland mountain areas for as long as possible and so tie down large American forces. Particularly in north Luzon this was the pattern that the fighting took on. Baguio, where Yamashita had had his HQ, was not taken until 27 April and when he surrendered at the end of the war Yamashita still had some 50,000 fighting men under his command.

Undoubtedly the most bitterly contested part of the campaign was the recapture of Manila. The city garrison died almost to a man in the defense and the fighting left Manila in ruins. By the end of the war landing operations in cooperation with Filipino guerillas had taken control of most of the other islands of the Philippine group.

**Above: US Navy PT-Boats come under attack from Japanese bombers during the reoccupation of the Philippines.
Top right: GIs take cover from sniper fire during the fighting to recapture Clark Field airbase in the Philippines.**

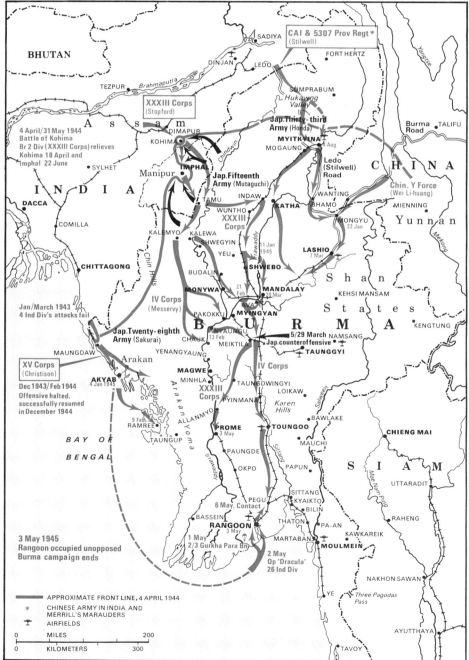

The map labels, reading within the figure:

BHUTAN

CAI & 5307 Prov Regt *
(Stilwell)

SADIYA
DINJAN
LEDO
FORT HERTZ
Yangtse

XXXIII Corps
(Stopford)

TEZPUR Brahmaputra
SUMPRABUM
Hukawng Valley
Burma TALIFU
Road

A s s a m
DIMAPUR
KOHIMA
Jap.Thirty-third
Army (Honda)
MYITKYINA 4 Aug
MOGAUNG
C H I N A

4 April/31 May 1944
Battle of Kohima
Br 2 Div (XXXIII Corps) relieves
Kohima 18 April and
Imphal 22 June

SYLHET
Manipur
IMPHAL
Chindwin
Jap.Fifteenth
Army (Mutaguchi)
INDAW
Ledo (Stilwell)
Road
WANTING
Chin. Y Force
(Wei Li-huang)
MIENNING
Y u n n a n

I N D I A
TAMU
WUNTHO
KATHA
BHAMO
MONGYU 22 Jan

DACCA
KALEMYO KALEWA
XXXIII
Corps
11 Jan
1945
Irrawaddy
LASHIO
7 Mar
S h a n

COMILLA
SHWEGYIN
YEU
SHWEBO

CHITTAGONG
BUDALIN
21 Feb
MANDALAY
20 Mar
KEHSI MANSAM
S t a t e s

MONYWA
AVA
MYINGYAN

IV Corps
(Messervy)
PAKOKKU
KENGTUNG

Jan/March 1943
4 Ind Div's attacks fail

B U R M A
NYAUNGU
13 Feb
MEIKTILA
5/29 March
Jap.counteroffensive
NAMSANG

Jap.Twenty-eighth
Army (Sakurai)
CHAUK
TAUNGGYI

MAUNGDAW Arakan
YENANGYAUNG
IV Corps

XV Corps
(Christison)
AKYAB
4 Jan 1945
MAGWE
MINHLA
XXXIII
Corps
TAUNGDWINGYI
LOIKAW
CHIENG MAI

Dec 1943/Feb 1944
Offensive halted,
successfully resumed
in December 1944

Arakan Yoma
PYINMANA
Karen
Hills
BAWLAKE
S I A M

9 Feb
RAMREE
ALLANMYO
PROME
3 May
TOUNGOO
MAUCHI
Mae Nam Ping
UTTARADIT

BAY OF
BENGAL
TAUNGUP
PAUNGDE
PAPUN
RAHENG

3 May 1945
Rangoon occupied unopposed
Burma campaign ends

OKPO
Pegu Yoma
Irrawaddy
Sittang
6 May. Contact
PEGU
SITTANG
KYAIKTO
BILIN
THATON
PA-AN
KAWKAREIK

BASSEIN
RANGOON
3 May
1 May
2/3 Gurkha Para Bn
MARTABAN
MOULMEIN

2 May
Op 'Dracula'
26 Ind Div

NAKHON SAWAN

YE
Three Pagodas
Pass

TAVOY
AYUTTHAYA

APPROXIMATE FRONT LINE, 4 APRIL 1944
* CHINESE ARMY IN INDIA AND
MERRILL'S MARAUDERS
AIRFIELDS

0 MILES 200
0 KILOMETERS 300

The Burma Campaign

To most of the Allied leaders the Burma theater came very low on the scale of priorities. Even when they agreed that resources could be sent there, the British and Americans rarely agreed on the strategy to be followed. The Americans thought that the main objective should be to reopen land communications with the Chinese Nationalists to help them against the large forces of the Japanese Army which were tied up in China. The British had far less respect for Chiang and the Nationalists (perhaps more realistically) and preferred to plan to recover the imperial territories lost to the Japanese in 1942.

Whatever strategy was to be followed it was first necessary to build a respectable fighting force from the shattered remnants that had retreated to the Indian border in April-May 1942. Much work had also to be done to improve communications between India and northern Burma. The first offensive move, an advance in the Arakan in early 1943, was decisively defeated by Japanese infiltration tactics. A new British commander, General Slim, took over at the end of this operation and developed new tactics. He laid down that, in future, encircled units should not retreat to restore their communications but hold out with the help of air supply while reserve units retook the rear areas. A further innovation based on the use of air supply was the establishment of independent units designed to operate behind the Japanese lines. The efforts of these Chindits or their American equivalent, the Maurauders, were not an unqualified military success but they made an important contribution to Allied morale by showing that it was possible to take on the Japanese in the jungle and win. The technique of supplying surrounded formations from the air helped stem a limited Japanese counteroffensive in the Arakan early in 1944 and played a vital part in defeating the major Japanese offensive that followed in the battles of Imphal and Kohima. This campaign was by far the heaviest defeat that the Japanese Army had suffered to that time. The Allied forces resumed their advance on all fronts in late 1944, after the monsoon, and the Japanese were again soundly beaten in the decisive battles around Meiktila and Mandalay. Rangoon was captured by a seaborne landing at the start of May 1945 after virtually all the Japanese forces had been expelled from Burma.

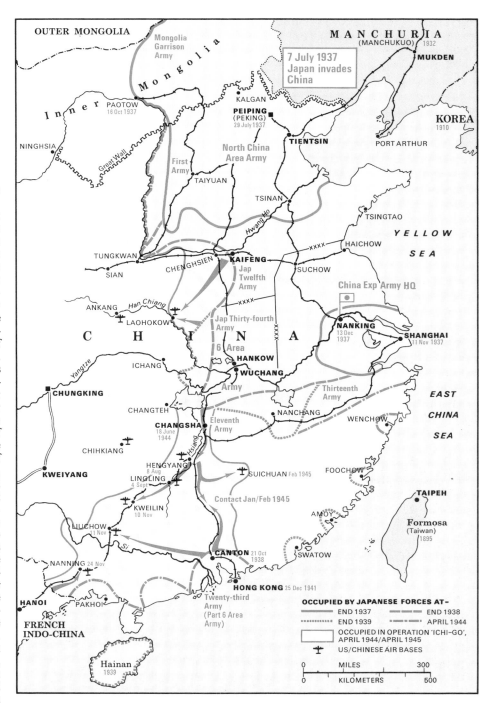

The War in China

Following Japan's establishment of Manchukuo in 1931–32, there was little fighting between Japan and China until 1937. The Chinese were absorbed in the struggle between the Nationalists and Communists while the Japanese government was opposed to further aggressive moves although it was not always in full control of the army. In July 1937 an incident between Japanese and Nationalist soldiers on the Peking–Tientsin railroad quickly escalated into a major Japanese invasion. There was no declaration of war by either side at this stage. Large areas of China were quickly overrun and Chiang Kai-shek was forced to move his capital to Chungking. Chiang did receive some help from Britain and America but neither country was able or willing to do much at this point.

By 1939 the Japanese advance had been stopped and the Japanese forces were consolidating their gains while it seemed that Chiang had been reduced to being a minor warlord. From then until 1944 the Japanese made no major forward moves apart from occasional 'rice offensives' to seize food supplies, and attacks against the mainly communist guerrilla forces. Chiang's position recovered to some degree with considerable help from the western allies although

Below: American Marines man forward positions on Iwo Jima facing Mount Suribachi. Casualties were very heavy on both sides in this operation.

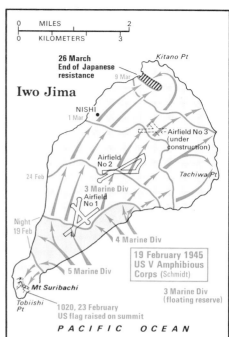

their supply efforts were hampered by the cutting of the Burma Road by the Japanese advance in 1942. From then until January 1945 all supplies to Chiang had to be flown 'Over the Hump' from India. Large quantities were sent, some to General Chennault's Fourteenth US Air Force. Corruption within the Kuomintang and Chiang's preoccupation with building up his forces to meet the Communists, meant that the Kuomintang did not make full use of the supplies against the Japanese.

However, the growing strength and activity of Fourteenth Air Force provoked the Japanese into renewing their attacks. Their initial efforts were by First and Twelfth Armies in April 1944 in the Kaifeng area

and, after some regrouping, the attacks were extended south later in the year. In the meantime Superfortress bombers based near Calcutta in India had attacked targets in the Japanese Home Islands using forward airfields in China. Despite the additional incentive this gave to the Japanese attacks the difficult communications and the demands of other areas meant that progress was very slow by early 1945. In the final months of the war the Nationalists recovered some territory near the Indo-China border.

Iwo Jima

After Saipan and Tinian in the Marianas Islands were taken by the US forces in June and July 1944 huge air bases were constructed there from which B-29 Superfortress bombers could begin an all-out strategic bombing attack on Japan. Although the Japanese air defense system was never as efficient as the German effort to ward off the Allied bomber offensive in Europe, losses were uncomfortably high. A base on Iwo Jima could be used to provide needed fighter support and an emergency landing ground for damaged bombers unable to complete the long journey back to the Marianas. This was the principal reason for the US attack but since it was a part of metropolitan Japan the capture of Iwo Jima would be good for morale too.

From the outset it was clear that a stubborn defense of the island could be expected and a massive preliminary air and naval bombardment was ordered. However, the 21,000-strong Japanese garrison led by General Kuribayashi had constructed an astonishingly elaborate and resilient defense system much of which survived the early attacks. The Japanese plan was to wait until the landings had just begun before showing their hand and opening fire. In the event they held off a little too long and the Marines were able to fight their way off the beaches. By the end of the first day 30,000 US troops were ashore. Although the battle could now have only one result the complex of trenches, tunnels and strongpoints and the fanatical determination of the defenders meant that the US forces had to fight for virtually every yard of the island. Casualties were very high. The US forces lost 6800 dead and 20,000 wounded.

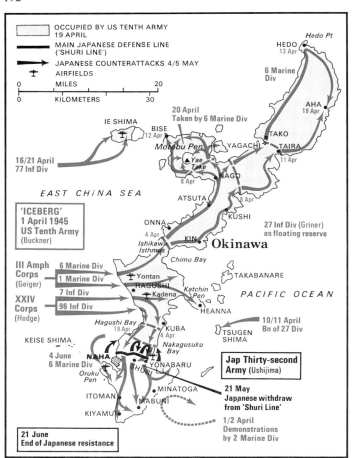

OCCUPIED BY US TENTH ARMY
19 APRIL
MAIN JAPANESE DEFENSE LINE
('SHURI LINE')
JAPANESE COUNTERATTACKS 4/5 MAY
AIRFIELDS

Okinawa

The attack on Okinawa was planned as the last major landing operation before the invasion of the Japanese home islands for which the capture of Okinawa was necessary to provide harbor and air base facilities. As was customary the campaign began with carrier and other air attacks to soften up the local defenses and the supporting air bases on Kyushu. The newly-active British Pacific Fleet joined in these operations. The carrier and bombardment groups continued to give support throughout the battle.

The Japanese Thirty-second Army defending Okinawa under General Ushijima's command was about 130,000 strong and had most of its forces concentrated at the southern end of the island behind a formidable position known as the Shuri Line. There was no intention of resisting the Americans on the beaches and the only heavily defended areas apart from the Shuri position were the Motobu Peninsula and the offshore island of Ie Shima.

The American landings began on 1 April and, as the map shows, most of the island was quickly overrun with little opposition. However, XXIV Corps made little progress once the Shuri Line defenses were met. Despite overwhelming air and bombardment support, gains were few until unsuccessful Japanese attacks in early May had

given away the locations of many of their defensive positions. From that time reinforced attacks by both US corps gradually pushed forward to finish the battle despite difficult ground and weather conditions.

The supporting naval forces had a fierce battle of their own to fight. The kamikaze attacks which had become a feature of Japanese tactics were here developed to their fullest extent. Several thousand Japanese aircraft were destroyed during the Okinawa operation, a great number of them kamikazes. The US and British naval forces had 36 ships sunk and 368 damaged, almost all of them by suicide attacks. Perhaps the most bizarre aspect of the campaign was the employment of the giant battleship *Yamato* which was sent off to Okinawa on what amounted to a suicide mission since too little fuel was carried to make a return journey possible. The *Yamato* was sunk by US carrier planes on 7 April long before she could reach the invasion area and without causing the hoped-for disruption to the American air defense system which would have allowed the simultaneous program of air attacks to achieve important successes.

The casualty lists on both sides were extensive. For the first time a significant number of Japanese troops, over 7000, was taken prisoner, but this still meant that over 120,000 died or committed suicide. In addition there were a great many civilian casualties. Okinawa was fairly densely populated and the local people had been in-

doctrinated with stories of American brutality. The US forces lost 12,500 dead, including the Army Commander General Buckner, and 35,000 wounded. As a rehearsal for the invasion of Japan these casualty totals were frightening to the Americans and could only support the case for bringing the war to an end by other means.

Left: Marines from the Sixth Division
reach the outskirts of Naha on Okinawa,
6 June 1945.
Bottom: F4U Corsair fighters are
silhouetted by antiaircraft fire during a
Japanese air raid on Yontan airfield,
Okinawa, April 1945.
Right: Soviet occupying forces in Harbin
Manchuria, August 1945.

Manchuria

After the end of the war in Europe strong Soviet forces were transferred to the Far East to face the Japanese in Manchuria. The USSR declared war on Japan on 8 August 1945 and the Soviet armies attacked on the following day. They employed about 1,500,000 men against the Japanese commander Yamada's 1,000,000 and had far superior tanks and other equipment as well as overwhelming air support. There was little real fighting and Manchuria and northern Korea were quickly overrun.

The possibility of Soviet participation in the Pacific War was first raised seriously at the inter-Allied Teheran conference in December 1943. Stalin promised to join the war against Japan as soon as the war in Europe was over and this promise was confirmed at Yalta in February 1945 in return for some territorial concessions and the promise of Soviet influence in the region being recognized. Roosevelt was the principal architect of these negotiations and he has been criticized for setting aside earlier promises to Chiang Kai-shek to gain this Soviet help. At the time, however, it was generally felt, bearing in mind the very large Japanese forces undefeated in China and the normal ferocity of Japanese resistance elsewhere in the Pacific, that Soviet participation in the war against Japan would be of vital help.

The Allied leaders met again at Potsdam in July 1945 and issued new calls on the Japanese to surrender. By this time also the atomic bomb had become available and President Truman ordered its use if the Japanese did not respond to the Potsdam Declaration. Although many Japanese leaders wanted peace and had tried to communicate with the Allies through still-neutral Russia, they were unwilling to consider capitulation unless the position of the Emperor was guaranteed and they therefore made no satisfactory reply to the Potsdam message. The first atomic bomb was therefore dropped on Hiroshima on 6 August 1945 and the second on Nagasaki on the 9th as the Soviet attacks began. It has been suggested that the Soviet attacks were started earlier than planned so that advantage could be gained before the bombs forced the Japanese to surrender. If this was the case then there is evidence that this was misguided since Japanese records lay as much stress on the Soviet attacks as on the atomic bombs as the final cause which brought about the surrender. The western Allies were able to celebrate victory over Japan on 15 August although some fighting continued in Manchuria for a few days longer.

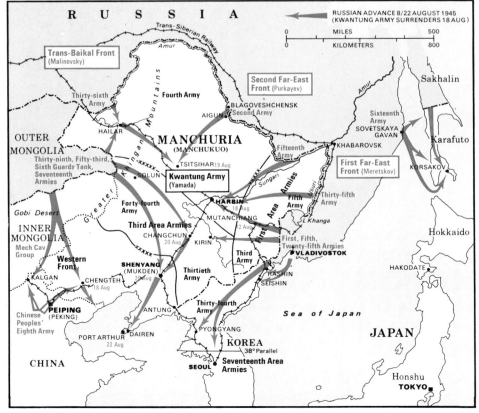

194

Tanzanian troops advance past a burning
Ugandan vehicle during the fighting to
depose General Amin in 1978.

The Postwar World

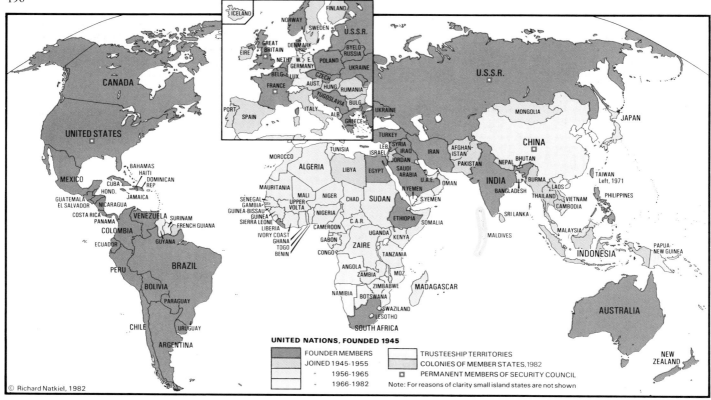

UNITED NATIONS, FOUNDED 1945

FOUNDER MEMBERS
JOINED 1945-1955
"   1956-1965
"   1966-1982

TRUSTEESHIP TERRITORIES
COLONIES OF MEMBER STATES, 1982
□ PERMANENT MEMBERS OF SECURITY COUNCIL
Note: For reasons of clarity small island states are not shown

© Richard Natkiel, 1982

The United Nations

Looking back at the failures of the League of Nations, the statesmen who in 1945 planned the United Nations Organization laid priority on two precautions: UNO was to have a membership of as near as possible all states, and the great powers had to be among that membership. Secondly, it had to have within itself a small group of powerful states which would not hesitate to act together against a threat to world peace. It was from these considerations that the concept of a General Assembly representing all nations, with a small Security Council as its executive branch, was embodied in the United Nations Charter.

Even though it was only the handful of victorious powers which had the initiative in composing the UN Charter, they could only reach overall agreement at the expense of compromise which weakened the Organization. Thus the concept of one-state-one-vote was weakened when the USSR was granted three seats in the General Assembly; Moscow had argued that if the British dominions each had a seat, so should the constituent republics of the USSR, and after some argument it was agreed that Byelorussia and the Ukraine should have their own representatives. The Security Council was to consist of five permanent members and six (later ten) short-term members. The five permanent members were the victorious powers (USA, USSR, Britain, France, China), each of which had the right to veto a resolution. In practice this

meant that the Council could be paralyzed and, with some exceptions, the peacekeeping activity of UNO depended on the agreement, all too rare, of the permanent members. In practice, therefore, its existence has facilitated rather than compelled conciliation of disputes.

Meanwhile, with decolonization, the number of new states grew and inside the General Assembly a loose alliance of Arab and African states, supported intermittently by the Soviet Bloc, and some Asian and South American states, began to emerge in the 1960s. This alliance could prevent certain questions, notably human rights, being properly discussed. The USA, in particular, resented this situation, especially as it was by far the biggest contributor to UN funds. This, and the increasing use made of the General Assembly not for true debate but for propaganda and counter-propaganda, meant that it did not become quite as respected as its founders had hoped.

The Partition of Eastern and Central Europe

The post-1945 map of Europe was decided at the three-power wartime conferences of Teheran, Yalta, and Potsdam and at rather more acrimonious post-war foreign ministers' conferences. Poland's frontiers were especially changed by these decisions. It was agreed that Poland should lose to Russia that part of its eastern territory which lay beyond the Curzon Line (a line suggested in 1920, but rejected by the Poles, who had gone on to conquer additional areas of the Ukraine). In exchange, Poland took from Germany the area east of the Oder and Neisse rivers, the southern part of East Prussia (the northern part went to the USSR), plus the international city of Danzig. Yugoslavia received the city of Fiume and its surrounding territory, and some Adriatic islands, from defeated Italy. Italy also sacrificed small parts of its territory to France and Greece.

In the far north Finland ceded Petsamo, and sundry strips along the Soviet-Finnish frontier, to the USSR. The latter was also confirmed in her possession of Northern Bukovina and Bessarabia, taken from Rumania in 1940, and of Estonia, Latvia and Lithuania.

At the close of hostilities in Germany, the Allied troops took up four previously agreed zones of occupation. The Americans were

COUNTRIES UNDER COMMUNIST
CONTROL AT DATES SHOWN

◈ UNDER 4-POWER CONTROL
(Vienna 1945-55)

▨ RUSSIAN CONTROL ZONE.
1945-55

0 MILES 250

0 KILOMETERS 400

© Richard Natkiel, 1982

Below left: an RAF Avro York transport aircraft's load brings the total weight of supplies airlifted into Berlin up to one million tons in February 1949.

Division of Berlin and Berlin Blockade

After the war both the USA and the USSR realized that Germany was pivotal for the control both of west and east Europe, and both feared that the other might take advantage of any concessions in order to strengthen its position there. Thus, although in the sterile debates which took place over two decades both the western Allies and the USSR demanded the reunification of Germany, neither really wanted this except on its own, unobtainable, terms.

In 1947 the western powers took the first steps toward the economic independence of their own zones, and this was cemented early in 1948 by a currency reform which excluded the Russian zone. In the same year, it was decided to establish a German government in the three western zones. The Soviet response was a blockade of Berlin.

Under the post-war arrangement Berlin, which was about 100 miles inside the Soviet

in the south, in Bavaria, Hesse, and Baden Wurtemburg, the British occupied the Ruhr industrial area and North Germany, while the French took the Rhine-Palatinate and the south west. These three zones contained about 45 million residents. Eastern Germany, with a 17 million population, was occupied by the USSR. In Austria, a similar pattern of occupation zones was set up which lasted until the Austrian Peace Treaty was signed in 1955. In Germany the USSR and the Western allies were unable to agree on a peace settlement and, in stages, the western occupation zones were transformed into the German Federal Republic, while the Soviet zone became the German Democratic Republic.

In the late 1940s, pro-Moscow communist regimes took power in Poland, Czechoslovakia, Hungary, Rumania, Albania, Bulgaria, East Germany and, for a time, in Yugoslavia. Soon after the war, therefore, there was a line running from Stettin to Trieste, dividing Soviet-controlled Europe from a western Europe orientated in varying degrees toward the USA. This line became known as the 'Iron Curtain.'

ACCESS ROUTES TO WEST BERLIN

AIR CORRIDORS
RAILROADS
ROADS
RIVER
CANAL
● CHECKPOINTS (RUSSIAN ZONE)

0 MILES 100

0 KM 150

© Richard Natkiel, 1982

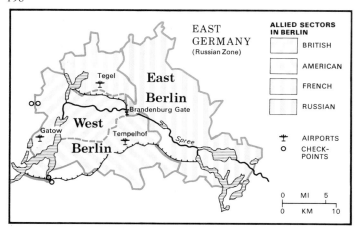

occupation zone, had been divided into four occupation zones, with the British, American and French occupying forces guaranteed road, rail and air access for supply and renewal. The Soviet blockade of Berlin took the form of barring all road and rail traffic to and from the western zones of the city. Its aim was to deprive not only the occupying forces, but also the population, of the necessities of life and thereby force the western powers to make concessions. The western zones of Berlin had about two and one-half million inhabitants and the Soviet government did not think it would be possible for the western powers to supply such a large population by air. On 24 June 1948 the Red Army put up its barricades.

For the western powers either the use of force, which it was feared might precipitate a wider conflict, or a submission to Soviet demands, seemed equally distasteful, so an airlift was the only possible reaction. It was calculated that the aircraft available could fly in 4000 tons of freight each day, on average. This was enough to provide basic rations, and coal for the power stations (but not for any other purpose). In the first weeks a total of 4000 tons was indeed achieved. West Berlin could live, but only in siege

conditions. In time, however, larger aircraft became available, and private charter companies gave considerable help. To the original receiving airports (Tempelhof in the US zone and Gatow in the British) was soon added a third, Tegel, in the French zone. A shuttle service was operated, mainly from five airfields in the western zones of Germany proper. The blockade was called off on 12 May 1949.

Soon after, the western zones of Germany were formally united to form the German Federal Republic, while the Russians established the German Democratic Republic in their zone. Both German governments progressively took over the functions previously carried out by the occupying forces, although the latter remained in Germany. While contact between the two Germanies had been sealed off by a highly militarized and mined frontier laid by the Russians, many East German citizens fled to the west through Berlin. This drain of its best citizens persuaded the East German government to erect a high, patrolled, wall to divide its part of Berlin from West Berlin in 1961. However, from the late 1960s, in fits and starts, the very tense relationship between the two Germanies eased to some degree.

Trieste

The post-war peace treaty with Italy, while it provided for the cession of the Venezia Giulia province to Yugoslavia, did not settle the fate of Trieste. This important port at the head of the Adriatic was demanded by Yugoslavia, but its population was four-fifths Italian. The treaty attempted, unsuccessfully, to solve this problem by assigning the port to neither claimant. Instead Trieste and its immediate surroundings were declared to be a Free Territory, guaranteed by the United Nations Security Council. Most of the non-urban area, having two-thirds of the territory but only a quarter of the population (mainly Slavic) was to be administered by Yugoslavia; this was Zone B. The Americans and British were to look after Zone A, where the bulk of the population, mostly Italian, lived.

Yugoslavia and Italy continued to advance their claims; the former was backed until its defection from the Soviet bloc in 1948, by the USSR. America and Britain supported Italy and in 1948, with France, declared that Trieste should be returned to

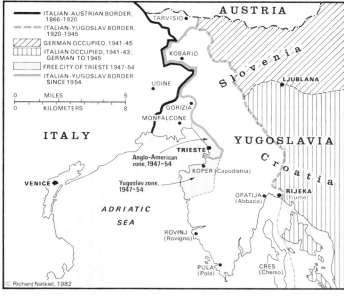

Left: the disputed area of Trieste
bedecked by Yugoslav propaganda in an
attempt to impress the Allied Control
Commission.
Bottom left: Berliners greet a bus which
has driven into the city from Hanover along
the recently reopened land route.

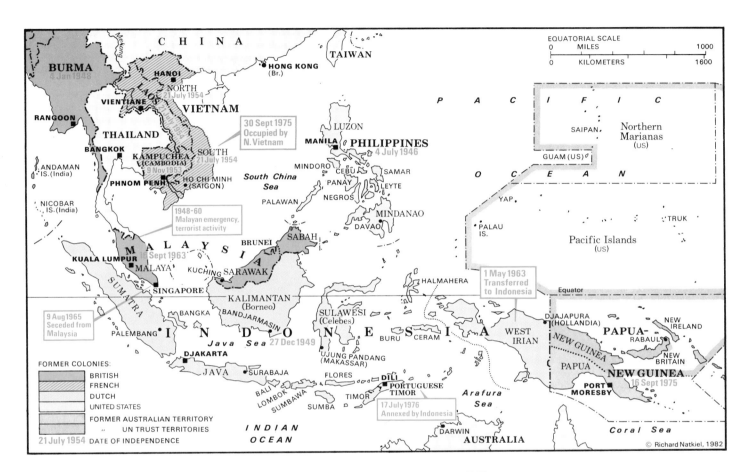

Italy. In Zone A, much of the administration was transferred to Italians. With the relaxation of tension between the West and the USSR, it was possible to reach a final agreement in 1954 which was not wholly to the liking of Yugoslavia. Zone A, less a few square miles around Crevatini, was handed to Italy. Crevatini and Zone B became part of Yugoslavia.

East Indies Independence

Because of the disturbance caused by Japanese wartime occupation, independence came to most southeast Asian nations sooner than it would otherwise have done. Nowhere was this more evident than in the Dutch East Indies, where strong nationalist guerrilla forces, led by Sukarno, were already in action in 1945, resisting the returning Dutch. The fighting went on for some years, many influential Dutch politicians being convinced, wrongly, that the Netherlands could not survive without the profits of the East Indies. In 1949 the new state of Indonesia was formed as a result of a settlement of this dispute. It comprised all the former Dutch territories except West New Guinea. The latter, much against the will of

its inhabitants, was transferred to Indonesia in 1963. Neighboring East New Guinea, under Australian tutelage, gained independence in 1975.

The federation of Malaysia was formed in 1963 of scattered former British possessions; Malaya, Penang, North Borneo (Sabah), Sarawak, and Singapore (Singapore left in 1965). This federation was not to the liking of Sukarno, who initiated a policy of violent 'confrontation' with Malaysia, until in 1965 the exertions of this policy brought him down himself. The federation was also troubled, although not violently, by the claims of the Philippine Republic (which gained independence from the USA in 1946) to Sabah. This dispute was an embarrassment, though not fatal, to the Association of South-East Asian Nations [ASEAN] organization, formed in 1967 to develop economic cooperation between Indonesia, Malaysia, Singapore, and the Philippines.

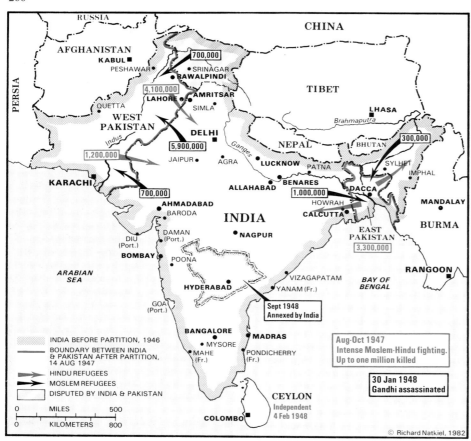

The Partition of Palestine

Independence for India and Pakistan

When in 1946 the British government announced its intention to grant complete independence to the Indian sub-continent, the leaders of the large Moslem population were already intent on disengaging themselves from an independent, predominantly Hindu, India and forming their own state, Pakistan. To enable independence to be granted in 1947 the concept of Pakistan was accepted. This Moslem state was in two parts. A large region, West Pakistan, including the port of Karachi and cities such as Lahore and Peshawar, lay between the new India and Afghanistan. Hundreds of miles to the east, across Indian territory, an eastern wing of Pakistan was established for the Moslems of Bengal. The boundary between India and West Pakistan was fixed a few days after independence, and unavoidably divided the Punjab, homeland of the Sikhs. Horrific massacres followed, as Sikhs and Hindus in the East Punjab attacked local Moslems, and Moslems attacked Sikhs in the West Punjab. These massacres were repeated in Delhi and elsewhere. Millions of refugees travelled in both directions across the newly-established Indo-Pakistani frontiers.

Under British rule the Indian princes had been allowed to rule their own states, but by the end of 1948 all except three of the approximately 350 princely states had joined the Indian Union in response to persuasion, concession, and implied threat. Of the three, Junagadh acceded to India after the entry of Indian troops. In Hyderabad, a large state of 17 million inhabitants, the prince was evasive and finally, not without provocation, the Indian government absorbed it by force. In Kashmir, lying uneasily between India and West Pakistan, there was a Hindu ruler, a Hindu majority around Jammu, but a predominantly Moslem population in the Vale of Kashmir. The ruler, alarmed by an incursion of Moslem tribesmen, finally opted for India and saved his capital, Srinagar. But opposing Indian and Pakistani forces were soon in action, and the dispute over the possession of Kashmir was to poison Indo-Pakistani relations for decades.

After World War I Britain had received the League of Nations mandate to rule Palestine. During the 1930s Jewish immigration increased the Jewish population there from 11 per cent of the total in 1922 to 29 per cent in 1939. Local Arabs resented this, so shortly before the outbreak of war Britain restricted immigration.

After 1945 the Jews' wartime experience hardened their resolve to found their own state of Israel, while at the same time world opinion had come to sympathize with them. The British government, realizing that a Jewish state could be created in Palestine only at the cost of antagonizing Arabs all over the Middle East, continued to oppose the large-scale admission of Jewish refugees. Illegal Jewish immigration began, and Jewish terrorists began to prey on Britons in Palestine. In 1947 Britain asked the United Nations to take over the problem. The UN decided to divide Palestine into an Arab state, a Jewish state, and an internationalized city of Jerusalem. This was impossible to put into practice. In December 1947 war started between the Jews and the armed forces of the Arab League, continuing until the spring. In May 1948 the independent state of Israel was proclaimed by the Jews. Jewish troops fought better than the Arabs and won additional territory for Israel, but the Arabs refused to negotiate unless one million Palestinian refugees were returned to their homes.

Left: Lord Mountbatten, the last British Viceroy of India, inspects a guard of honor shortly before independence.
Below: newly independent Israel celebrates Hagana Day to honor the dead freedom fighters, March 1949.

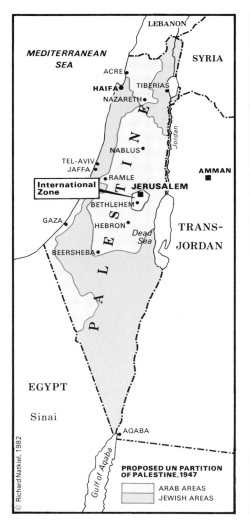

MEDITERRANEAN SEA
LEBANON
SYRIA
ACRE
HAIFA • TIBERIAS
NAZARETH •
NABLUS •
TEL-AVIV
JAFFA
RAMLE
International Zone
JERUSALEM
BETHLEHEM •
GAZA •
HEBRON •
Dead Sea
BEERSHEBA •
TRANS-JORDAN
AMMAN ■
P A L E S T I N E
Jordan
EGYPT
Sinai
AQABA
Gulf of Aqaba

PROPOSED UN PARTITION OF PALESTINE, 1947
☐ ARAB AREAS
☐ JEWISH AREAS

© Richard Natkiel, 1982

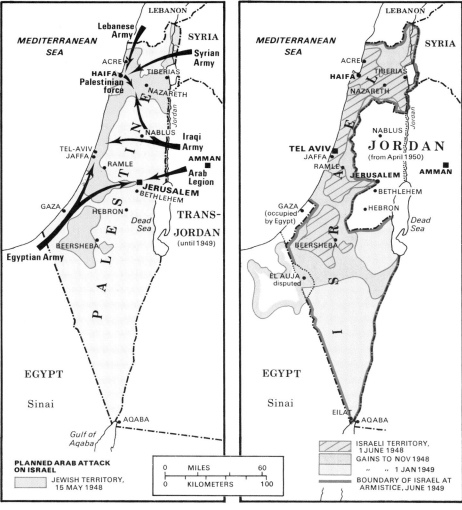

MEDITERRANEAN SEA
Lebanese Army
LEBANON
SYRIA
Syrian Army
ACRE
HAIFA
Palestinian force
TIBERIAS
NAZARETH •
NABLUS •
Iraqi Army
TEL-AVIV
JAFFA
RAMLE
AMMAN ■
Arab Legion
JERUSALEM
BETHLEHEM •
GAZA •
HEBRON •
Dead Sea
TRANS-JORDAN (until 1949)
BEERSHEBA •
Egyptian Army
P A L E S T I N E
Jordan
EGYPT
Sinai
AQABA
Gulf of Aqaba

PLANNED ARAB ATTACK ON ISRAEL
☐ JEWISH TERRITORY, 15 MAY 1948

MILES 0–60
KILOMETERS 0–100

MEDITERRANEAN SEA
LEBANON
SYRIA
ACRE
HAIFA • TIBERIAS
NAZARETH •
NABLUS •
JORDAN (from April 1950)
TEL AVIV
JAFFA
RAMLE
JERUSALEM
AMMAN ■
GAZA (occupied by Egypt)
BETHLEHEM •
HEBRON •
Dead Sea
BEERSHEBA •
EL AUJA disputed
I S R A E L
Jordan
EGYPT
Sinai
EILAT
AQABA

☐ ISRAELI TERRITORY, 1 JUNE 1948
☐ GAINS TO NOV 1948
" " 1 JAN 1949
— BOUNDARY OF ISRAEL AT ARMISTICE, JUNE 1949

AREAS OCCUPIED BY COMMUNIST FORCES
- 1934–1945
- 1945–JUNE 1946
- JULY 1946–JUNE 1947
- JULY 1947–JUNE 1948
- JULY 1948–JUNE 1949
- JULY–SEPT 1949

© Richard Natkiel, 1982

The Chinese Revolution

By April 1945 the Chinese communists had about one million men under arms, and looked forward to the post-war struggle for power against the Kuomintang with optimism, because although the latter was receiving American equipment its troops were believed to be of low morale. Stalin did not share this optimism and decided that Russian aid should be given to the communists. Despite the disappointment and resentment which this caused, the communists under Mao Tse-tung took the offensive and by mid-1946 a civil war was raging in Manchuria, where many of the Kuomintang troops deserted and others fought unenthusiastically. By late 1947 the Kuomintang's military superiority had declined from 4:1 to 2:1, and by the end of the civil war two million of the People's Liberation Army's troops were former Kuomintang soldiers. Having taken Manchuria in 1948, the communists drove southward and in 1949 the last remnants of the old regime took refuge in Formosa (Taiwan). There had been little foreign interference, although some British warships on the Yangtze were shelled and one of them,

Amethyst, was pinned down by artillery fire for a few days.

Having gained power, the communists set about the transformation of Chinese society. Mao Tse-tung, despite his mistrust of the Russians and the uneasy relations between Moscow and Peking, took a pro-Soviet line in foreign affairs; American policy-makers, who by this time included few who were willing or able to express an informed opinion, believed that China was simply a Soviet satellite, and behaved towards the new republic accordingly. Meanwhile the communist transformation was hampered by the dominance of Mao Tse-tung and his theories. There followed a series of mass campaigns like the Great Leap Forward (for rapid economic development in 1957–59) and the Cultural Revolution (for a replacement of old attitudes by new in 1965–67). These campaigns were accompanied by violence, bloodshed, and blind and exaggerated adherence to centrally laid-down theories; their results reflected the Chinese saying, 'They drained the pond to catch a fish.'

The Korean War

When Japan surrendered in 1945, the Red Army occupied the northern and less populous part of Korea and the US Army the southern. By previous agreement the division was made at the 38th Parallel, but there was a loose understanding that the two halves would soon be reunited, and elections held. However, the United Nations commission sent to arrange a reunion of the two Koreas could make no progress because the Russians and Americans had very different concepts of what they meant by free elections. In the end, the elections were held only in the South, whose new government was recognized by the United Nations. In reply, the Russians established a communist government in North Korea and, unlike the Americans in the South, ensured that it had a large and well-equipped army.

In 1949, partly because the Republic of Korea (ROK) seemed secure, the US troops left South Korea. In early 1950 several US leaders seemed to express doubts as to whether it would be practicable for the USA to defend South Korea if the latter should be attacked. Perhaps with this encouragement, on 25 June 1950 the North Korean army invaded South Korea at several points and made a rapid advance. While efforts, soon successful, were made to obtain the UN Security Council's recommendation that member states should aid South Korea, American troops were sent from Japan to stem the rout. The troops were only partially successful, both they and the surviving ROK divisions ending their retreat inside a perimeter enclosing a small area in the south which, however, included the vital port of Pusan.

More American troops, fighting under the United Nations flag, soon began to arrive, joined afterward by units from other countries, of which Britain sent the largest contingent. The US Commander in Chief, MacArthur, against the advice of almost all his colleagues, decided to turn the tide with an amphibious assault at Inchon, on the west coast not far from the 38th Parallel. Despite extensive mudbanks and difficult tides, this operation was a complete success and the North Koreans, with their supply lines threatened, began to withdraw. Soon the American and ROK forces recaptured the South Korean capital of Seoul,

Below: a tank goes into action in support
of infantry fighting in Korea during the
second winter of the war, January 1952.
Bottom left: President Harry S Truman
proved to be a tough and uncompromising
war leader during the Korean War.

FRONT LINES
— — — 4 JULY 1950
·········· 14 JULY
— · — · — 25 JULY
———— 5 AUG
— — — 26 AUG
———— 10 SEP
▓▓▓ PUSAN PERIMETER,
10-15 SEPT
→ NORTH KOREAN ATTACKS

© Richard Natkiel, 1982

25 June 1950
Korean attack
begins

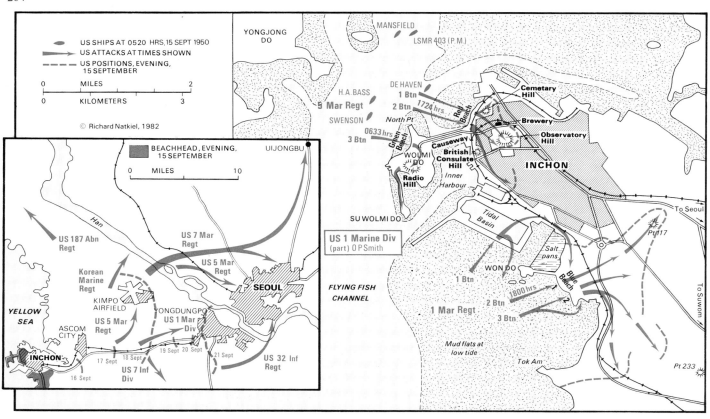

US SHIPS AT 0520 HRS, 15 SEPT 1950
US ATTACKS AT TIMES SHOWN
US POSITIONS, EVENING,
15 SEPTEMBER

MILES
0   2
KILOMETERS
0   3

© Richard Natkiel, 1982

BEACHHEAD, EVENING,
15 SEPTEMBER

MILES
0   10

YONGJONG
DO

MANSFIELD

LSMR 403 (P.M.)

DE HAVEN
1 Btn
2 Btn   1724 hrs.

H.A. BASS
5 Mar Regt
SWENSON
3 Btn   0633 hrs

Cemetary
Hill

Red
Beach

North Pt

Green
Beach

Brewery

Observatory
Hill

Causeway

British
Consulate
Hill

WOLMI
DO

INCHON

Radio
Hill

Inner
Harbour

SU WOLMI DO

To Seoul

FLYING FISH
CHANNEL

Tidal
Basin

Pt 117

US 1 Marine Div
(part) O P Smith

WON DO

1 Btn

Salt
pans

Blue
Beach

1800 hrs

2

To Suwom

1 Mar Regt

2 Btn

3 Btn

Mud flats at
low tide

Tok Am

Pt 233

UIJONGBU

Han

US 187 Abn
Regt

US 7 Mar
Regt

Korean
Marine
Regt

US 5 Mar
Regt

SEOUL

KIMPO
AIRFIELD

YELLOW
SEA

ASCOM
CITY

INCHON

16 Sept

17 Sept

US 5 Mar
Regt

18 Sept

US 7 Inf
Div

YONGDUNGPO
US 1 Mar
Div

19 Sept   20 Sept

21 Sept

US 32 Inf
Regt

and pushed on to the 38th Parallel. Here a decision had to be made whether to pursue the invaders inside North Korea itself. MacArthur was among those who favored this, despite a warning from Communist China that if the UN forces approached closer to the River Yalu, the China-Korea frontier, they would intervene. By this time there were about 50,000 US troops in Korea, and more were on their way.

Having linked up with the forces that had broken out northward from the Pusan perimeter and with authorization from Washington, on 27 September MacArthur moved his troops across the 38th Parallel. In October the North Korean capital, Pyongyang, was captured. Many North Korean soldiers began to desert or surrender, and on 26 October ROK forces reached the Yalu, but were soon confronted by massed Chinese troops who crossed the Yalu and routed the outnumbered UN forces. The Chinese moved south along the high ground, enabling them to take UN units from the flank or rear; a great advantage. The Americans, in particular, were dependent on road transport and made easy targets as they moved along the valley highways. By the end of the year the UN forces had withdrawn behind the 38th Parallel, and Seoul was lost. However, in early 1951 the UN command launched a series of counter offensives. Because the Americans had command of the air, and the Chinese troops had long supply lines, these offensives were immediately successful, Seoul being recaptured in March. A final Chinese effort was made in April, at the Imjin River, but this had limited success and it was clear to the Chinese that this war, if continued, would be very costly. An armistice commission had its first meeting in July 1951, but, largely because of Chinese stalling tactics, it was not until 27 July 1953 that an armistice was actually signed. In the intervening period hostilities continued, although at a lower level and in conditions of trench warfare as each side tried to improve its defensive line. After the armistice things continued much the same as they had before, with the two Koreas developing separately and in mutual dislike and distrust.

Left: General MacArthur inspects the Inchon bridgehead following the successful amphibious assault in September 1950. Right: landing craft head in for the sea wall at Inchon.

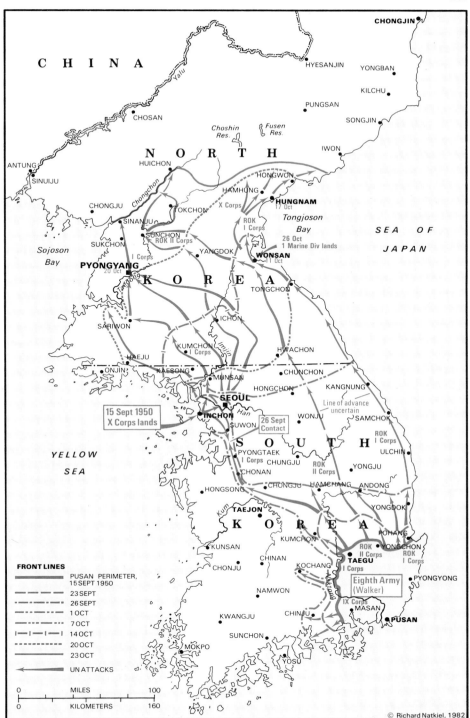

206

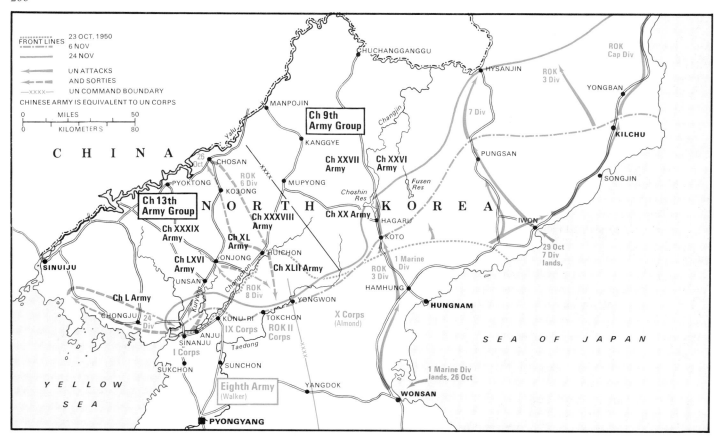

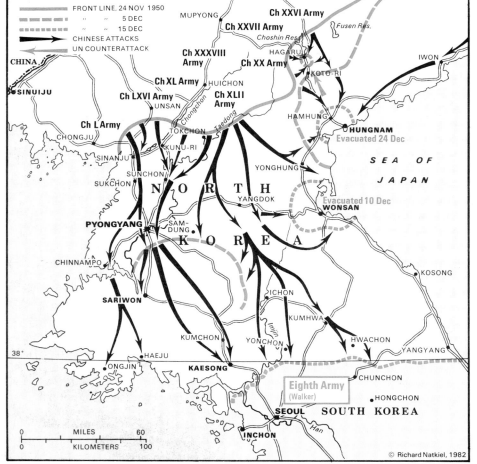

Above right: Vietnamese peasants during road building operations near Dien Bien Phu.
Right: the Hwachon Dam is attacked by US Navy Skyraider aircraft with torpedoes. The aim of the attack was to release floodwater which would disrupt enemy positions downstream.

Revolution in Indo-China

In 1945 the first Allied troops to arrive in French Indo-China were British. In Saigon they encountered confusion, as nationalist groups tried to take advantage of the situation to assert their own control, and Free French detachments arrived to support the French settlers. At one point the British were using, to maintain order, the same Japanese troops whose surrender they had come to accept.

By the end of 1946 the French seemed to have re-established themselves although, realizing the strength of national feeling, they had agreed in principle to the establishment of an independent Vietnam in a proposed Indo-Chinese Federation within the French Union. The leader of the most powerful nationalist organization, the Viet Minh, was the communist Ho Chi Minh, whose status had risen during the war, partly because of US support; the Americans had no love for French colonialism. But by the end of 1946 Ho Chi Minh, with his military commander, the former schoolmaster Giap, had realized that the French were determined to hold on to what they had, and retired to the mountains to develop guerrilla activities. In the following two years the French sent more troops to Vietnam, and instituted a native but highly-supervised government under the titular Emperor, Bao Dai.

The victory of the Chinese communists in 1949 changed the situation, because Viet Minh forces could now obtain supplies over a friendly frontier. Giap began a campaign of attacks, usually successful, on isolated French garrisons and on the relief columns sent to help them. The French responded with the use of mobile columns and parachute troops. In 1950 Ho Chi Minh claimed to be the head of the true Vietnam government, and was recognized by China and the USSR. The USA, deciding that communism was worse than colonialism, granted Bao Dai military aid to fight the Viet Minh. Nevertheless, Giap was in sufficient strength to force the French to abandon most of the Red River Delta in October 1950. By this stage Giap had progressed beyond guerrilla warfare and possessed full-scale and properly equipped regular divisions. Overconfident, he made attacks on French strongholds at Vinh Yen, Mao Khe, and Phat Diem which were unsuccessful and costly. Guerrilla warfare continued throughout 1951–53.

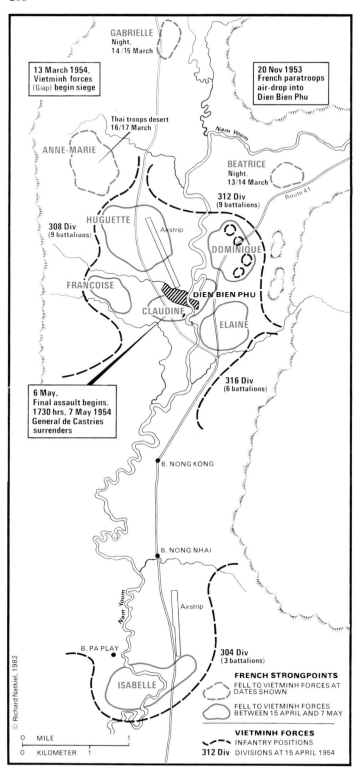

Dien Bien Phu

The war between the French and the com-
munist-led Viet Minh in French Indo China
took a new turn in April 1953 when Giap's
forces, instead of pursuing the war in Vietnam, invaded another French territory,
Laos. French reinforcements poured in and
Giap withdrew, having demonstrated that

he had the French on the run. Later in the
year the French decided to block Giap's
expected renewal of the attack in Laos. The
settlement of Dien Bien Phu was selected as
a French defensive strongpoint, rudimentary
fortifications were built there, and fresh
troops flown in. When the Viet Minh did
attack, in March 1954, it had about 18,000
defenders, of whom about 3,000 were French
and the rest colonial troops. But Giap had
an overwhelming numerical superiority, and

was well-supplied with artillery, including
anti-aircraft guns supplied by China. When
the encirclement closed in, the airstrip could
no longer be used: supplies could be para-
chuted in, at some risk, but wounded could
not be moved out. The defense was genuinely
heroic, and ended only when the Viet Minh
divisions broke into the center of the
position.

When Dien Bien Phu fell the conference
to end this war was already in progress at

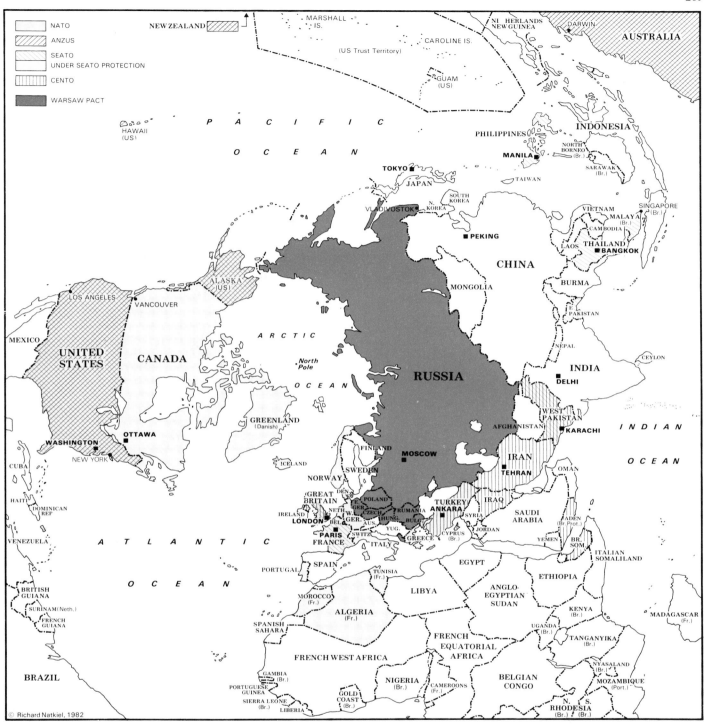

Legend:

- NATO
- ANZUS
- SEATO
- UNDER SEATO PROTECTION
- CENTO
- WARSAW PACT

© Richard Natkiel, 1982

Geneva. Here the French agreed to the provisional formation of a Viet Minh North Vietnam and a French-orientated South Vietnam, with internationally supervised elections in both within two years. The independence of Cambodia and Laos, formerly parts of French Indo-China, was also recognized.

Above left: Vietnamese porters carry supplies to the front by bicycle during the build-up to Dien Bien Phu.

Encirclement of the USSR in 1955

Soviet expansion into Eastern Europe in 1945 was virtually completed by the absorption of Czechoslovakia into the Soviet bloc in 1948. The establishment of the North Atlantic Treaty Organization (NATO) in 1949 was a direct response to the Berlin blockade and the Czech coup. The ANZUS Pact (Australia, New Zealand, USA) in

1951, which accompanied the peace treaty with Japan, as well as the US-Philippine treaty signed at the same time, linked these three countries with the United States.

Eisenhower's Secretary of State, John Foster Dulles, sought to respond to the collapse of French Indochina and the end of the Korean War by forming the South East Asia Treaty Organization in 1954. SEATO's basic weakness lay in the fact that most of its membership was already linked to the United States in the Alliance already, and the treaty called for no automatic response to overt Communist aggression, unlike

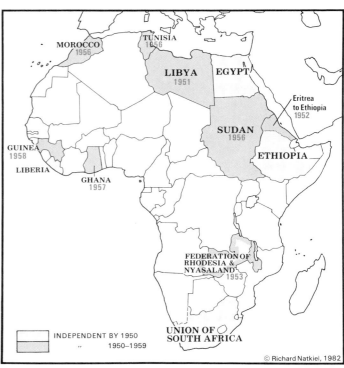

NATO. Pakistan and Thailand were the only two new states added, as Malaya, British North Borneo, Brunei and Sarawak were still parts of the British Empire in 1954. The so-called protocol states of South Vietnam, Laos and Cambodia, were not in fact members of SEATO, but were able to call upon the aid of SEATO in case of overt Communist aggression. This never was done because SEATO required unanimity among its members, and usually France or Pakistan was unwilling to be committed to the defense of Southeast Asia. Therefore SEATO, unlike NATO, was a weak reed in the bundle of American alliances meant to surround the Communist bloc.

The Central Treaty Organization (CENTO) was originally known as the Baghdad Pact. Its lynchpin was Great Britain, the only member of all the alliances, and it included Turkey, Iraq, Iran and Pakistan. The United States was only an observer in the Baghdad Pact. Since Turkey was a NATO member as was Britain, Pakistan was included only because she was a member of SEATO. Iraq was a reluctant member of the alliance and dropped out of it after the assassination of King Faisal, and therefore CENTO was based on Iran.

Although appearing formidable on such a map as this, the strength of the encirclement policy lay in NATO, the ANZUS Pact, and in the bilateral treaties the United States had with Japan, the Philippines and South Korea. Nonetheless, from a Soviet perspective, these encircling alliances and the United States' great nuclear superiority, must have seemed formidable indeed. It is not surprising therefore that the suspicious attitudes of the Cold War and the concurrent arms race were the dominant factors in US-Soviet relations.

Africa in 1950s

In the mid-1950s four-fifths of the African population lived under some kind of European rule, genuinely independent native governments being found only in Egypt, Libya, Ethiopia and Liberia. But all over the continent the scene was being set for upheavals that would, within a decade, mean that four-fifths of the Africans would have their own independent states. Already, in 1956, the French relinquished Tunisia. In 1958 another French colony, Guinea, became the next part of French West and Equatorial Africa to gain independence, the other parts reaching that stage in 1960. In the English-speaking parts, the Gold Coast ceased to be a crown colony and became independent Ghana in 1957.

Top left: armed native police set out in their truck to search a Kenyan village for Mau Mau terrorists. The colonial authorities defeated the terrorist campaign. Top right. French troops during an advance against Algerian rebel forces in the course of the Challe offensive in August 1959. Right: troops patrol the European quarter of Algiers in March 1962 to guard against terrorism.

Algeria

In response to developing nationalism, in 1947 the French government introduced a constitution for Algeria which gave all residents French citizenship. But the European minority had as many seats in the legislative assembly as the native majority, and the nationalists' drive was hardly weakened. However, until 1954 the different nationalist groups attacked each other as much as they attacked the French. In that year, the terrorist FLN (National Libration Front) was formed.

The terrorists' bombing campaign caused many casualties and brought a strong French reaction. Soon there were half a million French troops, with aircraft, attempting to control a population which was becoming increasingly hostile in response to reprisals, particularly in Algiers. European settlers, fearing that the French government might negotiate with the rebels, staged, in collusion with army officers, a coup which so discredited the government that de Gaulle returned to power. At first intent on defeating the Algerian terrorists, de Gaulle in 1959 acknowledged that Algerians had the right to choose their future. This caused the settlers to rebel again in January 1960 but, lacking army support this time, they were dispersed. Negotiations between France and the FLN were long and intermittent and in April 1961 four French generals, fearing a 'sell-out,' tried to seize power in Algiers; this unsuccessful coup was organized by the OAS (Secret Army Organization). Nevertheless, after a referendum in Algeria, de Gaulle proclaimed Algerian independence on 3 July 1962.

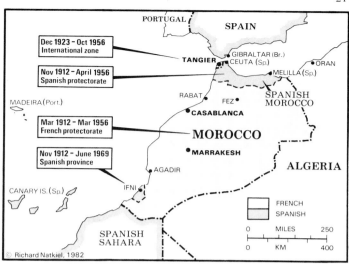

Map legend:

| Dec 1923 – Oct 1956 International zone |
| Nov 1912 – April 1956 Spanish protectorate |
| Mar 1912 – Mar 1956 French protectorate |
| Nov 1912 – June 1969 Spanish province |

© Richard Natkiel, 1982

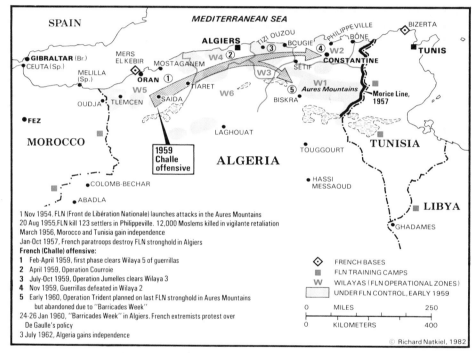

1 Nov 1954, FLN (Front de Libération Nationale) launches attacks in the Aures Mountains
20 Aug 1955, FLN kill 123 settlers in Philippeville. 12,000 Moslems killed in vigilante retaliation
March 1956, Morocco and Tunisia gain independence
Jan-Oct 1957, French paratroops destroy FLN stronghold in Algiers
French (Challe) offensive:
1 Feb-April 1959, first phase clears Wilaya 5 of guerrillas
2 April 1959, Operation Courroie
3 July-Oct 1959, Operation Jumelles clears Wilaya 3
4 Nov 1959, Guerrillas defeated in Wilaya 2
5 Early 1960, Operation Trident planned on last FLN stronghold in Aures Mountains
    but abandoned due to "Barricades Week"
24-26 Jan 1960, "Barricades Week" in Algiers. French extremists protest over
   De Gaulle's policy
3 July 1962, Algeria gains independence

◇ FRENCH BASES
■ FLN TRAINING CAMPS
W WILAYAS (FLN OPERATIONAL ZONES)
▢ UNDER FLN CONTROL, EARLY 1959

© Richard Natkiel, 1982

Morocco

At the beginning of the century Morocco seemed a tempting object for French colonial expansion and in 1904, France and Spain settled on an eventual partition of the country between themselves. Britain and France were by then aligned in the *Entente Cordiale* and Britain recognized French interest in Morocco in return for acceptance of British pre-eminence in Egypt and the Sudan. In an effort to weaken the Entente the Germans twice, in 1905–06 and 1911, disputed the French influence in Morocco but although they gained some concessions from the French in Equatorial Africa the French hold on Morocco was maintained. This was followed, in 1912, by most of Morocco becoming a French protectorate, with Spanish territories in the north and south. Marshal Lyautey, the first Resident-General, brought large areas under French control fairly quickly.

In the mid-50s nationalist groups began violent resistance to French rule. The French were preoccupied by Algerian problems and rather than add to these France recognized Moroccan independence in 1956. Tangier, which the great powers had 'international-ized' in 1923, was returned to Morocco in the same year. The new state, a monarchy, soon laid claim to the Spanish Sahara, the Spanish enclave of Ifni, Spanish Morocco, Mauritania, and parts of southwest Algeria. At Independence Spain had agreed to hand over Spanish Morocco, excluding the two cities of Cueta and Melilla and, after skirmishes Spain agreed to give up most of her southern territories too, with the exception of Ifni and most of the Spanish Sahara. In 1962 Moroccan troops crossed the undemarcated frontier with southern Algeria but a ceasefire in 1963 brought this conflict to an end although Algerian-Moroccan relations remained poor. Ifni was ceded by Spain in 1969 and in the same year the claims to the now-independent Mauritania were abandoned.

The Middle East, 1956

After the Arab-Israeli War of 1948–49 border battles, guerrilla activity, and terrorism continued. In 1955 President Nasser of Egypt, having earlier secured by agreement the evacuation of British troops from the Suez Canal Zone, announced that the Canal would be closed to Israeli commerce. Soon the Egyptian government also announced that ships using the Israeli port of Eilat might be shelled by guns commanding the Tiran Strait, and a British steamer was indeed hit by Egyptian shells. All this persuaded the Israeli government that some counterstroke was necessary.

Nasser, meantime, had projects both for a new Aswan dam on the Nile and for rearmament. Britain and the USA had expressed willingness to help with the dam but not with arms. Nasser therefore turned to the eastern block for arms, which so alarmed Washington and London that they announced that they would no longer help with the Aswan Dam. In retaliation, Nasser announced the nationlization of the Suez Canal. This action, while directly affecting France and Britain, the principal shareholders, was also a threat to international commerce, or so it was thought. Since international support for the Anglo-French rights over the Canal was more vocal than substantial, the US government being especially lukewarm, Britain, France and Israel evolved a plan for the invasion of Sinai and the Canal Zone. Israel commenced

hostilities on 29 October 1956, and Britain and France then announced that they were going to occupy, forcibly, the Canal Zone in order to protect it from the damage it might suffer in the course of Israeli-Egyptian hostilities.

The Anglo-French invading forces had little difficulty in getting ashore near Port Said and advancing down the Canal; Egyptian forces had already been demoralized by defeats inflicted by Israel in the Sinai Desert. However, pressure exerted by the USA, and in the United Nations, persuaded Britain and France to halt their advance and soon, in December, to begin a withdrawal. The situation returned to normal, except that the Canal, blocked by Nasser, took several months to clear. British and French prestige had been irreparably damaged in the Middle East.

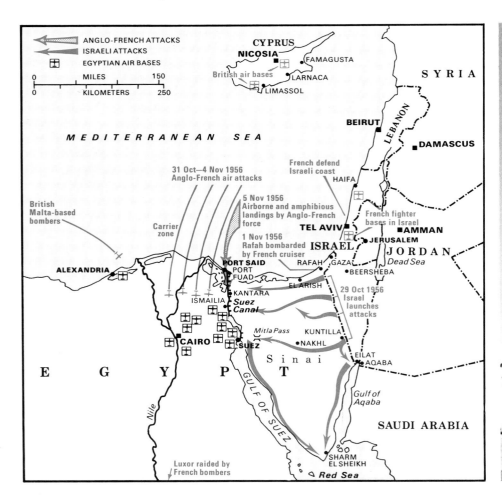

Right: this Soviet-built tank of the
Egyptian army was captured by Israeli
forces in Sinai.
Below: British troops of the 3rd Battalion
the Parachute Regiment assault El Gamil
airfield, near Port Said on 5 November
1956.
Bottom: French Noratlas transport aircraft
drop paras on Fuad during the Suez
operation, November 1956.

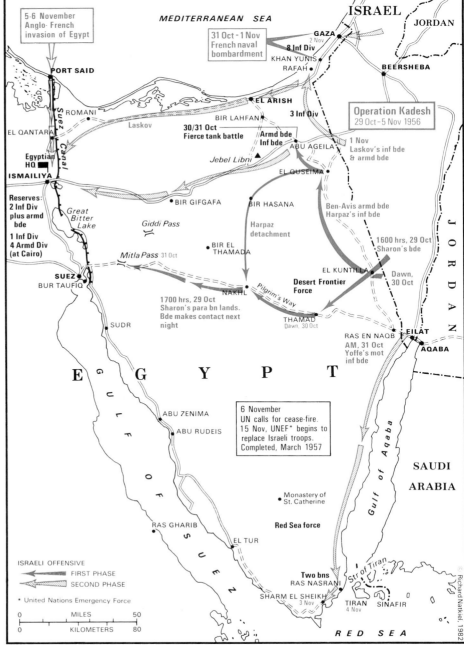

5-6 November
Anglo-French
invasion of Egypt

MEDITERRANEAN SEA

31 Oct - 1 Nov
French naval
bombardment

ISRAEL

JORDAN

GAZA
2 Nov
8 Inf Div
KHAN YUNIS
RAFAH

BEERSHEBA

PORT SAID

ROMANI

EL ARISH

3 Inf Div

Operation Kadesh
29 Oct–5 Nov 1956

EL QANTARA

Laskov

BIR LAHFAN

30/31 Oct
Fierce tank battle

Armd bde
Inf bde

Jebel Libni

ABU AGEILA

1 Nov
Laskov's inf bde
& armd bde

Egyptian
HQ

ISMAILIYA

EL QUSEIMA

Reserves:
2 Inf Div
plus armd
bde

*Great
Bitter
Lake*

BIR GIFGAFA

BIR HASANA

Ben-Avis armd bde
Harpaz's inf bde

1 Inf Div
4 Armd Div
(at Cairo)

Giddi Pass

Harpaz
detachment

1600 hrs, 29 Oct
Sharon's bde

Mitla Pass 31 Oct

BIR EL
THAMADA

EL KUNTILLA

Dawn,
30 Oct

**Desert Frontier
Force**

JORDAN

SUEZ
BUR TAUFIQ

NAKHL

Pilgrim's Way

1700 hrs, 29 Oct
Sharon's para bn lands.
Bde makes contact next
night

THAMAD
Dawn, 30 Oct

RAS EN NAQB
AM, 31 Oct
Yoffe's mot
inf bde

EILAT

AQABA

SUDR

E G Y P T

6 November
UN calls for cease-fire.
15 Nov, UNEF* begins to
replace Israeli troops.
Completed, March 1957

Gulf of Aqaba

ABU ZENIMA

ABU RUDEIS

SAUDI
ARABIA

*Monastery of
St. Catherine*

Red Sea force

RAS GHARIB

EL TUR

ISRAELI OFFENSIVE
FIRST PHASE
SECOND PHASE

* United Nations Emergency Force

Two bns
RAS NASRANI

Str of Tiran

SHARM EL SHEIKH
3 Nov

TIRAN
4 Nov

SINAFIR

© Richard Natkiel, 1982

0   MILES   50
0   KILOMETERS   80

RED SEA

Gulf of Suez

Africa in 1960s

It was not until the 1960s that big changes were made in Africa south of the Sahara. In 1960 the French and Belgian Congos became independent, as well as Nigeria and Tanganyika, the latter uniting with the island of Zanzibar to become Tanzania in 1964. Also in 1960 independent Somalia was created from British and Italian Somaliland. In Kenya, independence was delayed until 1963, the Mau-Mau guerrilla and terrorist movement of 1952–55 having soured the atmosphere. Uganda, which became independent in 1962, kept its tribal monarchies until 1967, but that did not solve its tribal problems. After the failure of the short-lived Rhodesian Federation, former Northern Rhodesia became independent Zambia, while Nyasaland became Malawi. These were both states in which the predominant, black, population provided the government. In neighboring Southern Rhodesia, however, the white minority did not relish the prospect of majority (that is, black) government, and made a 'unilateral declaration of independence' which resulted in the *de facto*

end of colonial status and the preservation of a white government.

By the end of the 1960s European rule had been confined to South Africa and Rhodesia, together with the Portuguese colonies, principally Angola and Mozambique, the Spanish Sahara, and French Djibouti. Meanwhile in 1963 the Organization of African Unity was established. This had a general council in which each non-European African government was represented. One of its most intelligent decisions was to agree that the colonial frontiers, unsatisfactory though they were, should be regarded as fixed, thereby sterilizing many potential disputes. The OAU also helped to solve conflicts between Algeria and Morocco, and between Somalia and its neighbors Ethiopia and Kenya, but the Nigerian Civil War was too much for it, although it tried hard.

Below right: Jomo Kenyatta became president of newly-independent Kenya in 1964.

The Congo

In 1960 the Belgian Congo gained its independence and a new government headed by the nationalist Lumumba took office in the capital Leopoldville (later Kinshasa). An army mutiny led to general disorder and at the request of the government a UN force was sent, but in the confusion a prominent member of the Lunda tribe, Tshombe, with the help of Belgian residents and of Anglo-Belgian companies, declared the mineral-rich province of Katanga to be an independent state. Tshombe hired white mercenary troops to block any attempt by UN forces to subdue him, while Lumumba, despairing of obtaining real UN help to eject Tshombe, appealed to the USSR for aid. But the UN did secure Tshombe's agreement to the entry of UN forces into Katanga. Meanwhile, the confusion in the Congo was reflected in political life at Leopoldville, where Prime Minister Lumumba and President Kasavubu dismissed each other. Kasavubu prevailed with support from the army led by Colonel Mobutu. Lumumba was later murdered, in February 1961, probably by Katangan

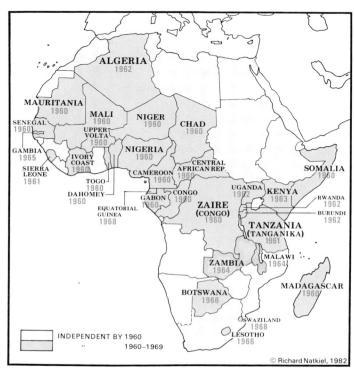

ALGERIA 1962
MAURITANIA 1960
SENEGAL 1960
MALI 1960
NIGER 1960
CHAD 1960
UPPER VOLTA 1960
GAMBIA 1965
NIGERIA 1960
IVORY COAST 1960
SIERRA LEONE 1961
TOGO 1960
DAHOMEY 1960
CAMEROON 1960
CENTRAL AFRICAN REP. 1960
SOMALIA 1960
GABON 1960
CONGO 1960
EQUATORIAL GUINEA 1968
UGANDA 1962
KENYA 1963
RWANDA 1962
ZAIRE (CONGO) 1960
TANZANIA (TANGANIKA) 1961
BURUNDI 1962
ZAMBIA 1964
MALAWI 1964
BOTSWANA 1966
MADAGASCAR 1960
SWAZILAND 1968
LESOTHO 1966

INDEPENDENT BY 1960
1960–1969

© Richard Natkiel, 1982

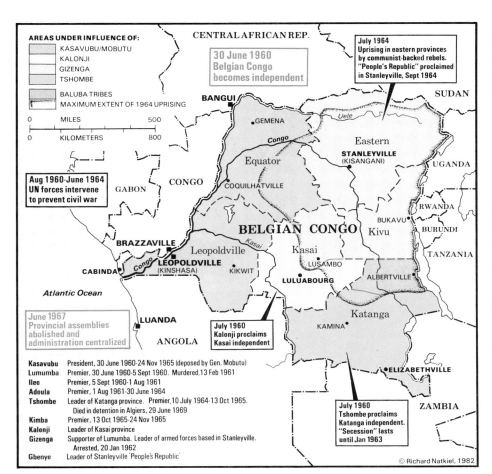

AREAS UNDER INFLUENCE OF:
KASAVUBU/MOBUTU
KALONJI
GIZENGA
TSHOMBE
BALUBA TRIBES
MAXIMUM EXTENT OF 1964 UPRISING

0 MILES 500
0 KILOMETERS 800

30 June 1960 Belgian Congo becomes independent

July 1964 Uprising in eastern provinces by communist-backed rebels. "People's Republic" proclaimed in Stanleyville, Sept 1964

Aug 1960-June 1964 UN forces intervene to prevent civil war

June 1967 Provincial assemblies abolished and administration centralized

July 1960 Kalonji proclaims Kasai independent

July 1960 Tshombe proclaims Katanga independent. "Secession" lasts until Jan 1963

CENTRAL AFRICAN REP.
BANGUI
GEMENA
Uele
Congo
Equator
STANLEYVILLE (KISANGANI)
Eastern
SUDAN
UGANDA
COQUILHATVILLE
BELGIAN CONGO
Kivu
RWANDA
BUKAVU
BURUNDI
BRAZZAVILLE
Leopoldville
Kasai
LEOPOLDVILLE (KINSHASA)
KIKWIT
LUSAMBO
Kasai
TANZANIA
CABINDA
Congo
LULUABOURG
ALBERTVILLE
Atlantic Ocean
LUANDA
KAMINA
Katanga
ANGOLA
KAMINA
ELIZABETHVILLE
ZAMBIA
GABON
CONGO

Kasavubu President, 30 June 1960-24 Nov 1965 (deposed by Gen. Mobutu)
Lumumba Premier, 30 June 1960-5 Sept 1960. Murdered, 13 Feb 1961
Ileo Premier, 5 Sept 1960-1 Aug 1961
Adoula Premier, 1 Aug 1961-30 June 1964
Tshombe Leader of Katanga province. Premier, 10 July 1964-13 Oct 1965. Died in detention in Algiers, 29 June 1969
Kimba Premier, 13 Oct 1965-24 Nov 1965
Kalonji Leader of Kasai province
Gizenga Supporter of Lumumba. Leader of armed forces based in Stanleyville. Arrested, 20 Jan 1962
Gbenye Leader of Stanleyville 'People's Republic'

© Richard Natkiel, 1982

Below: President Tshombe of the Congo inspects a guard of honor at Stanleyville airport after the suppression of the 'People's Republic.'
Bottom: President Kasavubu's Congolese troops parade through Leopoldville in 1961.

mercenaries. Following Lumumba's fall his supporter Gizenga began a rising based on Stanleyville which was, however, put down in January 1962 after periods of fighting and negotiation. The province of Kasai had also been declared independent under the leadership of Kalonji but he was reconciled to the Kasavubu-Ileo government in 1961.

The Katanga problem remained unresolved and after negotiations had failed, there was fighting in September 1961 between the Katanga army and the UN forces. The fighting was resumed in December 1961 and again in October 1962 after the failure of talks. However, in January 1963 Tshombe agreed to end the secession, going into exile a few months later.

As the last UN troops were leaving the country in mid-1964 communist-supported rebel forces gained increasing strength in the eastern provinces. Tshombe returned in July to become premier of a compromise government and, with western help and the use of mercenaries, suppressed the Stanleyville 'People's Republic' in late 1964.

Political troubles continued until November 1965 when General Mobutu led a further coup and himself took over the presidency. Mobutu was almost ousted by the mercenaries in his turn but his rule survived. Though the new government was neither incorrupt nor wholly efficient it did enable the Congo to settle down to solve its pressing economic and social problems. In 1971 the name of the state was changed to Zaire.

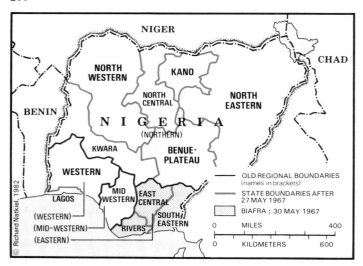

Biafra

Before the British colony of Nigeria obtained its independence in October 1960, a federal constitution was evolved which, with its three largely autonomous regions (North, West and East), attempted to balance the conflicting interests of the various groups and tribes. These groups were already represented by their own political parties. The NCNC Party represented the better-educated East, and especially the Ibo people. The NPC was the party of the Moslem North, which was the most populous but less educated region, while the Action Group represented the West, and especially the Yoruba people. With party divisions repeating regional and hence tribal divisions, electoral democracy failed to produce governments which were both effective and respected, and in 1966 junior army officers staged a coup, killing the Prime Minister and various North and West leaders. Senior army officers intervened and installed a military government under Major General Ironsi.

The Ironsi regime was at first popular, but its use of Ibo civil servants all over the country helped to provoke discontent in the West and North. Oil, meanwhile, had been discovered in the East, which promised to become the richest region. After thousands of Ibo professionals in the North and West were killed in disorders, the East, under Lieutenant Colonel Ojukwu, announced its secession. By this time Lieutenant General Gowon headed the Federal Government, and he proposed a re-division of the country into 12 regions (plus the federal territory of Lagos). But this did not remove the East's fears of northern domination. Civil War broke out in July 1967, the East calling itself the state of Biafra, with its capital at Enugu.

The fighting went well for the Biafran forces at first but a Nigerian counter-offensive soon seized Enugu. Nigerian gains continued with the capture of the important base at Port Harcourt and the Biafrans be-

came confined to a small embattled enclave. Food supplies in Biafra had become very short and a dreadful famine ensued. Nonetheless, the Biafrans held out until January 1970. The peace settlement was not ungenerous but the old problems remained and provoked a series of coups throughout the 1970s.

Above right: Nigerian Federal troops stop and search a car on the road to Onitsha.
Right: an RAF Hercules transport aircraft prepares to fly medical supplies to Nigeria in the closing days of the war.
Below right: an apprehensive Biafran officer is interrogated by Federal troops.

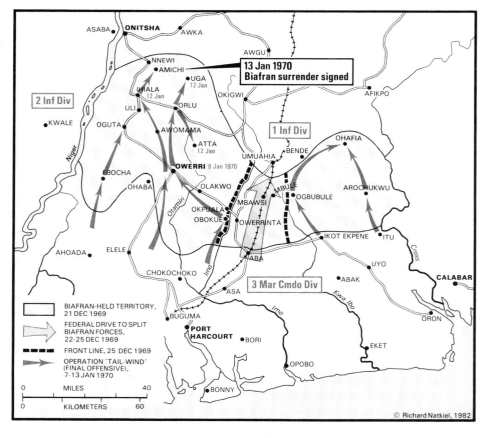

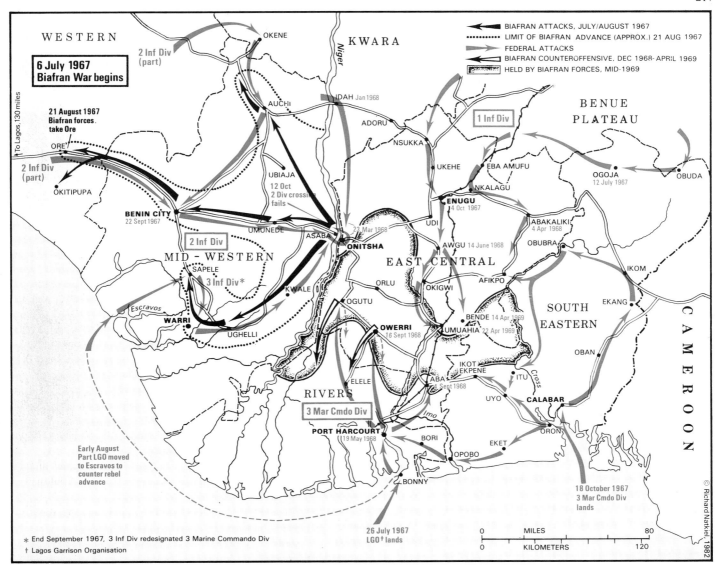

WESTERN

KWARA

**6 July 1967
Biafran War begins**

BIAFRAN ATTACKS, JULY/AUGUST 1967
LIMIT OF BIAFRAN ADVANCE (APPROX.) 21 AUG 1967
FEDERAL ATTACKS
BIAFRAN COUNTEROFFENSIVE, DEC 1968-APRIL 1969
HELD BY BIAFRAN FORCES, MID-1969

2 Inf Div
(part)

OKENE

Niger

IDAH Jan 1968

ADORU

NSUKKA

1 Inf Div

BENUE
PLATEAU

**21 August 1967
Biafran forces
take Ore**

AUCHI

UKEHE

EBA AMUFU

OGOJA
12 July 1967

OBUDA

ORE

UBIAJA

NKALAGU

**2 Inf Div
(part)**

OKITIPUPA

12 Oct
2 Div crossing
fails

ENUGU
4 Oct 1967

ABAKALIKI
4 Apr 1968

OBUBRA

BENIN CITY
22 Sept 1967

UMUNEDE

ASABA

23 Mar 1968

UDI

2 Inf Div

ONITSHA

AWGU 14 June 1968

EAST CENTRAL

IKOM

MID - WESTERN

SAPELE

3 Inf Div*

KWALE

ORLU

OKIGWI

AFIKPO

SOUTH
EASTERN

EKANG

Escravos

WARRI

OGUTU

BENDE 14 Apr 1969

UMUAHIA 22 Apr 1969

OBAN

UGHELLI

OWERRI
16 Sept 1968

IKOT
EKPENE

ITU

Cross

ELELE

ABA
7 Sept 1968

UYO

CALABAR

RIVERS

3 Mar Cmdo Div

Imo

ORON

**Early August
Part LGO moved
to Escravos to
counter rebel
advance**

PORT HARCOURT
(19 May 1968)

BORI

EKET

OPOBO

**18 October 1967
3 Mar Cmdo Div
lands**

C
A
M
E
R
O
O
N

BONNY

**26 July 1967
LGO† lands**

0   MILES   80

0   KILOMETERS   120

* End September 1967, 3 Inf Div redesignated 3 Marine Commando Div
† Lagos Garrison Organisation

© Richard Natkiel, 1982

To Lagos, 130 miles

China-India Border Disputes

In colonial times the frontier between China and India had been fixed sufficiently for most purposes by the MacMahon Line, which ran through largely uninhabited terrain and was not precisely delineated, nor really accepted by the Chinese. In the 1950s the Indians' readiness to discuss certain obvious frontier difficulties was dampened by the Chinese insistence on reopening the question of the entire frontier. Moreover, when, after a revolt of Tibetans against the Chinese, the Dalai Lama was offered refuge in India, the Chinese began to doubt Indian goodwill. In 1960, however, the Chinese offered to accept the MacMahon Line in its entirety if the Indians would accept that the existing Chinese occupation of Aksai Chin was legitimate and permanent. Nehru, the Indian prime minister, would have agreed to this, but a powerful press campaign in India so aroused public opinion against the proposal that he was unable to pursue it.

Meanwhile, the Indian Army's request for re-equipment to enable it to match the Chinese was refused, and the generals were told by the defense minister, Menon, that a Chinese attack was out of the question and should not even be discussed. However, after continuing reports of a Chinese build-up around Dho La, Nehru incautiously said that the Indian Army would throw them out. He said this on 13 October 1962, and eight days later the Chinese army attacked. Indian troops were poorly prepared, many units being sent into battle before they were properly acclimatized for mountain warfare. An Indian withdrawal was inevitable, even though some of the regular mountain troops acquitted themselves creditably. Having gained ground in the Ladakh area and defeated the Indians in the eastern part of the frontier, threatening the Brahmaputra the Chinese withdrew, implying that the Indians had been taught a lesson.

After this the Indian army chief of staff lost his job, but the real culprit, Menon, was unable to withstand popular outrage and was soon dismissed. The frontier question remained unsettled.

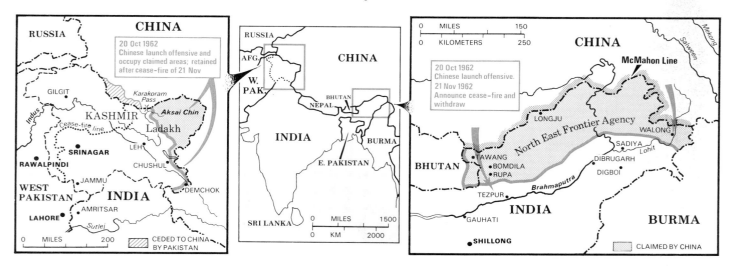

5 September, 1965
Cross-border skirmishes
develop into full scale war

© Richard Natkiel, 1982

CEASE-FIRE LINE

| | MILES | 200 |
| | KMS | 300 |

1	5 Aug 1965	: 5 Pakistanis killed in clash with Indian police	7	1 Sept	: Pakistani brigade launches major attack in Chhamb/Jammu Sector
2	9 Aug	: Widespread clashes along cease-fire line			
3	14-15 Aug	: Pakistani battalion attacks near Chhamb	8	6 Sept	: Indian forces cross border towards Lahore and Sialkot
4	16 Aug	: Indian troops take two Pakistani outposts			
5	25 Aug	: Indian forces take outposts in Tithwal area	9	8 Sept	: India launches attack on Gadra
6	26-30 Aug	: Indian attack on the Uri-Poonch salient		10-19 Sept:	Fighting fades into stalemate
				20 Sept	: UN Security Council calls for cease-fire

The Kashmir Dispute, 1965

The relations between India and Pakistan had been soured, above all, by their dispute over the ownership of Kashmir. In pursuing this quarrel both had allowed themselves to be drawn into the affairs of the great powers in order, especially, to obtain modern arms. Pakistan had become a member of the US-sponsored Central Treaty Organization (CENTO) and had also drawn closer to China. India had moved closer to the Soviet orbit. In a brief campaign in the Himalayas, fought over a disputed frontier, Indian forces had been clearly beaten by the Chinese in 1962, and this encouraged the Pakistani forces in their belief that, although outnumbered, they could defeat India.

The war which broke out in January 1965 between the two countries had no real aims. Both sides simply thought it was a good time to have a battle. The ostensible cause was a minor infringement of a poorly demarcated frontier in the barren Rann of Kutch. This occurred in January, and by April the resulting skirmishes had developed into large-scale warfare. Hostilities were interrupted by an agreement made in June.

Independently of the Rann of Kutch dispute there was increasing unrest in Kashmir from May following the arrest of a Moslem leader. Throughout the succeeding weeks there were various incidents in the Indian held part of Kashmir and along the border in which Pakistani and irregular forces were involved. To prevent infiltration over the cease-fire line the Indians, who had three divisions in Kashmir, advanced in late August to capture the Haji Pir Pass, threatening Muzafarabad, the capital of Pakistan-Kashmir. On 1 September Pakistan made a diversionary offensive around Chhamb and Bhimbar which threatened Indian communications with Srinagar. The conflict now escalated into a full-scale war and the Pakistani threat was countered with an Indian attack toward Lahore which was strongly held. When this petered out the Indians launched another attack toward Sialkot, and after a big tank battle they remained in well-defended positions close to that town.

Meanwhile both sides were coming to the end of their resources. The USA and Britain had stopped arms supplies to both sides, and although the USSR had not taken this step, it also was in favor of peace. A cease fire was imposed on 23 September and in January 1966 both governments agreed to return to their pre-August positions.

The Caribbean

The political situation of the Caribbean, and indeed of the Americas, was transformed in 1959, when revolutionaries led by Fidel Castro won a long guerrilla war against the US-supported Batista regime in Cuba. Soon Castro declared himself a Marxist, and by the early 1960s Cuba was part of the Soviet bloc. In 1961 a US-supported landing by Cuban exiles at the Bay of Pigs was a pathetic failure, but the following year the US emerged from the Cuban Missile Crisis with restored prestige, having obliged the USSR to forswear the installation of medium-range nuclear-armed missiles on Cuban soil.

Meanwhile decolonization, especially by the British, resulted in many Caribbean islands becoming independent states. Britain had hoped, in the late 1950s, that these would join in the West Indian Federation, but soon Jamaica, Trinidad and Tobago and Barbados left this, robbing it of any significance. Of the smaller newly-independent islands, Anguilla was the scene in 1969 of a revolt against its government, and similar disturbances followed over the years in neighboring islands. One of the last British colonies to be decolonized was British Honduras, whose independence was granted late because of Guatemalan claims on its territory. British Guyana, part of which was claimed by Venezuela, did, however, receive independence in 1970 despite the mutual fears dividing its black and Indian population.

From time to time the USA, usually quietly, intervened in the interests of stability, especially in Haiti and the Dominican Republic. Puerto Rico became a part of the USA, while in 1979 the long dispute over the ownership of the Panama Canal Zone was settled in a compromise treaty between the USA and Panama. US fears of communist subversion continued and in the early 1980s led to support for the troubled government of El Salvador.

ERECTOR

3 MISSILE TRANSPORTERS

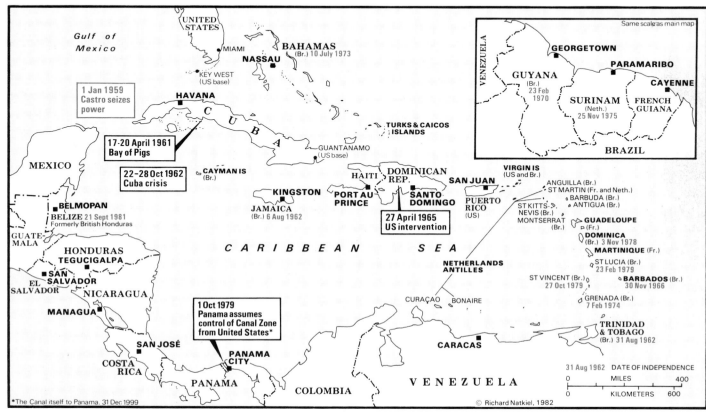

Below left: missile-carrying Soviet cargo ships were photographed at the Cuban port of Mariel by USAF reconnaissance aircraft. Right: Soviet ballistic missiles were established in Cuba in October 1962, leading to a serious international crisis.

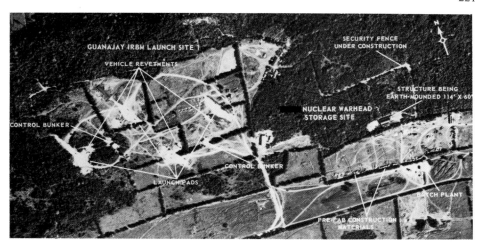

The Six-Day War, 1967

The Suez War of 1956 had seen Israeli military successes in Sinai but her strategic position did not improve, despite the presence of a United Nations peacekeeping force in the buffer zone of the Sinai Desert. A new Iraqi regime quit the Western-sponsored Baghdad Pact in 1959 and allied itself with Egypt, while Egypt and other Arab countries began to receive armaments from the Soviet Union, as well as more diplomatic support. The Suez Canal was still blocked to Israeli commerce, and the Gulf of Aqaba was covered by Egyptian artillery, while the Palestinian refugees remained unsettled and presented a threat to Israel's security. Israel's frontier with Syria was especially troubled. Here, the Syrians' possession of the Golan Heights facilitated frequent bombardment of Israeli settlements close to the border.

In May 1967 Egypt, claiming that Israel was about to launch a reprisal attack against Syria, deployed its army on the frontier with Israel and at Sharm el Sheikh, meanwhile requesting the United Nations to remove its 3,000-strong peacekeeping force from Sinai. The UN, because it had no authority to station troops on Egyptian soil without Egyptian consent, complied with this demand. Statements by Egyptian and other Arab leaders seemed to indicate that another attack on Israel was imminent. Israel appealed to the United Nations and to various powers but did not obtain the reassurances which she requested. Moreover, on 25 May, Iraq, Jordan, Syria and Saudi Arabia deployed their forces along Israel's frontiers. The Strait of Tiran was declared by Egypt to be closed to Israeli shipping on 22 May.

By the beginning of June Israeli leaders calculated that they were outnumbered on the frontiers by about three to one and that they could be invaded any moment. Rather than wait for this to happen, they had planned a pre-emptive attack, and this was launched on the morning of 5 June, when Egyptian air bases, some as far distant as Cairo and even Luxor, were the victims of destructive surprise attacks by the Israeli air force. These attacks were well-planned and well-executed and resulted in the virtual removal of the Egyptian air force from the

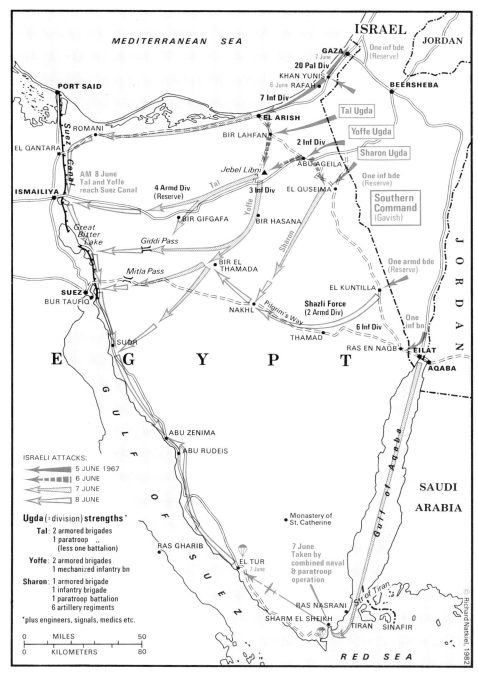

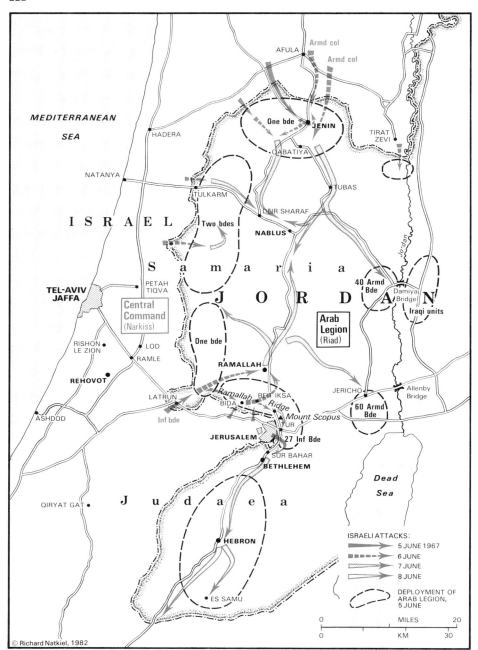

Map labels:

MEDITERRANEAN SEA

AFULA
Armd col
Armd col
HADERA
One bde
JENIN
TIRAT ZEVI
QABATIYA
NATANYA
TULKARM
TUBAS
DEIR SHARAF
ISRAEL
Two bdes
NABLUS
Samaria
JORDAN
TEL-AVIV JAFFA
PETAH TIQVA
Central Command (Narkiss)
40 Armd Bde
Damiya Bridge
Iraqi units
RISHON LE ZION
LOD
One bde
RAMLE
REHOVOT
Arab Legion (Riad)
RAMALLAH
Ramallah
BEIT IKSA
JERICHO
Allenby Bridge
LATRUN
BIDA
Ridge
60 Armd Bde
Inf bde
Mount Scopus
TUR
ASHDOD
JERUSALEM
27 Inf Bde
SUR BAHAR
BETHLEHEM
Dead Sea
QIRYAT GAT
J u d a e a
HEBRON
ISRAELI ATTACKS:
5 JUNE 1967
6 JUNE
7 JUNE
8 JUNE
DEPLOYMENT OF ARAB LEGION, 5 JUNE
ES SAMU
0   MILES   20
0   KM   30
© Richard Natkiel, 1982

Below: Egyptian prisoners under guard at El Arish on the second day of the 1967 Arab-Israeli War.
Bottom: the Israeli army advances to the outskirts of Suez.
Right: an Israeli armored column advances into the Sinai Desert.
Bottom right: an Arab soldier surrenders to Israeli forces in Sinai.

following days' hostilities. Having won command of the air, the rout of the Egyptian army in Sinai followed almost automatically. On 9 June the Syrian Golan Heights were assaulted by Israeli forces, and after a day's fighting were captured. Israeli troops entered Kuneitra. Meanwhile, Israeli forces were also throwing back the Jordanians from west of the Jordan and in Jerusalem.

In these victorious circumstances, Israel was able to obtain ceasefire agreements within a week of the commencement of hostilities. As a result of this 'Six-Day War,' the whole of Sinai remained in Israeli hands, as well as the 'West Bank' (Jordan's territory west of the River Jordan) and the Golan Heights. Thus Israel had gained new frontiers which were more easily defensible than the old but the basic causes of hostility remained.

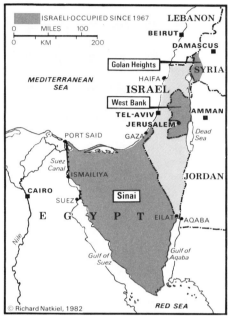

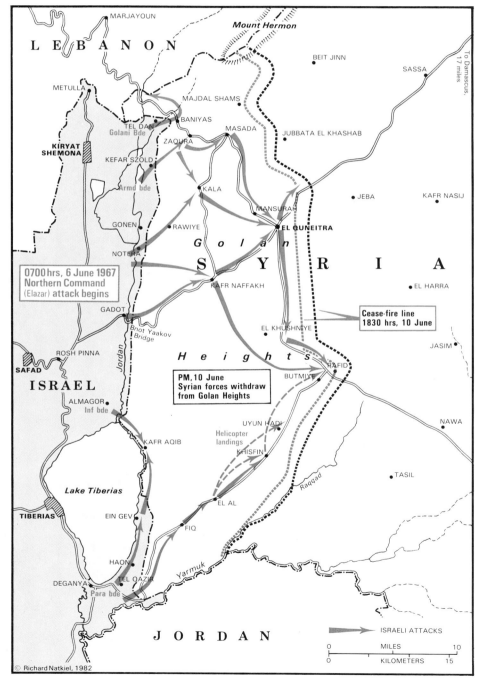

0700 hrs, 6 June 1967
Northern Command
(Elazar) attack begins

Cease-fire line
1830 hrs, 10 June

PM, 10 June
Syrian forces withdraw
from Golan Heights

ISRAELI ATTACKS

© Richard Natkiel, 1982

Bottom: Egyptian air force MiG-17s
attack an Israeli truck convoy in the
vicinity of the Suez Canal.
Bottom right: Soviet border guards take up
a defensive position on the disputed
Sino-Soviet frontier in 1969.

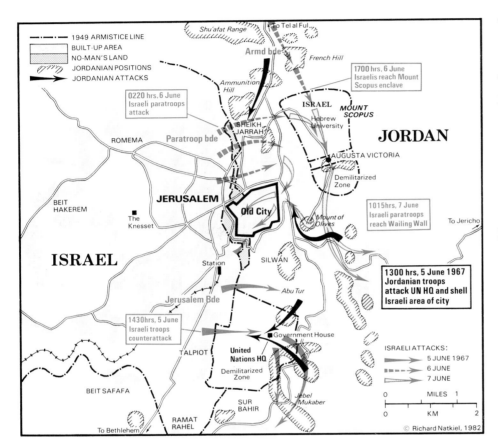

1949 ARMISTICE LINE
BUILT-UP AREA
NO-MAN'S LAND
JORDANIAN POSITIONS
JORDANIAN ATTACKS

Shu'afat Range
To Tel al Ful
Armd bde
French Hill

1700 hrs, 6 June
Israelis reach Mount
Scopus enclave

Ammunition Hill

0220 hrs, 6 June
Israeli paratroops
attack

ISRAEL
MOUNT SCOPUS

ROMEMA
Paratroop bde
SHEIKH JARRAH
Hebrew University

JORDAN

AUGUSTA VICTORIA
Demilitarized Zone

BEIT HAKEREM

JERUSALEM
The Knesset
Old City

Mount of Olives

1015hrs, 7 June
Israeli paratroops
reach Wailing Wall

To Jericho

ISRAEL
Station
SILWAN

Abu Tur

1300 hrs, 5 June 1967
Jordanian troops
attack UN HQ and shell
Israeli area of city

Jerusalem Bde

1430hrs, 5 June
Israeli troops
counterattack

TALPIOT
United Nations HQ
Demilitarized Zone

Government House

ISRAELI ATTACKS:
5 JUNE 1967
6 JUNE
7 JUNE

BEIT SAFAFA

SUR BAHIR
Jebel Mukaber

0   MILES   1
0   KM   2

RAMAT RAHEL
To Bethlehem

© Richard Natkiel, 1982

Sino-Soviet Border Disputes

From the end of the 1950s Soviet-Chinese relations, which had been close ever since the Chinese communists gained power, deteriorated. China, among other responses, began to demand revision of the 'unfair' treaties in which a weak Chinese Empire had ceded territory to tsarist Russia. In 1858 China had ceded the north bank of the Amur and in 1860 the east bank of the Ussuri. Taken together, this was an enormous expanse, forming a new Russian province. Then, in 1864, in the far west, much of Sinkiang became part of tsarist Turkestan. After the Bolshevik revolution the Soviet government had steadily advanced in Mongolia, annexing part of it and sponsoring a pro-Soviet government in the remainder. In the 1930s, when the Japanese were occupying north China, they tried to 'rectify' the frontiers by force, but were beaten back, in large-scale battles, by the Red Army. The heaviest fighting was in the summer of 1939 when the Soviet forces were led by the future Marshal Zhukov.

In the 1960s, as tension mounted, there were numerous frontier incidents, and in 1969 this culminated in quite serious fighting between the frontier troops of the two powers. Frontier negotiations were begun, but their progress was intermittent, and in 1978 there was another serious incident on the Ussuri River.

Although navigation rights on the Amur and Ussuri were peacefully negotiated, agreement on the main issues seemed unobtainable, so long as there was no general improvement in Soviet-Chinese relations. Soon after the break with the USSR, the Chinese government placed the USSR and the USA together as aggressive superpowers and claimed leadership of the Third World countries against the domination of these two. By the mid-1970s, however, Chinese-American relations had been much improved. In the early 1980s, although there were occasional hints of a reconciliation, the Soviet-Chinese relationship was as unfriendly as ever and strong forces remained in position on both sides. That underpopulated Siberia was so close to well-populated China was one cause of Soviet mistrust.

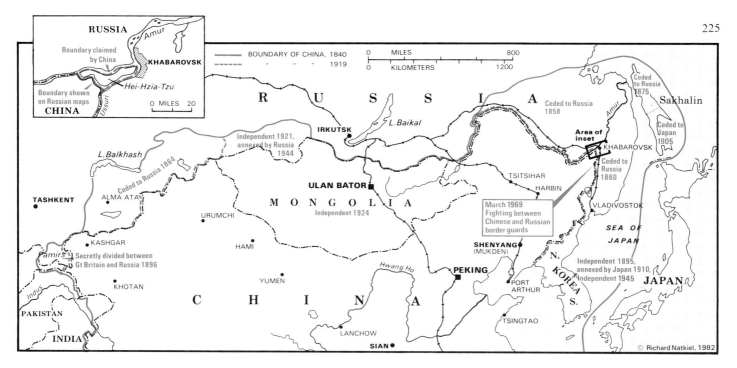

RUSSIA
Boundary claimed by China
KHABAROVSK
Boundary shown on Russian maps
CHINA
Hei-Hzia-Tzu
Amur
Ussuri
0 MILES 20

BOUNDARY OF CHINA, 1840
" " " 1919
0 MILES 800
0 KILOMETERS 1200

R U S S I A
L. Baikal
IRKUTSK
Ceded to Russia 1858
Area of inset
KHABAROVSK
Sakhalin
Ceded to Russia 1875
Ceded to Japan 1905
L. Balkhash
Ceded to Russia 1864
Independent 1921, annexed by Russia 1944
TSITSIHAR
HARBIN
Ceded to Russia 1860
TASHKENT
ALMA ATA
ULAN BATOR
M O N G O L I A
Independent 1924
VLADIVOSTOK
URUMCHI
KASHGAR
HAMI
March 1969 Fighting between Chinese and Russian border guards
SHENYANG (MUKDEN)
SEA OF JAPAN
Pamirs
Secretly divided between Gt Britain and Russia 1896
YUMEN
Hwang Ho
PEKING
PORT ARTHUR
Independent 1895, annexed by Japan 1910, Independent 1945
JAPAN
Indus
KHOTAN
N. KOREA
S.
PAKISTAN
C H I N A
TSINGTAO
INDIA
LANCHOW
SIAN
© Richard Natkiel, 1982

Right: South Vietnamese refugees are escorted across the flight deck of USS *Hancock* during Operation Frequent Wind, the evacuation of Saigon.

Vietnam: the Tet Offensive

After the French disengagement from Vietnam, the Americans tried to encourage the development of a local Vietnamese government which would have the support of its people and thereby be in a position to defend the country against the communists. The American government considered that the elections, promised by the Geneva agreements for 1956, would produce a communist victory, and therefore had no intention of holding them until a date far in the future. But, step by step, the USA found itself drawn into the conflict in Vietnam.

In the late 1950s, while the Vietcong movement in South Vietnam gradually extended its control to almost all the country areas, the US-backed governments proved ineffective, unpopular, and often corrupt. Coups and the occasional assassination did remove the most-disliked government leaders, but each seemed to be followed by a man who was no better. American aid, including advisers, began to create an army for South Vietnam (the ARVN), but at first this was no match for the increasingly large Vietcong formations. In 1959 North Vietnam took control of the anti-government operations in South Vietnam, but it was not until 1964, after incidents in the Gulf of Tonkin, that the US president obtained congressional authority for committing large numbers of US troops to Vietnam. In December of that year Vietcong attacks intensified, and some US air bases were struck. The US Air Force began to bomb North Vietnam and in January 1965 the North Vietnamese Army was committed to action inside South Vietnam.

By 1967 about half a million American troops were in Vietnam, and the ARVN was becoming an effective force. At the end of the year a painstaking operation was begun, aimed at totally eliminating Vietcong from a limited area around Saigon. Extension of this drive, however, was interrupted by the Vietcong's Tet Offensive. This took the form of attacks on cities and towns by small formations which, using infiltration tactics, launched assaults on key government buildings. Although these tactics worked, the attackers were in due course thrown out with very heavy losses.

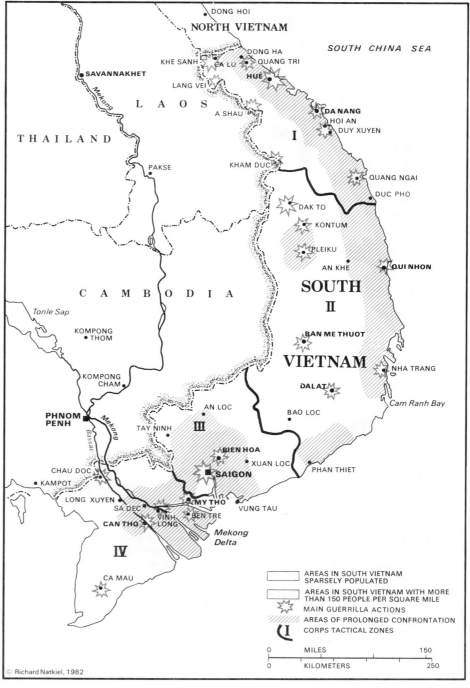

Below: a Marine patrol moves along the dike of a rice paddy during operations against the Viet Cong in 1965.

Vietnam: the Fall of Saigon

The Tet Offensive was victory concealed in a failure. Although beaten militarily, the Vietcong had made a great impression in the USA. Americans asked themselves how it was that, after so much American blood and money had been spent, the enemy could install himself for a few hours or days in almost all the towns and cities. The key town of Hué had been held by the Vietcong for 25 days, and they had even penetrated into the US Embassy in Saigon. Also, as a preliminary to the Tet Offensive, North Vietnamese divisions had heavily attacked Khe Sanh, defended by American Marines. Although it had held out, it was a reminder of the great fear in Washington that the USA, too, could suffer a Dien Bien Phu. It was from this time, January 1968, that the American government, and perhaps most Americans, came to believe that this was a war they could not win and the best thing to do was to get out in as dignified a manner as possible. The request by the American commander in Vietnam, Westmoreland, for reinforcements to exploit what he rightly saw as the enemy's failure during the Tet Offensive, was unsuccessful. Only a few thousand troops were sent, while at the same time American bombing was limited to the enemy's supply routes through Laos and a small part of North Vietnam close to the border.

The morale of American troops was deteriorating, and they began to be progressively withdrawn from 1969 as the US government sought to extricate itself from

Vietnam by negotiation. But in the end the terms it wanted were unobtainable, despite periodic flurries of activity including a US invasion of Cambodia and a renewal of bombing attacks on Hanoi. In January 1973 the US signed an agreement by which its troops finally quit Vietnam, and in exchange North Vietnam merely agreed to release US prisoners of war. The ARVN was left to fight on alone. In late 1974 the North Vietnamese Army began an offensive in the Mekong Delta, followed in January 1975 by another in the Central Highlands. Meanwhile the ARVN had to deal with a successful revolt in Cambodia by the Khmer Rouge revolutionaries. It could not cope with so many crises, and was soon making its last stand before Saigon. This did not last long. At the end of April Saigon fell, bringing the 30-year struggle to a close.

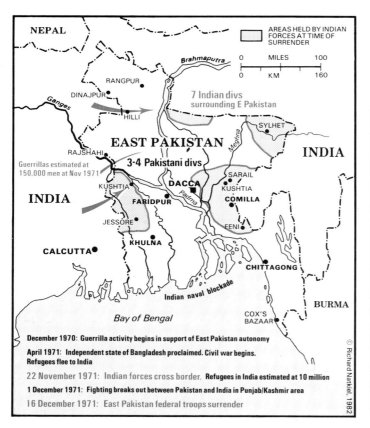

NEPAL

AREAS HELD BY INDIAN FORCES AT TIME OF SURRENDER

Brahmaputra

0 MILES 100
0 KM 160

RANGPUR
DINAJPUR
Ganges
HILLI

7 Indian divs surrounding E Pakistan

SYLHET

EAST PAKISTAN

Meghna

RAJSHAHI

3-4 Pakistani divs

INDIA

Guerrillas estimated at 150,000 men at Nov 1971

KUSHTIA

DACCA

Padma

SARAIL
KUSHTIA
COMILLA

INDIA

FARIDPUR

JESSORE

FENI

KHULNA

CALCUTTA

CHITTAGONG

Indian naval blockade

BURMA

COX'S BAZAAR

Bay of Bengal

December 1970: Guerrilla activity begins in support of East Pakistan autonomy

April 1971: Independent state of Bangladesh proclaimed. Civil war begins. Refugees flee to India

22 November 1971: Indian forces cross border. Refugees in India estimated at 10 million

1 December 1971: Fighting breaks out between Pakistan and India in Punjab/Kashmir area

16 December 1971: East Pakistan federal troops surrender

© Richard Natkiel, 1982

The Creation of Bangladesh

The Bengali population of East Pakistan had become steadily disenchanted with its political situation because, although nominally equal with the West as a constituent of the state of Pakistan, in reality the East was dominated by numerically inferior West Pakistan. In 1970 the East's Awami League, which demanded greater independence for the East, won an overwhelming election victory, giving it a considerable majority in the all-Pakistan Assembly. Faced with this, the leader of the next largest, and mainly West Pakistan, party, Bhutto, decided to boycott the Assembly. There were protest demonstrations in East Pakistan. Bit by bit, the army took up the role of an oppressive army of occupation while the Awami League strengthened its resistance movement, the Mukti Bahini.

The Mukti Bahini began conventional terrorist and guerrilla activity, concentrated near the frontier with India, which was becoming increasingly cooperative. Meanwhile the flow of refugees from East Pakistan to India grew to perhaps 15 million, or no fewer than one in five of the population. In November, in a further step toward open war, the Indian and Pakistan governments announced that their troops were authorized to cross the frontiers in case of need.

On 3 December an excuse to go to war was provided by Pakistan, which began to make attacks on Indian positions in the west and in Kashmir. These attacks were small, and presumably intended as warnings; Pakistan was ruled by a general, Yahia Khan, whose political understanding was unsophisticated. The Indian forces destined for East Pakistan were given extra complements of engineering troops in order to speed the crossing of the many rivers and streams of the region, the plan being to make quickly for the towns and railroad junctions, relying on the Mukti Bahini to

hold down the Pakistanis' defensive positions. One Indian corps attacked from the west, around Hilli, while another made three thrusts from the east to capture the capital Dacca and cut off Chittagong. The third corps attacked from the southwest to capture Jessore and reach the Padma River. On 6 December India recognized the independence of the new state of Bangladesh, and ten days later Indian troops reached Dacca, bringing the war to a close and guaranteeing independence. Internal political problems and recurrent famine continued to unsettle Bangladesh throughout the 1970s and beyond.

EEC, EFTA, and COMECON

The success of the European Coal and Steel Community, established in 1951 to co-ordinate coal and metallurgical industries and also to bring France and Germany, enemies for decades, into a healthier relationship, led to the European Economic Community (EEC). There was a growing opinion that the west European states, in order to survive in a difficult world economy, needed to join together in mutual support. But, initially, its main effect was the elimination of tariffs and other trade barriers between its members, which is why it became known as the Common Market. However, it steadily developed many other functions; its main bodies are the EEC Commission, the Council of Ministers, the Court of Justice, the European Parliament, and the Economic and Social Committee. The six original members which signed the 1958 Treaty of Rome were the members of the Iron and Steel Community; that is, France, West Germany, Italy and the Benelux trio (BElgium, the NEtherlands, LUXembourg).

Neighboring European states, led by Britain, formed another free trade organization, largely as protection against tariff barriers and other restrictions which were expected to limit trade between themselves and EEC countries. This new organization, the European Free Trade Area (EFTA) comprised Britain, Sweden, Switzerland, Austria, Norway, Denmark, and Portugal. These agreed to remove trade barriers between themselves but to maintain them against other nations. For Britain, EFTA had the advantage that it could maintain its preferential trading arrangements with Commonwealth countries. But when Britain's links with the Commonwealth were seen to be weakening in any case, her government decided to ask for membership of the EEC. At first rebuffed, Britain later succeeded, and became a member in 1973, together with Denmark and Ireland. The other EFTA nations continued with the existing free trade agreement.

In communist Europe there had existed since 1949 a Council for Mutual Economic Assistance, later known in the west as COMECON. Originally intended to oversee the sovietization and the exploitation of the economies of communist eastern Europe, it was later developed to coordinate the communist bloc economies, with some specialization of production so that, for example, Czechoslovakia supplies street-cars to the whole bloc while the USSR provides oil. In course of time extra-European members were admitted, although the entry of Vietnam was resented by some of the original members as it seemed to be part of the struggle between the USSR and China for influence in that new state.

© Richard Natkiel, 1982

EEC		**EFTA**			**COMECON**		
APPLICATION PENDING		ASSOCIATE MEMBER			AFFILIATED		

DATE OF JOINING AND POPULATION IN 1979 (MILLIONS)

West Germany	1958	61.34	Portugal	1960	9.87	Russia	1949	264.11
Italy	1958	56.91	Sweden	1960	8.29	Poland	1949	35.23
France	1958	53.48	Austria	1960	7.50	Rumania	1949	22.05
Netherlands	1958	14.03	Switzerland	1960	6.36	Czechoslovakia	1949	15.25
Belgium	1958	9.85	Norway	1960	4.07	Hungary	1949	10.70
Luxembourg	1958	0.36	Iceland	1960	0.23	Bulgaria	1949	8.98
Britain	1973	55.88				Albania (Left 1961)	1949	2.67
Denmark	1973	5.12	Finland	1961	4.76	East Germany	1950	16.75
Ireland	1973	3.37				Mongolia	1962	1.62
Greece	1981	9.44				Cuba	1972	9.78
						Vietnam	1978	51.08
Turkey		44.31						
Spain		37.18				Yugoslavia	1964	22.16
Portugal		9.87						

Right: the opening of the 1972 Common Market summit conference in Paris.

OPEC

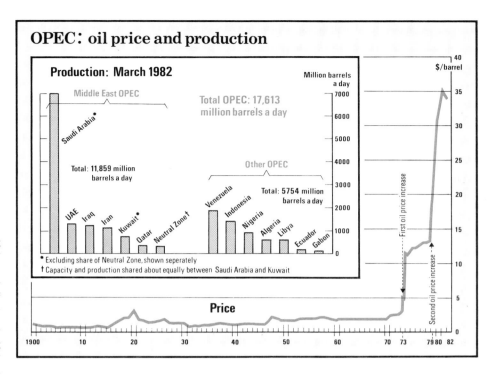

OPEC: oil price and production

Production: March 1982

Middle East OPEC

Total OPEC: 17,613 million barrels a day

Saudi Arabia

Total: 11,859 million barrels a day

Other OPEC

UAE Iraq Iran Kuwait Qatar Neutral Zone† Venezuela Indonesia Nigeria Algeria Libya Ecuador Gabon

Total: 5754 million barrels a day

Million barrels a day

* Excluding share of Neutral Zone, shown seperately
† Capacity and production shared about equally between Saudi Arabia and Kuwait

$/barrel

First oil price increase

Second oil price increase

Price

1900 10 20 30 40 50 60 70 73 79 80 82

The Organization of Petroleum Exporting Countries (OPEC) was formed in 1960 by five founder-members (Iran, Saudi Arabia, Iraq, Kuwait, Venezuela). At the time, its purpose was to slow and perhaps halt the decline in oil prices which the international oil companies had been powerful enough to impose. Thanks to the accession of new members, it did consolidate itself as a strong bargaining body and by 1970, aided by increased world demand, was able to obtain somewhat higher prices.

The very sharp price rises which OPEC enforced in 1973 had a damaging effect not only on the western economies, but throughout the world. Eastern Europe, for example, although mainly supplied by a non-OPEC member, the USSR, found itself faced with price increases as the USSR brought its oil prices closer to world prices. Third World countries in the early stages of economic growth were faced with enormously inflated import expenditures; OPEC did establish a special fund in 1976 to help them, but it was only a palliative.

In the advanced economies the immediate effect of the 1973 and subsequent price rises was an increase in the general price level, since most production depended directly or indirectly on energy. These higher prices were accompanied by a decline of output in specific sectors. There was, therefore a general decline of growth rates and

this entailed a decline of oil imports. The exploitation by the energy-consuming nations of alternative fuels, including oil deposits outside the OPEC countries, and various energy-saving measures, led to a further diminution of oil imports and a situation where several OPEC members preferred to lower prices in order to increase their exports rather than maintain high prices which could result in their oils losing a market.

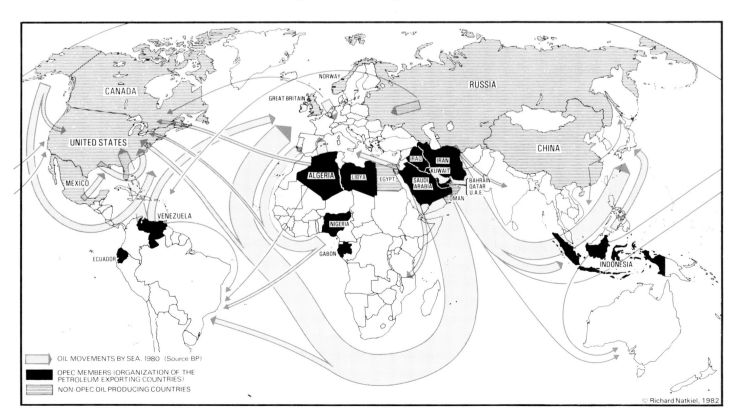

OIL MOVEMENTS BY SEA, 1980 (Source BP)

OPEC MEMBERS (ORGANIZATION OF THE PETROLEUM EXPORTING COUNTRIES)

NON-OPEC OIL PRODUCING COUNTRIES

© Richard Natkiel, 1982

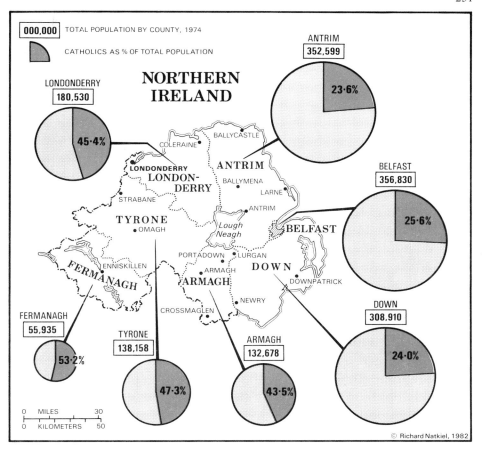

000,000 TOTAL POPULATION BY COUNTY, 1974

CATHOLICS AS % OF TOTAL POPULATION

NORTHERN IRELAND

LONDONDERRY **180,530** **45·4%**

ANTRIM **352,599** **23·6%**

BELFAST **356,830** **25·6%**

DOWN **308,910** **24·0%**

FERMANAGH **55,935** **53·2%**

TYRONE **138,158** **47·3%**

ARMAGH **132,678** **43·5%**

0 MILES 30
0 KILOMETERS 50

© Richard Natkiel, 1982

Northern Ireland

In Ulster the Catholic population has usually not exceeded a third of the total, largely because so many Catholics emigrate. Hence the Protestants, helped by careful manipulation of electoral boundaries, retained control of the Ulster government and were able to discriminate against Catholics in the allocation of cheap public housing, in jobs and in other areas.

Londonderry was a city where these grievances of the Catholics were most intense, and in 1968 a civil rights march there, banned by the authorities, nevertheless took place, and was violently dispersed. In August 1969 the traditional Protestant, and provocative, Apprentice Boys' march was not banned, and was followed by rioting by the inhabitants of Londonderry's Bogside quarter. Rioting spread through the Province, violently countered and sometimes provoked by the Protestant police reservists, the B Specials, and British troops were sent in. The British government promised that reforms would be introduced, and soon established 'direct rule' from London.

The August riots led to a split in the Irish Republican Army [IRA], an underground organization, with those of its members who favored violent tactics leaving to form the Provisional IRA, or Provos. Gradually the British army lost the confidence of the Catholic population, which had initially welcomed its protection, and in February 1971 the first soldier was killed by the Provos. The leader of the Protestant ruling party, the Unionists, despite internal opposition, intro-

duced limited 'power-sharing,' in which two other parties, wholly or partly representing Catholic interests, could take part. In the face of increasing terrorism, and much to the indignation of an aroused Catholic population, he also introduced internment. This was the arrest, all too often bungled, of known IRA members. In 1972 a London-sponsored proposal for a Council of Ireland, in which Dublin, London, and the Northern Ireland Executive would work together, at first seemed likely to succeed, but failed to receive enough support from Unionist politicians, and foundered. Attempts of the powersharing Northern Ireland Executive to govern the Province came to an end when a strike staged by Protestant organizations brought ordinary life to a halt. The British government's weakness in allowing the

Protestants to thereby put an end to any hope of compromise was later severely criticized. In the following years, various political initiatives failed, although attempts to improve conditions by the encouragement of new industries in the Province were partly successful. Killings continued, by Provos, by a new Irish National Liberation Army, and by Protestant, or 'Loyalist,' groups. The political temperature was further raised in 1981 by the deaths of Provo hunger-strikers in Northern Ireland prisons, and at the end of that year a solution was still not in sight. The level of violence had declined from its peak in the early 1970s and improved relations between the London and Dublin governments offered some prospects for the future although such contacts with the Irish Republic were anathema to Loyalist leaders.

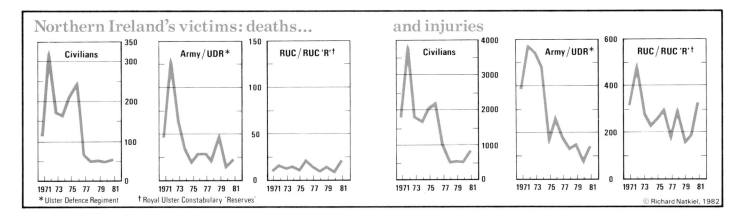

Northern Ireland's victims: deaths...   and injuries

Civilians

Army/UDR*

RUC/RUC 'R'†

Civilians

Army/UDR*

RUC/RUC 'R'†

1971 73 75 77 79 81
* Ulster Defence Regiment   † Royal Ulster Constabulary 'Reserves'

© Richard Natkiel, 1982

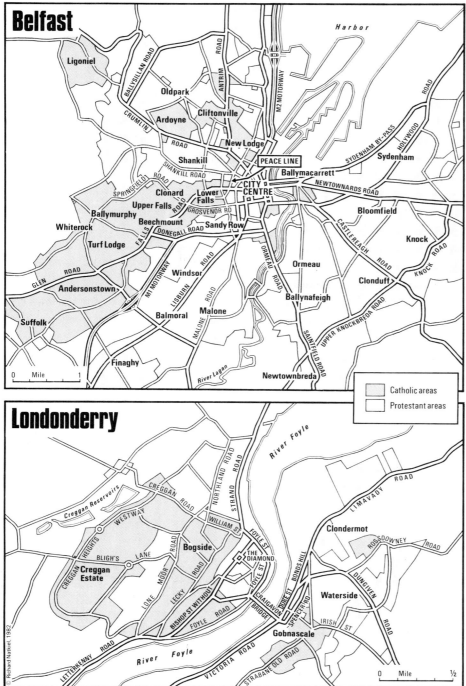

Belfast

Londonderry

Catholic areas
Protestant areas

© Richard Natkiel, 1982

Left: a remotely-controlled bomb-disposal apparatus goes into action in Belfast.
Below: rioters pelt British troops with stones as they attempt to control the mob in the Bogside area of Londonderry in April 1971.
Bottom: Turkish occupation forces in position near Famagusta, Cyprus, August 1974.

Cyprus

After World War II in the British colony of Cyprus the patriarch of the Orthodox Church, Archbishop Makarios III, became the moral leader of the *Enosis* movement, which sought union with Greece. However, it was the local Greek terrorist organization, EOKA, instigator of murderous attacks on British servicemen and colonial officials, which had the main effect on British policy. In 1957 negotiations were begun which led to a 1959 agreement granting the island independence. Thirty percent of key positions were reserved for Turks, who amounted to 18 percent of the population. Any suggestion of union with Greece was rejected, and Britain retained sovereign rights in two military base areas.

Makarios, retaining religious authority as Archbishop and having won secular authority as President, proved less enthusiastic for *Enosis* than expected, so EOKA made a new start, abetted by the Greek government. Some pro-Greece bishops attempted to depose Makarios from his archbishopric, but were outmaneuvered and unfrocked. More serious were the several unsuccessful attempts to assassinate Makarios. Then, on 15 July 1974, a coup organized by *Enosis* and EOKA elements was successful, and Nikos Sampson, a local Greek Cypriot, was placed in the presidency. In response, and surprisingly promptly, Turkey dispatched an invasion force to Cyprus, which landed near Kyrenia on 20 July and steadily moved inland. The covert but plain-to-all involvement of the Greek government as instigator of this new international crisis led to the dismissal of the Greek cabinet on 23 July and Sampson, after a week of fame, was deposed by the Cyprus National Guard. The three guarantor-powers of the Republic of Cyprus (Britain, Turkey, Greece) met at Geneva, but a lasting ceasefire was obtained only on 16 August. This left the Turkish Army in control of the northern third of the island, mainly inhabited by Turks. Late in 1974 Makarios returned to the presidency in the capital, Nicosia, but he had no authority in the Turkish zone, which became increasingly linked with the Turkish mainland. A UN peacekeeping force patrolled a buffer zone between the two parts, and there were sporadic attempts to arrive at a settlement under UN auspices. Talks between Turkish Cypriot and Greek Cypriot leaders were successful in avoiding further violence but unsuccessful in ending the *de facto* partition of the island. Makarios died in 1977, and five years later the 'Cyprus Problem' was still unsolved.

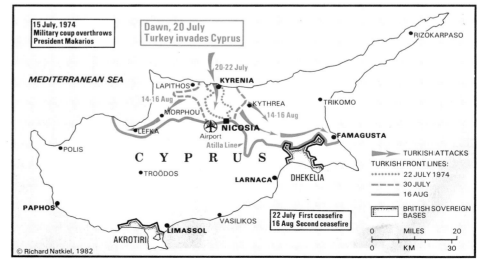

The October War, 1973

The ceasefire after the Six-Day War of 1967 was followed by six years of tension in the Middle East. Arabs and Israelis resorted to terrorism and counter-terrorism, with the occasional air battle punctuating the situation, as the Arab states bordering Israel continued to demand a restoration of the pre-1967 frontiers. By 1973 President Sadat of Egypt had enhanced, with Soviet help, the battleworthiness of his army, but he had then invited the Soviet military specialists to leave, thereby freeing himself from a possible restraining Soviet influence over his military ambitions.

On the Jewish Day of Atonement (*Yom Kippur*), 6 October 1973, Egyptian and Syrian forces launched a coordinated surprise attack on Israel, with the stated intention of regaining the 1967 frontiers. The Egyptian crossing of the Suez Canal, thanks to the surprise achieved, was successful, and the Israeli forces defending Sinai were put into disarray. In the north, too, the Israelis were thrown back, losing much of the Golan Heights. Help for both sides soon began to arrive. Iraq sent tanks to help the Syrians, and so did Jordan, while Kuwait and Saudi Arabia sent token forces to the same front. Egypt received some aircraft from Iraq, while Moroccan and Algerian troops arrived to release more Egyptian troops for the front. Meanwhile, the USA airlifted military supplies to Israel, while Soviet aid was sent by air and by sea to

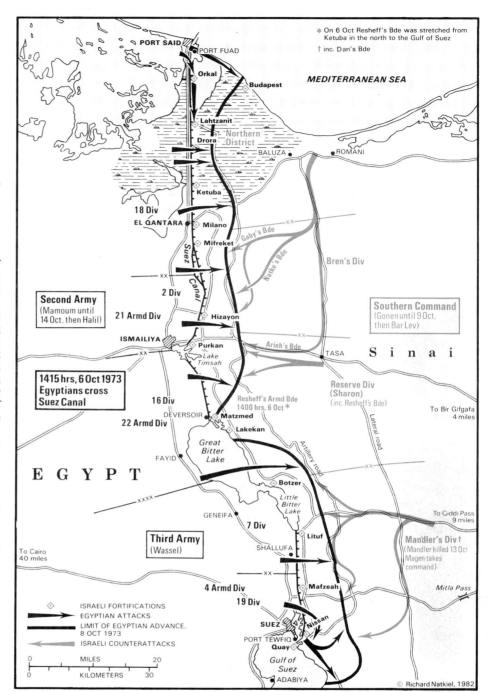

* On 6 Oct Resheff's Bde was stretched from Ketuba in the north to the Gulf of Suez

† inc. Dan's Bde

MEDITERRANEAN SEA

Second Army
(Mamoum until 14 Oct, then Halil)

1415 hrs, 6 Oct 1973
Egyptians cross
Suez Canal

Third Army
(Wassel)

Southern Command
(Gonen until 9 Oct, then Bar Lev)

S i n a i

Reserve Div (Sharon)
(inc. Resheff's Bde)

Resheff's Armd Bde
1400 hrs, 6 Oct *

To Bir Gifgafa
4 miles

To Giddi Pass
9 miles

Mandler's Div †
(Mandler killed 13 Oct Magen takes command)

Mitla Pass

E G Y P T

To Cairo
40 miles

◇ ISRAELI FORTIFICATIONS
➤ EGYPTIAN ATTACKS
━ LIMIT OF EGYPTIAN ADVANCE, 8 OCT 1973
➤ ISRAELI COUNTERATTACKS

0 — MILES — 20
0 — KILOMETERS — 30

© Richard Natkiel, 1982

PORT SAID, PORT FUAD, Orkal, Budapest, Lahtzanit, Drora, Northern District, BALUZA, ROMANI, Ketuba, 18 Div, EL QANTARA, Milano, Mifreket, Gaby's Bde, Natke's Bde, Bren's Div, 2 Div, 21 Armd Div, Hizayon, Suez Canal, ISMAILIYA, Purkan, Lake Timsah, Arieh's Bde, TASA, 16 Div, DEVERSOIR, Matzmed, 22 Armd Div, Lakekan, Great Bitter Lake, FAYID, Botzer, Little Bitter Lake, GENEIFA, 7 Div, Lituf, SHALLUFA, Artillery road, Lateral road, 4 Armd Div, 19 Div, Mafzeah, SUEZ, Nissan, PORT TEWFIQ, Quay, Gulf of Suez, ADABIYA

Left: the ceasefire line in the town of Suez at the end of the Yom Kippur War, October 1973.
Top right: Israeli troops cross the Suez Canal over a temporary causeway.
Right: Israeli soldiers relax during a lull in the fighting in Sinai.

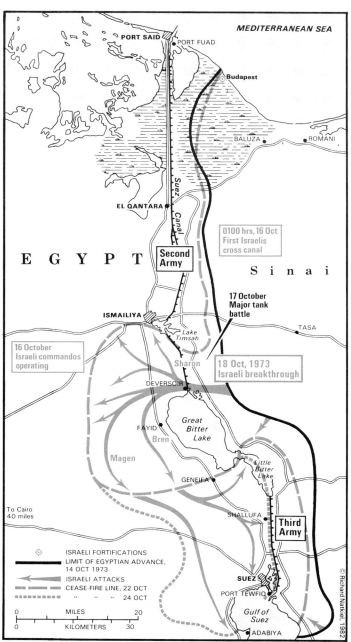

MEDITERRANEAN SEA

PORT SAID • PORT FUAD

Budapest

BALUZA • ROMANI

EL QANTARA

EGYPT

Second Army

S i n a i

0100 hrs, 16 Oct
First Israelis
cross canal

17 October
Major tank
battle

TASA

ISMAILIYA

Lake Timsah

16 October
Israeli commandos
operating

Sharon

18 Oct, 1973
Israeli breakthrough

DEVERSOIR

Great Bitter Lake

FAYID

Bren

Magen

Little Bitter Lake

GENEIFA

SHALLUFA

Third Army

To Cairo
40 miles

SUEZ

PORT TEWFIQ

Gulf of Suez

◇ ISRAELI FORTIFICATIONS

━━ LIMIT OF EGYPTIAN ADVANCE,
      14 OCT 1973

◄━ ISRAELI ATTACKS

▬ ▬ CEASE-FIRE LINE, 22 OCT

· · · "   "   "   24 OCT

ADABIYA

MILES   20
0

KILOMETERS   30
0

© Richard Natkiel, 1982

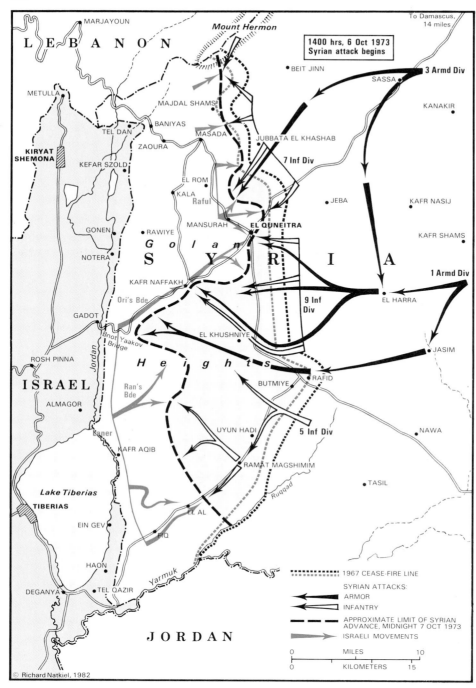

Map legend:
- **1400 hrs, 6 Oct 1973 Syrian attack begins**
- 1967 CEASE-FIRE LINE
- SYRIAN ATTACKS:
  - ARMOR
  - INFANTRY
- APPROXIMATE LIMIT OF SYRIAN ADVANCE, MIDNIGHT 7 OCT 1973
- ISRAELI MOVEMENTS

© Richard Natkiel, 1982

Egypt and Syria. Israel was again out-numbered, having about 300,000 troops against Egypt's 650,000 and Syria's 150,000.

By 10 October the Israelis had beaten back the Syrians in the north, and were just holding the Egyptians in Sinai. Israeli air-craft, which had been vulnerable to Soviet-made missiles while attacking the Suez Canal bridges and the Syrian and Egyptian troops, were now free to deal with their opponents' own air forces. A strong counter-offensive was launched against the Syrians, whose defense line was pushed back. A threat to Damascus was avoided as this, it was feared, might have brought the USSR into the war in support of her protégé Syria. Having weakened the Syrian position, the Israelis concentrated their next effort on the Suez Front. Egyptian tanks, attempting to push eastward and especially toward the vital Mitla Pass, were routed in an enormous tank battle by Israeli armor and aircraft. This victory encouraged the Israeli generals, who were rarely in agreement with each other, to launch a decisive counterblow. The aim was to cross the Suez Canal in the area of the Great Bitter Lake, and thereby trans-form the situation. Despite some difficulty, when unexpectedly strong Egyptian action was encountered east of the Canal, a bridge-head was established and this was progres-sively enlarged until the Egyptian Third Army found itself almost cut off. A USSR delegation to Cairo realized that Egypt was facing total defeat, and with US and Soviet help the United Nations Security Council arranged a ceasefire, effective from 24 October.

Although Israel had emerged triumphant from this new ordeal, the war had shown

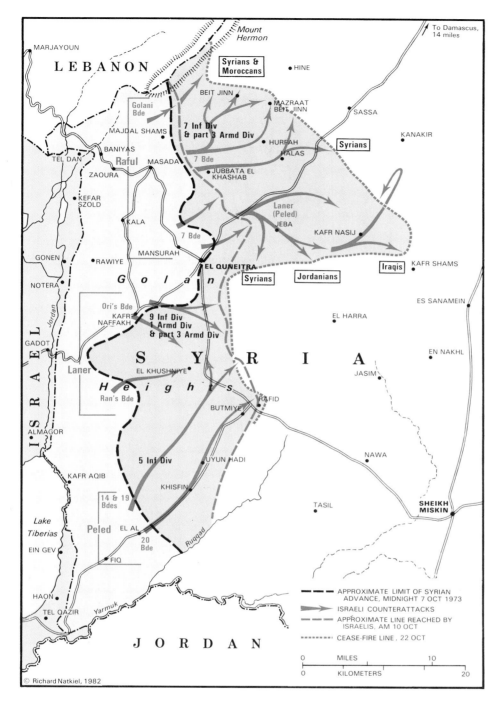

LEBANON

Mount Hermon

To Damascus, 14 miles

MARJAYOUN

Syrians & Moroccans

HINE

BEIT JINN

MAZRAAT BEIT JINN

SASSA

Golani Bde

MAJDAL SHAMS

7 Inf Div & part 3 Armd Div

HURFAH
HALAS

KANAKIR

Syrians

BANIYAS

TEL DAN

Raful

MASADA

7 Bde

JUBBATA EL KHASHAB

ZAOURA

KEFAR SZOLD

KALA

Laner (Peled)

JEBA

KAFR NASIJ

GONEN

RAWIYE

MANSURAH

7 Bde

Golan

EL QUNEITRA

Syrians

Jordanians

Iraqis

KAFR SHAMS

NOTERA

ES SANAMEIN

Ori's Bde

KAFR NAFFAKH

9 Inf Div 1 Armd Div & part 3 Armd Div

EL HARRA

EN NAKHL

GADOT

S Y R I A

Laner

EL KHUSHNIYE

Heights

Ran's Bde

BUTMIYE

RAFID

JASIM

ISRAEL

ALMAGOR

5 Inf Div

UYUN HADI

NAWA

KAFR AQIB

KHISFIN

Lake Tiberias

14 & 19 Bdes

Peled

EL AL

TASIL

SHEIKH MISKIN

EIN GEV

20 Bde

Jordan

FIQ

HAON

Ruqqad

TEL QAZIR

Yarmuk

J O R D A N

— — — APPROXIMATE LIMIT OF SYRIAN ADVANCE, MIDNIGHT 7 OCT 1973

ISRAELI COUNTERATTACKS

APPROXIMATE LINE REACHED BY ISRAELIS, AM 10 OCT

········· CEASE-FIRE LINE, 22 OCT

© Richard Natkiel, 1982

0   MILES   10

0   KILOMETERS   20

that the Egyptian Army was more battle-worthy than had been believed, and that Israel was more vulnerable to surprise attack than had been thought. UN forces were sent to Sinai, while Israeli forces were withdrawn east of the passes. Egyptian forces remained on the right bank of the Canal, but the UN force separating the two armies was equipped to issue early warning of troop movements to both sides.

Below left: Egyptian troops load supplies aboard amphibious craft, which were used to ferry food and ammunition across the Suez Canal to the encircled Third Army. Below: these Palestinian terrorists were killed when the explosives they were carrying into Israel across the Golan Heights accidentally detonated.

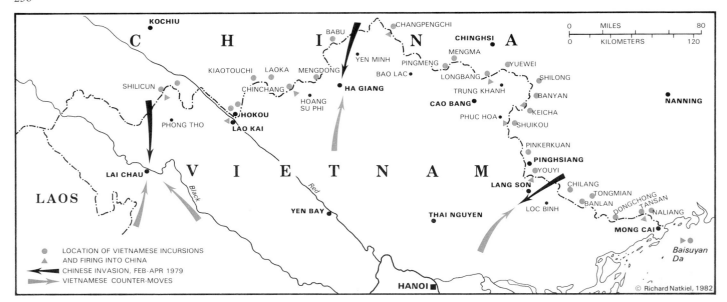

CHINA

KOCHIU
BABU
CHANGPENGCHI
CHINGHSI
NANNING

KIAOTOUCHI LAOKA MENGDONG
YEN MINH PINGMENG MENGMA
YUEWEI
SHILONG

SHILICUN
CHINCHANG
BAO LAC
LONGBANG
BANYAN

HOKOU
HOANG SU PHI
HA GIANG
TRUNG KHANH
KEICHA

PHONG THO
LAO KAI
CAO BANG
PHUC HOA
SHUIKOU

LAI CHAU

VIETNAM

PINKERKUAN

LAOS

Black

Red

PINGHSIANG
YOUYI
LANG SON
CHILANG
TONGMIAN
DONGCHONG
TANSAN
NALIANG

YEN BAY

THAI NGUYEN
LOC BINH
BANLAN
MONG CAI
Baisuyan Da

HANOI

- LOCATION OF VIETNAMESE INCURSIONS
- AND FIRING INTO CHINA
→ CHINESE INVASION, FEB–APR 1979
→ VIETNAMESE COUNTER-MOVES

0 MILES 80
0 KILOMETERS 120

© Richard Natkiel, 1982

Vietnam versus China

After the establishment of the Socialist Republic of Vietnam, following the over-running of South Vietnam in 1975, the new state had serious policy differences with China. The Vietnamese wished to draw the neighboring states of Kampuchea (Cambodia) and Laos into close association, whereas China wished them to be independent and orientated toward Peking. In 1977 Vietnamese forces invaded Kampuchea and, despite Chinese help for the Cambodian government, captured the capital, Phnom Penh, and installed a new, friendly government, which agreed to the stationing of Vietnamese troops on its territory.

Meanwhile the tough socialist measures introduced in newly-conquered south Vietnam affected Chinese residents especially, since they were the trading and managerial class. In the summer of 1978 up to 200,000 fled into the Chinese provinces across the frontier. Chinese technical and economic aid to Vietnam was cut off. For this and other reasons Vietnam drew closer to the USSR, raising the possibility of Soviet bases close to China inside Vietnam. In early 1979 there were clashes on the Chinese-Vietnamese frontier and on 17 February the Chinese Army invaded in considerable strength. The town of Lang Son was captured; this opened the direct route to Hanoi, across flat country, but the Chinese, who had not, and did not wish, to deploy their full strength, called a halt and began to withdraw, claiming that they had done enough to 'teach Vietnam a lesson.' Although they had gained ground, and no doubt alarmed the Vietnamese government, their casualties had been heavy, the month's fighting having been quite fierce. In April negotiations began, and in May the two sides began to exchange prisoners. However, Vietnam continued to treat its Chinese citizens with hostility.

Below left: Vietnamese gunners bombard Chinese invading forces in 1979. The fine fighting qualities of the Vietnamese troops more than compensated for the numerical strength of the Chinese.

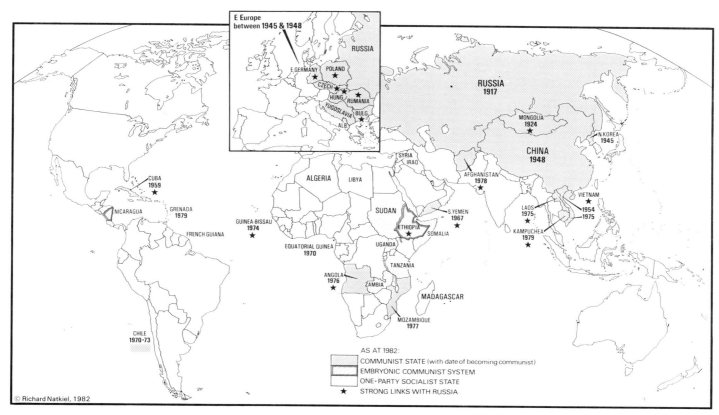

© Richard Natkiel, 1982

AS AT 1982:
- COMMUNIST STATE (with date of becoming communist)
- EMBRYONIC COMMUNIST SYSTEM
- ONE-PARTY SOCIALIST STATE
- ★ STRONG LINKS WITH RUSSIA

The Spread of Communist Influence

After 1945 the spread of Moscow's influence was largely a matter of consolidating control of the newly-established people's democracies. Elsewhere the policy was to help local communist parties, while ensuring that they did not deviate from the Moscow line which, briefly, was that the Russian way to communism was the only possible way and that Moscow was and would remain the ideological and inspirational centre of the communist world. In France and Italy there were very large communist parties, and in the late 1940s these staged disturbances, which included sabotage, but were unable to create the revolutionary opportunity for which Moscow had hoped. However, the communist victory in China seemed a great success.

This situation changed after the mid-1950s, when a new policy of supporting, and thereby influencing, non-communist nationalist movements in overseas territories was adopted, even though this meant Soviet support for newly-installed 'bourgeois' regimes in the Third World. In some cases these devices worked well. In Cuba, especially, Soviet help for Castro's revolutionary regime soon created a Soviet-orientated communist government in that island. In other cases, however, Soviet hopes were dramatically disappointed. Egypt, for example, at the time it was receiving substantial Soviet economic aid, had no hesitation in keeping its local communists safely in gaol, and later invited Soviet military advisers to leave. Almost always, Third World governments were skilled in obtaining what they wanted by playing off east against west while making irrevocable concessions to neither. The USSR did establish shore facilities for its navy in several countries, a vital need for a country intent on becoming a world naval power, but these bases were dependent on local goodwill which was not always long-lived.

Meanwhile the strong communist parties in Italy, France and Spain steadily moved from a position of servility to one of open hostility in their relationship with Moscow, while the emergence of China as an ideological and political opponent of the USSR made it easier for the smaller communist states to act more independently. Suppression of popular movements in eastern Europe further lowered Moscow's prestige, while the establishment of loyal communist regimes in Cuba and, later, Afghanistan, involved a heavy economic drain which was resented by Soviet citizens still living in conditions of scarcity. In general, western attempts to halt Soviet expansion by backing unpopular regimes which happened to be anti-communist were self-defeating, and certainly less important than local nationalisms and the provision of economic and technical aid to governments which, without necessarily being anti-communist, did not sympathize with Russian aspirations.

Africa in the 1970s

During the 1970s there was a growing tendency for the independent African states to take a stronger attitude toward the richer, industrialized, countries. This change became evident at a Commonwealth conference of 1971, in which Zambia, Tanzania, and Uganda threatened to impose economic penalties on Britain if the latter should export substantial arms and munitions to South Africa. The South African issue dominated the continent's outlook, as it was evident that the South African government not only intended to continue its restrictive attitude toward its black inhabitants at home, but also would interfere in its neighbors' affairs; South Africa's continued blocking of a majority-rule solution for Namibia, its incursions into Angola, and its aid to the rebel white regime of Rhodesia were regarded as examples of this. An informal alliance developed in which Arab states declared their hostility to South Africa in return for African states breaking off relations with Israel. However, South Africa continued on its course despite the attainment of black rule in Angola and Mozambique and, in 1980, in Zimbabwe (formerly Rhodesia).

In East Africa the situation was disturbed as the new Marxist regime in Ethiopia sought to consolidate its position and beat off the hostility of Eritrean nationalists and Somalia. There were several regional economic cooperation schemes but an old one, the East African Community, broke up because of animosity between its members, Kenya, Uganda and Tanzania. Here and there hostilities over border issues, or civil wars, broke out. At the beginning of the decade there were about seven million Africans under arms, but this soon increased. At the same time, of the world's 25 poorest nations, 18 were in Africa. Many Africans blamed the power of big international companies for their slow economic development and it seemed likely that, with the process of decolonization almost complete, the stronger states, like Nigeria, would begin to assert their economic independence.

Right: a UNITA soldier seen in Lobito during the civil war in Angola.
Below: UNITA forces on the attack in Southern Angola, February 1977.

Angola

In the 1950s and 1960s three competing organizations opposed the Portuguese administration in Angola. They all aimed at independence, but had different philosophies and different foreign backers. The MPLA (The Popular Movement) represented revolutionary nationalism and was Marxist. The FNLA (The National Front) defended the interests of northern tribes and had the tacit sympathy of the USA and Belgium. Curiously, the UNITA movement in the south depended on Portuguese tolerance; such tolerance was forthcoming because UNITA seemed likely to cause more damage to the MPLA than to the Portuguese.

When, in 1974, an army coup in Portugal made an opening for political parties which were willing to grant independence to the colonies, the MPLA, FNLA and UNITA continued their fight against each other. City-dwellers, especially in the capital Luanda, were largely in favor of the MPLA. This gave the latter an advantage, but FNLA and UNITA received much support from and through Zaire. Moreover, in August 1975 South African forces advanced into south Angola, where their effect was to strengthen the UNITA movement. But by July the MPLA had succeeded in gaining control of Luanda, through which military supplies were received from eastern Europe, helping the MPLA to

control 12 of the 16 Angolan districts. However, in October South African units advanced and helped FNLA and UNITA forces to capture Moçâmedes, Sá da Bandeira, Benguela, Lobito and Novo Redondo. But troops sent by Cuba were now arriving and these helped the MPLA to regain the initiative, and in February 1976 to proclaim Angolan independence and form a government.

Right: an MPLA soldier mounts guard at the Cuanda River, near the town of Dondo, Angola 1976.

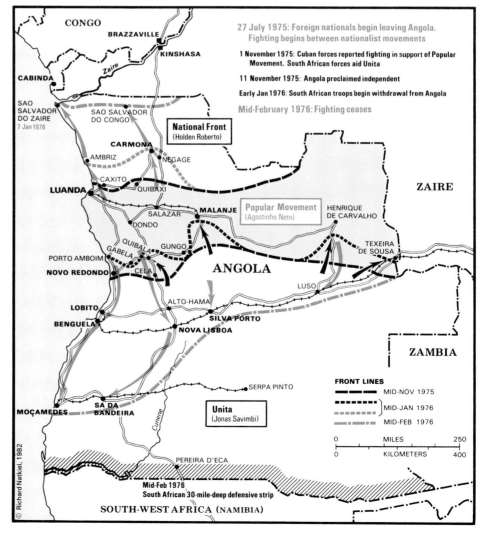

242

Eritrea, the Ogaden, and Ethiopia

In 1950 the United Nations Assembly approved the federation of the former Italian colony of Eritrea with Ethiopia. Eritrea had a mainly Moslem population, whereas Ethiopia was Christian, and this, with Ethiopia's 1962 termination of Eritrea's federal status, gave edge to Eritrean resistance. Farther south, in 1960 the former British and Italian Somaliland colonies were united, becoming independent Somalia with its capital at Mogadishu. However, the colonial frontiers were such that many Somalians remained outside, in Kenya and

Ethiopia. After a few unsettled years, frontier agreements were made with Ethiopia and Kenya, but Somalia did not obtain the Somali-speaking area of the Ogaden, in southern Ethiopia.

Eritrean nationalist guerrillas received much support from Arab countries, and the Ethiopian Army was still fighting them, unsuccessfully, when a revolution deposed Haile Sellassie and installed a Marxist government in Addis Ababa in 1974. Profiting by the confusion, the Eritrean Liberation Front, (ELF) almost captured the Eritrean capital Asmara. By 1977 the Ethiopians were being pursued by the ELF, and by the Eritrean People's Liberation Front (EPLF) in the north. Disunity between these two movements, and the rebuilding of the Ethiopian Army with Soviet help, helped

the Ethiopians to regain the initiative in 1978 and relieve Asmara and Massawa. But, reduced to a small area of difficult country, the ELF continued to hold out, as did the EPLF in the far north.

Meanwhile from 1973, the Western Somali Liberation Front (WSLF) was active in the Ogaden, and from July 1977 was supported by regular Somali forces. The USSR, previously supporting Somalia, switched its support to Ethiopia and, with the help of Cuban troops, saved the Ethiopian Army from rout. The Somali Army withdrew from the conflict while its government turned to the USA for help. Somalian guerrillas remained active in the Ogaden, while Somalia continued to . demand a frontier revision, and remained, technically at least, in a state of war.

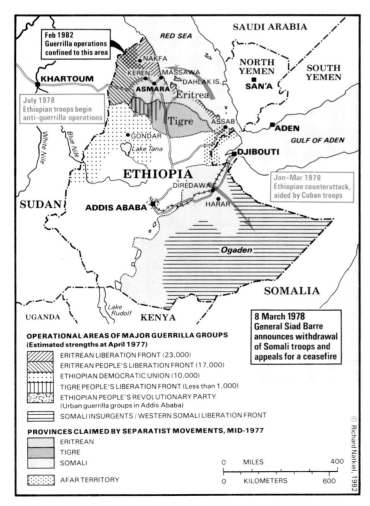

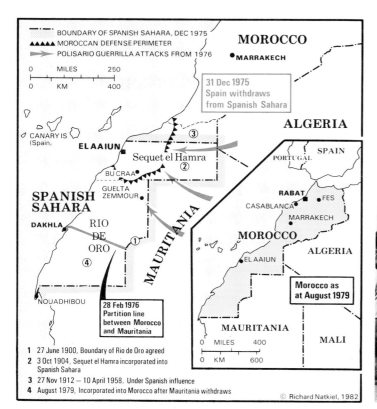

© Richard Natkiel, 1982

Map legend:
- BOUNDARY OF SPANISH SAHARA, DEC 1975
- ▲▲▲▲ MOROCCAN DEFENSE PERIMETER
- ➤ POLISARIO GUERRILLA ATTACKS FROM 1976

31 Dec 1975
Spain withdraws
from Spanish Sahara

Morocco as
at August 1979

28 Feb 1976
Partition line
between Morocco
and Mauritania

1 27 June 1900, Boundary of Rio de Oro agreed
2 3 Oct 1904, Sequet el Hamra incorporated into Spanish Sahara
3 27 Nov 1912 – 10 April 1958, Under Spanish influence
4 August 1979, Incorporated into Morocco after Mauritania withdraws

The Western Sahara

By the early 1970s it was clear that Spain was unlikely to maintain her hold on the Spanish Sahara for long. Morocco, Mauritania and Algeria each had interests in the colony. Algeria supported the Polisario movement (formed in 1973) which was nationalist and Marxist oriented whereas in October 1974 Morocco and Mauritania secretly agreed to partition the country between themselves. This they duly did when Spain withdrew and were immediately opposed by Polisario guerrillas.

From May 1976 the Polisario attacks were concentrated on Mauritania, very much poorer and weaker than Morocco, and despite the presence of Moroccan troops, a coup in Mauritania in July 1978 led to an agreement between Polisario and Mauritania in 1979. Mauritania then withdrew from the occupied territory. The fighting between Polisario and Morocco continued into the 1980s and was a heavy burden on the Moroccan economy. Although Algeria became less active in support of Polisario after the death of President Boumedienne in 1978 Polisario did receive arms from Libya and formal recognition from a number of other countries.

Right: a display of weapons which Ethiopian soldiers were carrying when they fled across the border into Sudan following fighting with the ELF in 1977.
Above right: Enthusiastic WSLF guerrillas on their way to the front, November 1977.

HOMELANDS
- BOPHUTHATSWANA
- CISKEI
- GAZANKULU
- KWAZULU
- LEBOWA
- QWAQWA
- SOUTH NDEBELE
- KANGWANE
- TRANSKEI
- VENDA

'INDEPENDENT' BY 1982

© Richard Natkiel, 1982

The South African Homelands

In 1948 in the Union of South Africa the hitherto minority Nationalist Party won an electoral majority, which it gradually increased over the following three decades. Thus the Union (since 1960 the Republic) found itself ruled by an Afrikaner ('Boer') party, advocating *apartheid*. *Apartheid*, or separation, implied that each race should have its own homeland where it could develop economically and culturally in accord with its own desires and capabilities. *Apartheid* also implied the concept of 'white supremacy,' although this term was later avoided, 'separate development' being favored instead.

In theory, the African majority was to live in its own homelands, while the white minority would occupy other parts of the territory. The first of the homelands, the Transkei, was granted internal self-government in 1963 and, with support from the Republic's government, Chief Matanzima became its first prime minister. Other homelands were subsequently given their own

legislative assemblies. In addition, earlier British colonial policy had created the independent black states of Swaziland and Lesotho; these were not part of the South African homelands strategy, but because of their geography had close connections with it. A further step was taken in 1976, when the South African government declared the Transkei to be independent, followed by Venda (1979), Bophuthatswana (1977) the Ciskei (1981), and others.

Most countries did not recognize the independence of these new so-called states, claiming that they were not truly independent. Criticis emphasized that the planned homelands could not possibly support the entire African population, while the forcible removal of many Africans from the white areas to the homelands aroused international criticism. The homelands possessed no ports and no industry and had few economic resources. In practice, they seemed to serve as reservoirs of cheap migrant labor for use by the white economy.

South America

Most countries of South America experienced accelerated industrial development during the two world wars and some, in the interwar years, strove to attain self-sufficiency in oil production. The exploitation of Mexican oil had led to over-rapid development and the 1910 Mexican revolution, but Venezuela became a major oil exporter and avoided this situation. Nevertheless the growth of the middle and working classes in many South American countries, together with the Mexican example, meant that changes of government by traditional coups sometimes developed into real revolutions seeking to change the social balance. Uruguay's constitutional revolution of 1919, the post-1945 Peronist movement in Argentina, and the Bolivian revolution of 1952 (that country's 179th), had much in common. In most cases these revolutions lost impetus, as did moves toward democracy,

Below: Gold miners in Johannesburg. Most of the black labor on which South Africa relies is imported from tribal territories. Bottom: National Guards patrolling a village street in war-torn El Salvador, 1979.

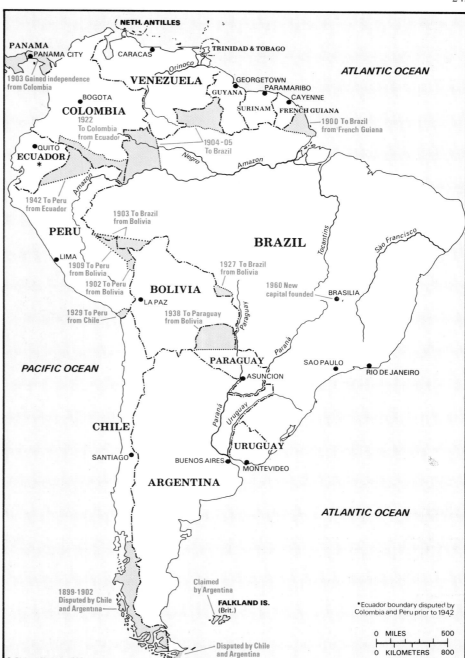

and in the early 1980s most South Americans lived under military regimes, or governments under military influence. Population continued to increase in the twentieth century, although this was less a result of continued immigration (especially from Italy, Spain and Portugal) than of improved public health. By the 1960s Brazil seemed set to be the future economic giant of the continent, a development symbolized by the construction of an expensive new capital at Brasilia.

The nineteenth century struggles for independence had left many indefinite frontiers, and disputes over these continued to plague the continent. The Chaco War (1932–1935) between Paraguay and Bolivia was the most destructive of these disputes, and resulted in Bolivia losing most of the Chaco territory. In the early 1980s Venezuela still had a territorial claim on Guyana (formerly British Guiana) and Argentina remained bellicosely dissatisfied with an arbitration award which confirmed Chilean possession of three islands in the Beagle Channel.

Uganda

The former British colony of Uganda had great difficulty in reconciling its new independent style of government with the strong tribal loyalties of its peoples. In 1971 the army commander, Idi Amin, in a coup which was largely tribal in its aspirations, deposed and then succeeded President Obote. Amin's eight-year rule was characterized by the elevation of his cronies to high office, the imprisonment, torture and murder not only of his enemies, real or suspected, but of any Ugandan who had the courage to criticize, the expulsion of the large Asian community and the takeover of the Asian-run businesses by Amin's supporters, the alienation of almost all Uganda's friends, including fellow-members of the British Commonwealth and of the Organization for African Unity, and a general run-down of the economy. Lacking other friends outside the country, and increasingly distrustful of his compatriots, Amin began to rely increasingly on Libya and Palestinians.

Having achieved all this, Amin declared 1978 to be a year of peace and reconciliation. But this proved to be wishful thinking for in July the army, hitherto cossetted by Amin in return for its support, staged a mutiny which was suppressed only by Palestinians flown in from Libya. In October Amin accused Tanzania of invading southwestern Uganda and dispatched three battalions, with tanks and artillery, to cross the frontier into Tanzania. Within a few days, however, Tanzanian troops and Ugandan exiles were advancing in south Uganda toward the capital, Kampala, which fell in April.

The Falklands Crisis

Although the Argentine invasion of the Falkland Islands on 2 April 1982 came as a complete surprise to the people of Britain and the rest of the world, the status of the islands had long been a source of dispute between Britain and Argentina. Despite the British military victory which ultimately ensued most Argentinians were and remain convinced that the islands, which they know as the Malvinas, ought rightfully to be part of Argentina. In negotiations over many years Britain had gone some way toward recognizing this claim. One suggestion had been to transfer sovereignty over the islands to Argentina but for Britain to continue to administer them on a 'lease-back' arrangement giving them a similar status as Hong Kong *vis-à-vis* China. However, Britain was unwilling to enforce such a deal against the wishes of the islanders who vehemently insisted that they wanted to remain British.

Negotiations in early 1982 made no new progress and, presumably after careful preparation, the invasion of the Falkland Islands and South Georgia followed. It has been suggested that a major motive for the Argentine military junta's decision was a desire to distract the Argentinian people from the country's appalling economic problems. The Argentinians were certainly surprised by the speed and anger of the British response. Britain was able to mobilize extensive diplomatic support in the UN and among her EEC partners who joined in imposing economic sanctions on Argentina. The USA at first remained neutral in the dispute and tried to mediate but after Secretary Haig's diplomatic efforts had failed America also condemned the Argentine aggression. The UN Secretary General also attempted to resolve the dispute but he too was unsuccessful.

While the diplomatic efforts were continuing the British task force was making its way to the South Atlantic. As well as sending warships the British government also requisitioned a number of merchant vessels, including luxury liners, to carry troops and supplies and act as hospital

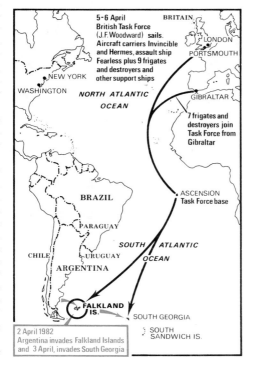

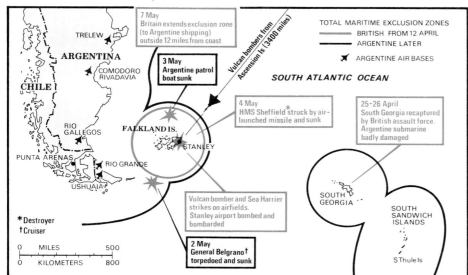

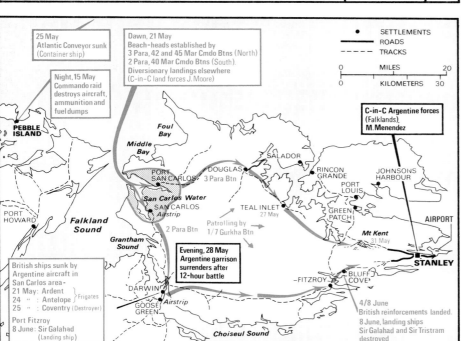

Dates and location of landings by Marine Commando battalions were not confirmed by Ministry of Defence at time of going to press

Far left: a portrait of Idi Amin, former president of Uganda, lies smashed on the floor of his residence in Kampala.
Below: loading a Tigerfish torpedo on the British nuclear submarine *Conqueror*. The *General Belgrano* was sunk by two of these weapons fired from *Conqueror*.

ships. The principal military problem for the British was in the air where the few Harrier aircraft carried by the two small aircraft carriers had, with help from missiles from the ships, to hold off the whole Argentine Air Force and support the troops in any landing. Although the Argentinian pilots fought very bravely and gained a number of successes as the maps show, they were unable, despite their own heavy losses, seriously to hinder the British operations. The Argentinian Navy had little chance to make any positive contribution and must have been deterred by the sinking of the cruiser *General Belgrano* by a British nuclear submarine.

South Georgia was quickly and easily recaptured by the British forces soon after they arrived but there then followed a delay, punctuated by air attacks by both sides before the main British landings at San Carlos. The first British formation to land was made up of elite Royal Marine and Parachute Regiment troops. Goose Green was captured after a hard fight and the British, reinforced by Ghurka and Guards units, pushed forward to surround, and eventually accept the surrender of Port Stanley. Although the Argentinian forces were numerically at least as strong as the British many of them were young conscripts, no match for the British regulars in morale or training.

In the aftermath of the surrender President Galtieri of Argentina was forced to resign but with the British seemingly more than ever determined to keep the islands any final settlement of the dispute remained unlikely.

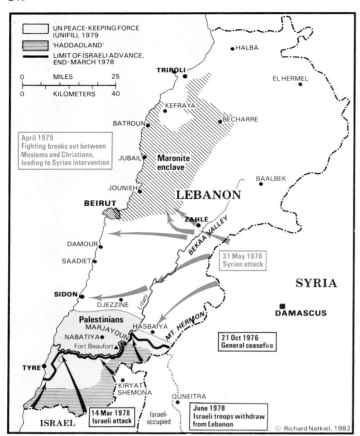

UN PEACE-KEEPING FORCE (UNIFIL), 1979
'HADDADLAND'
LIMIT OF ISRAELI ADVANCE, END-MARCH 1978

MILES 0 25
KILOMETERS 0 40

HALBA

TRIPOLI

EL HERMEL

KEFRAYA

BATROUN

BECHARRE

April 1975
Fighting breaks out between Moslems and Christians, leading to Syrian intervention

JUBAIL

Maronite enclave

JOUNIEH

BAALBEK

BEIRUT

LEBANON

ZAHLÉ

DAMOUR

BEKAA VALLEY

SAADIET

31 May 1976
Syrian attack

SYRIA

SIDON

DJEZZINE

Litani

Palestinians
MARJAYOUN
NABATIYA
Fort Beaufort
HASBAIYA

MT. HERMON

DAMASCUS

21 Oct 1976
General ceasefire

TYRE

KIRYAT SHEMONA

QUNEITRA

June 1978
Israeli troops withdraw from Lebanon

ISRAEL

14 Mar 1978
Israeli attack

Israeli-occupied

© Richard Natkiel, 1982

The Lebanon

Once part of the Ottoman Empire, and under French administration between the wars, the Lebanon emerged as an independent state after World War II. Socially it was finely balanced, for its population was divided between Moslems and Christians of various denominations, the delicacy of this situation being reflected in the practice of appointing a Maronite (Christian) president to balance the Moslem prime minister. Friction, however, was exacerbated by the presence of camps for Palestine refugees from Israel. These refugee camps provided both recruits and sanctuary for anti-Israeli guerrillas.

It became almost an Israeli custom to stage air attacks, military incursions, and assassinations in the Lebanon as reprisals for terrorist attacks on Israelis anywhere in the world. Against its will, therefore, the Lebanon became a battlefield in the Israeli-Arab struggle, and the resulting stress soon brought inter-communal violence; right-wing Christians began by attacking Palestinians but soon found themselves fighting their Moslem fellow-citizens. Syria intervened, at first quietly but finally, in summer 1976, with a full-scale invasion. Even after this officially ended in October, Syrian troops remained in a peace-keeping role which, by and large, was sincerely if clumsily executed.

In March 1978, in reprisal for continuing Palestinian guerrilla attacks, Israeli troops occupied the south part of the Lebanon. A United Nations force was sent as part of a peace settlement, but when the Israelis withdrew they handed over their positions to a friendly right-wing Christian Lebanese militia. In April 1979 this militia, under Major Haddad, declared the area to be 'Independent Free Lebanon.' Meanwhile, farther north, the Syrian peacekeeping troops were fighting Christian militia forces around Beirut, and besieging Zahlé. The alliances and alignments of the Syrians seemed highly flexible, but one constant factor were the Israeli raids. In summer 1981 a general war on Lebanese soil between Syria and Israel seemed imminent, but US mediation postponed the crisis. It was sometimes difficult to discern whether the activities of Palestinian guerrillas were a justification or merely a pretext for these incursions. Israeli pressure in the south intensified early in 1982. The Israelis mounted a full-scale invasion in June 1982 and there was renewed fierce fighting involving Syrian and Palestinian forces. The Israeli forces again had the best of the fighting and, although the Palestinians lost very heavily, it remained uncertain whether the Israelis would obtain their objective of settling with the Palestinians once and for all.

The Soviet Invasion of Afghanistan

In 1973 the King of Afghanistan was overthrown by Mohammed Daoud, who accepted Soviet military as well as economic assistance. Military help was required to back up Afghanistan's claim to territory on the Pakistan side of the frontier, provocatively called by the Afghans Paktoonistan. But in 1978, after attempting to limit Soviet influence, Daoud was overthrown in a Marxist coup and the new leaders were largely Soviet-trained army officers. The new government of Mohammed Taraki depended heavily on Soviet advisers, while the two wings (Parcham and Khalq) of the ruling communist party, the People's Democratic Party, remained in ideological and often violent conflict. In 1979 Taraki died in mysterious circumstances and the prime minister, Amin, became president and continued his hard-line policies. The latter aroused much resentment among the Afghans, many of whom had been arrested or had relatives arrested or executed. Amin pushed ahead with an attempt to transform social and economic life, but his attempt to end traditional feudal practices by land reforms, attacks on the priesthood and on landlords, abolition of the veil and dowries, intensified opposition. Rebels became bolder, and Amin called on Soviet-armed

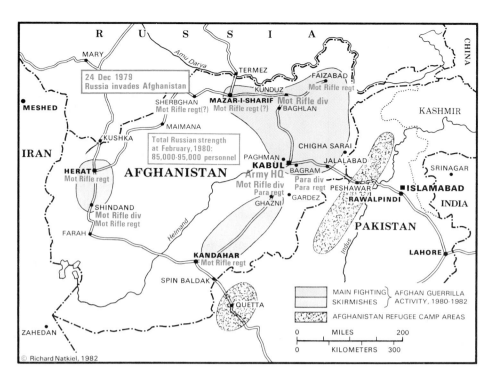

Left: Moslem rebels fight a guerrilla campaign of resistance against Afghan and Russian troops.

helicopters to bombard villages said to be harboring rebels. Armed conflict between rebels and government forces was marked by the ferocity employed by both sides.

Amin's presidency lasted only three months. His reliance on ever-increasing numbers of Soviet troops and advisers made it easy for the USSR to arrange a coup in which he was replaced by Babrak Karmal, a man regarded by the Soviets as a reliable communist who would tread more softly. This coup took place in December 1979, but did not bring peace. By the next summer former ministers who belonged to the Khalq faction had been executed, and the Red Army and Red Air Force were operating in Afghanistan in ever larger numbers. Only the capital Kabul, and cities like Jalabad, Herat, and Kandahar, could be considered safe by the government. The Afghan Army was demoralized, and large scale desertion made it ineffective. In the countryside the rebels were dominant, becoming quiet only when a Soviet punitive expedition was sent to the particular locality. The Soviet forces, which numbered as many as 100,000, used helicopters and armored vehicles, but were handicapped by the lack of roads. Raids by helicopter gunships and ground-support aircraft on rebellious villages produced little effect even though the rebels had no way of opposing them. Meanwhile refugees poured over the frontiers; about a million crossed to Pakistan in 1980, settling around Peshawar. Another half-million went to Iran. By 1981 one in every seven Afghans had fled his country. In 1982 the military situation was still a stalemate, with Soviet troops making the cities safe for the regime but holding little sway in the countryside. In this inhospitable environment the Karmal government was still attempting to introduce social reforms based on Marxist principles.

The Gulf War

In April 1969, when the Shah of Iran enjoyed US backing and possessed powerful forces, he decided to abrogate a 1937 treaty defining the Iran-Iraq frontier in which the waterway known as the Shatt-el-Arab was entirely allocated to Iraq. Iran sent ships, flying the national flag, along this waterway, but this show of strength was followed by armed clashes in the area and in January 1970 the two countries severed diplomatic relations. However, relations were restored in 1973, and in 1975 the two countries declared themselves back on a brotherly footing, with an agreement that their frontier would pass along the center of the deepest main shipping channel of the waterway. Iran also agreed to stop helping the Kurds of Iraq, who had been fighting Iraqi government forces in the hope of establishing their own independent state. The Shah's annexation of the Persian Gulf islands of Abu Musa and the Greater and Lesser Tumbs, which had occurred in 1971, by threat in the first place and by invasion in the second, was, however, still resented by Iraq and other Gulf states. The Shah regarded these islands, command-

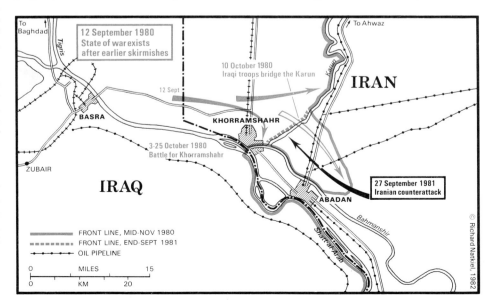

ing strategically-important straits, as vital and had lost no time in taking them after Britain's withdrawal from this region.

To Iraq's wish to regain control of the entire Shatt-el-Arab and to secure the withdrawal of Iranian forces from the Musa and Tumb islands, was added fear of Shi'ite Moslem influence. After the fall of the Shah and his replacement in Iran by a priestly (Shi'ite) government it seemed quite likely that the latter might encourage resistance of the Shi'ite majority in Iraq against the established Sunni leadership. In the meantime, Iraq had supported Arab demands that Iran should give autonomy to its Arabian territory of Khuzestan.

The Iranian revolution, its antagonizing of the USA by its detention of the US Embassy staff in Teheran, the murderous purge of the Iranian officer class, all suggested by mid-1980 that Iran was militarily weak. There were small frontier skirmishes, and on 22 September, following Iran's refusal to accept Iraq's demand that Iranian forces should be withdrawn from

one disputed area, the Iraqi Army crossed the frontier on a 300-mile front. Iraq had announced its abrogation of the Shatt-el-Arab agreement on 16 September.

Iran's resistance proved stronger than expected. Its first response was to bomb not only the advancing Iraqis, but also the port of Basra. The hostile capitals, Baghdad and Teheran, also came under air attack in September. By the end of that month the Iraqi army was besieging the ports of Abadan and Khorramshahr and the town of Susangerd. But Iraq was unable to capture these objectives before winter.

Mediation attempts failed during the winter and after the rains ceased in April 1981 full-scale warfare recommenced. In early June the Iranians fought some bloody battles to regain parts of their lost territory. But at the close of the dry season in 1981 the campaign was still a stalemate, although the vigor of Iranian counterattacks on the Iraqi salient toward Abadan suggested that time was not on Baghdad's side. Iranian attacks in 1982 made important gains.

The Antarctic

After Captain Cook became the first European to cross the South Polar Circle, scientific curiosity, love of adventure, and the quest for national prestige ensured that there would be a succession of expeditions to the Antarctic. Meanwhile seal-hunters and others who made their living from the seas visited and explored the coasts. The late nineteenth century and the early twentieth was a period of heroism and rivalry. Expeditions were mounted as much for the prestige of planting national flags in virgin territory as for the purpose of scientific discovery. Nevertheless, and perhaps because the Antarctic is the land most remote from the great powers, in recent decades it has become the scene of international harmony rarely encountered elsewhere in the world.

The age of rivalry, which was really the age of colonization, resulted in several territorial claims being staked out in Antarctica. Such claims were based on exploration or on propinquity, the nearness of a sector of the Antarctic to a claimant state. Claims of the latter type, made by Chile and Argentine, have brought them into dispute with Britain, which claims the same territory by right of exploration and discovery. Norway and France also have claims based on exploration, while New Zealand and Australia defend their claim to other sectors of the continent on both counts.

Apart from the investigation of Antarctica itself, scientific research conducted there has made very useful contributions to studies of the world's climate. Realizing that scientific research would progress more rewardingly in an atmosphere of cooperation, free of territorial acrimony, the different nations began to associate more closely and in the International Geophysical Year of 1957–58 ten nations set up coordinated research bases in the continent. From this cooperation was developed the Antarctic Treaty of 1961 in which a dozen states agreed that the continent should be used only for peaceful purposes, and that every part would be open to observers from all countries to ensure that this agreement was not being violated. The Treaty carefully sidestepped the subject of various nations' claims to sovereignty: it neigher recognized nor questioned any of these claims, either directly or implicitly.

0	MILES	2000
0	KILOMETERS	3000

COAST EXPLORED BY 1900

SOUTH PACIFIC OCEAN

CHILE ARGENTINA

Falkland Islands (Br., claimed by Argentina)

(Claimed by Chile)

Scotia Sea

(Claimed by Argentina)

S. SHETLAND IS. (Br.)

S. GEORGIA (Br.)

PETER 1st I. (Norway)

S. ORKNEY IS. (Br.)

S. SANDWICH IS. (Br.)

Antarctic Circle

60°S

Amundsen Sea

Marie Byrd Land (Unclaimed)

Weddell Sea

(Britain)

SOUTH ATLANTIC OCEAN

Coats Land

SCOTT I. (N.Z.)

Ross Sea (New Zealand)

South Pole

Queen Maud Land (Norway)

King Haakon VII Sea

BOUVET I. (Norway)

CAMPBELL I. (N.Z.)

BALLENY IS. (N.Z.)

Victoria Land (Australia)

(Australia)

AUCKLAND I. (N.Z.)

MACQUARIE I. (Australia) (France)

Adélie Land

Enderby Land

Wilkes Land

Queen Mary Coast

SOUTH AFRICA

Davis Sea

PRINCE EDWARD IS. (S.Africa)

AUSTRALIA

INDIAN OCEAN

HEARD I. (Australia)

McDONALD I. (Australia)

CROZET IS. (France)

KERGUELEN IS. (France)

© Richard Natkiel, 1982

The Formation of Senegambia

In colonial times, The Gambia was a British crown colony while Senegal, which surrounded it on three sides, was part of the French Empire, sending a deputy to the French parliament from 1848. Geographically, both countries are really one unit, with a common economic interest in the Gambia River, but politically they were split by accidents of the colonization process. The Gambia, with a population of only about 600,000, is simply two narrow strips on either side of the river, with a small port, Banjul, which is also the capital. Although it is about 200 miles long, it is only about twenty miles wide. Senegal is much bigger and has the largest port in West Africa, Dakar.

Both Senegal and The Gambia encountered social and economic problems following independence. Senegal at first joined with French Sudan, in 1959, to form the Mali Federation, but a year later seceded. Economic difficulties led to social unrest which in 1968 came to a head in strikes and demonstrations which, however, were quelled by a show of military force. French capital saved the economy from collapse but did little to help it become economically independent. Meanwhile, The Gambia was attempting in the 1970s to rescue its economy by the creation of a big tourist industry, but the signs were that this was creating many problems.

In June 1981 a left-wing coup just failed to overthrow the Gambian president, the situation being saved by the intervention of the Senegalese Army. Some of these troops stayed in Gambia, and this may have helped persuade the president of Gambia to accept the merger of Senegal and The Gambia, which had been sporadically discussed for at least 20 years. On 7 September 1981 it was announced that the merger would take place on 1 January 1982, and that the new state would call itself Senegambia.

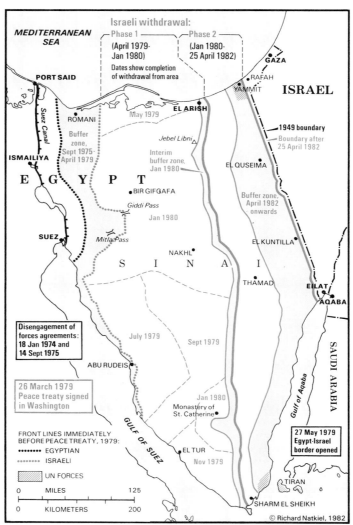

Israeli Withdrawal from Sinai

In November 1977 President Sadat of Egypt unexpectedly visited Israel and addressed the *Knesset* and almost a year later the leaders of Israel and Egypt, hitherto uncompromisingly hostile, signed what became known as the Camp David Agreements in the USA. The first of the two agreements envisioned a five-year transitional period in which the inhabitants of two territories, occupied by Israel during the Arab-Israeli conflict, would be granted self-government and autonomy. These were the Gaza Strip and the West Bank, hotly disputed areas, and in the years since the agreement there has been little sign of progress toward their promised liberation. The second agreement arranged for a peace treaty between Israel and Egypt (signed in 1979, much to the distaste of other Arab governments) and for an Israeli withdrawal from Sinai. This, which did go according to plan, was to be made in several stages.

A strip alongside the Suez Canal had been recaptured by Egypt in the 1973 war, and this was bordered on the east by a wide buffer zone, which was Israeli territory occupied by the UN Peacekeeping Force. The first stages of the new Israeli withdrawal were from the latter zone, the withdrawal being not so much military as civil. By the end of January 1980 rather more than half of Sinai had been handed over, the boundary running almost directly north to south from east of El Arish to the southern tip of Sinai. For Israel, these withdrawals meant, among other things, the relinquishment of oilfields in southwest Sinai. The final stage was to a frontier stretching from just west of Rafah, in the north, to a point west of the Israeli port of Eilat at the head of the Gulf of Aqaba. In early 1982, as the final evacuation drew nearer, Israeli settlers in Sinai began to resist the withdrawal, but the Israeli Army controlled the situation and the process was completed by May.

The World Today

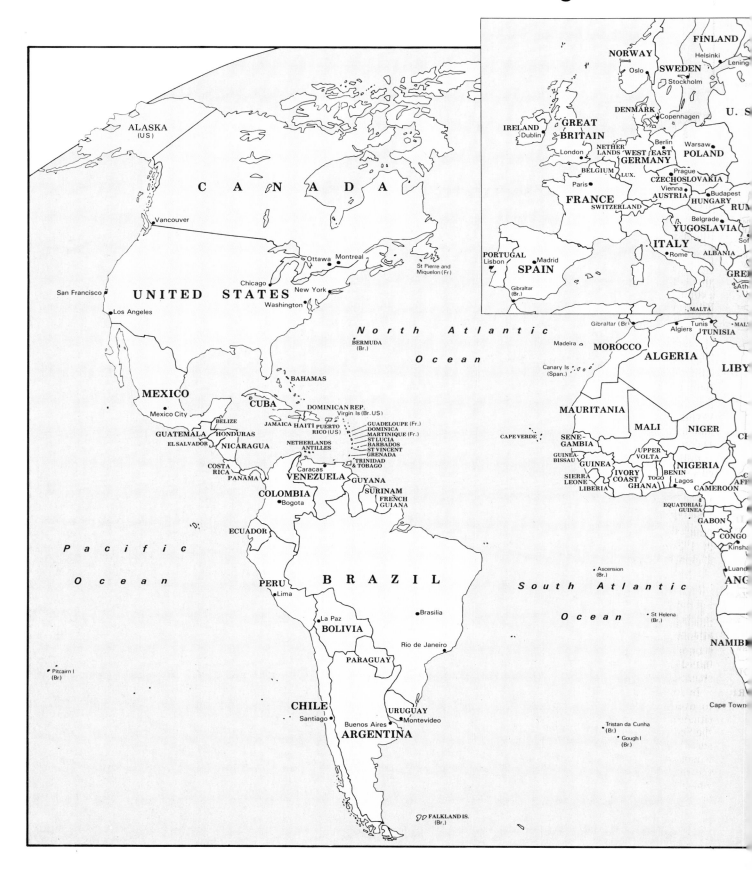

ALASKA (US)

C A N A D A

Vancouver

UNITED STATES

San Francisco
Los Angeles

Ottawa · Montreal
Chicago · New York
Washington

St Pierre and Miquelon (Fr.)

MEXICO
Mexico City

North Atlantic
Ocean

BERMUDA (Br.)

BAHAMAS

CUBA
DOMINICAN REP.
Virgin Is (Br. US)
GUATEMALA BELIZE
JAMAICA HAITI PUERTO
EL SALVADOR HONDURAS RICO (US)
NICARAGUA
COSTA RICA
PANAMA

GUADELOUPE (Fr.)
DOMINICA
MARTINIQUE (Fr.)
ST LUCIA
BARBADOS
ST VINCENT
GRENADA
NETHERLANDS
ANTILLES
TRINIDAD
& TOBAGO

Caracas
VENEZUELA GUYANA
COLOMBIA SURINAM
Bogota FRENCH GUIANA

ECUADOR

P a c i f i c
O c e a n

PERU
Lima

B R A Z I L

La Paz · Brasilia
BOLIVIA
Rio de Janeiro

PARAGUAY

Pitcairn I (Br.)

CHILE URUGUAY
Santiago Montevideo
Buenos Aires
ARGENTINA

CAPE VERDE

South Atlantic
Ocean

Ascension (Br.)

St Helena (Br.)

Cape Town

Tristan da Cunha (Br.)
Gough I (Br.)

FALKLAND IS. (Br.)

NORWAY
Oslo SWEDEN
Stockholm

FINLAND
Helsinki
Lening

DENMARK
Copenhagen
U. S

IRELAND GREAT
Dublin BRITAIN
London NETHER-
LANDS WEST EAST
GERMANY
BELGIUM LUX. Prague
Paris Vienna
FRANCE AUSTRIA
SWITZERLAND

Berlin
Warsaw
POLAND
CZECHOSLOVAKIA
Budapest
HUNGARY RUM
Belgrade

PORTUGAL Madrid
Lisbon SPAIN
Gibraltar (Br.)

YUGOSLAVIA
ITALY ALBANIA
Rome GRE
Ath

MALTA
Gibraltar (Br) Tunis MAL
Algiers TUNISIA
Madeira MOROCCO
Canary Is (Span.) ALGERIA LIBY

MAURITANIA
MALI NIGER CH
SENE-
GAMBIA
GUINEA- UPPER
BISSAU VOLTA NIGERIA
GUINEA BENIN
SIERRA IVORY TOGO Lagos CAMEROON
LEONE COAST GHANA C
LIBERIA AFR
EQUATORIAL
GUINEA
GABON
CONGO
Kinsha

Luand

ANG

NAMIBI

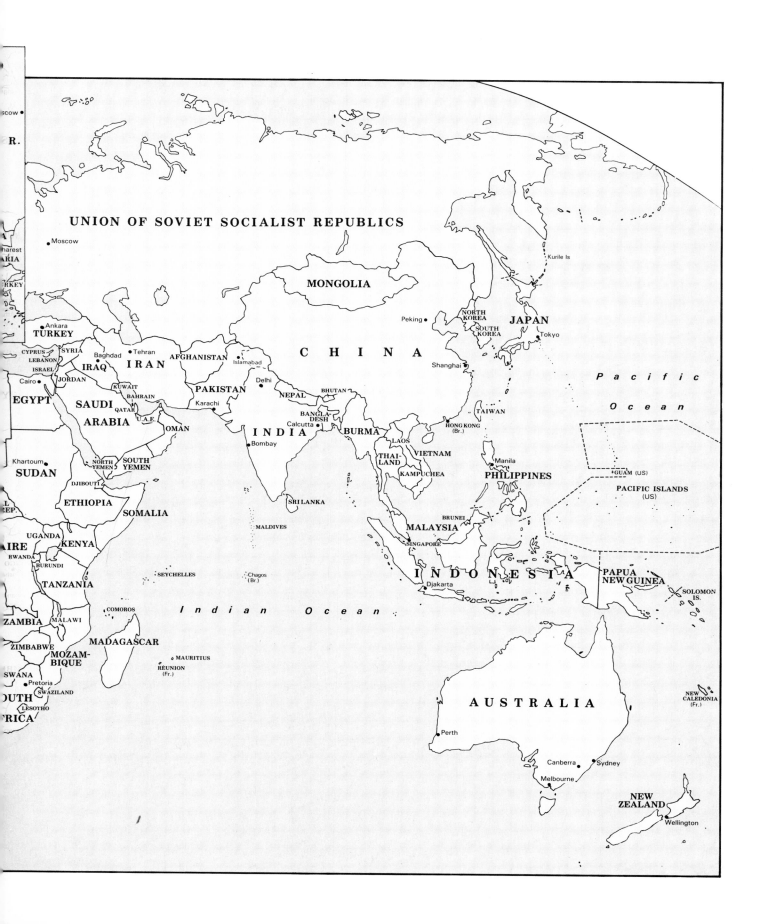

UNION OF SOVIET SOCIALIST REPUBLICS

Moscow

MONGOLIA

Peking

NORTH KOREA
JAPAN

Tokyo

SOUTH KOREA

C H I N A

Shanghai

Pacific

Ocean

Ankara
TURKEY

CYPRUS
LEBANON
ISRAEL

SYRIA
Baghdad
Tehran
IRAQ

AFGHANISTAN

IRAN

Islamabad

Delhi

Kurile Is

TAIWAN

Cairo
JORDAN

KUWAIT
BAHRAIN
QATAR
U.A.E.

PAKISTAN

NEPAL

BHUTAN

HONG KONG
(Br.)

EGYPT

SAUDI
ARABIA

OMAN

Karachi

BANGLA-
DESH
Calcutta

I N D I A

BURMA

LAOS

VIETNAM

Khartoum

NORTH
YEMEN

SOUTH
YEMEN

Bombay

THAI-
LAND

KAMPUCHEA

Manila

PHILIPPINES

GUAM (US)

SUDAN

DJIBOUTI

SRI LANKA

PACIFIC ISLANDS
(US)

ETHIOPIA

SOMALIA

MALDIVES

BRUNEI

UGANDA
KENYA

IRE

RWANDA
BURUNDI

SEYCHELLES

Chagos
(Br.)

MALAYSIA

SINGAPORE

TANZANIA

I N D O N E S I A

Djakarta

PAPUA
NEW GUINEA

SOLOMON
IS.

ZAMBIA
MALAWI

COMOROS

Indian   Ocean

ZIMBABWE

MADAGASCAR

MOZAM-
BIQUE

MAURITIUS

RÉUNION
(Fr.)

NEW
CALEDONIA
(Fr.)

SWANA

Pretoria
SWAZILAND

OUTH
RICA

LESOTHO

A U S T R A L I A

Perth

Canberra
Sydney

Melbourne

NEW
ZEALAND

Wellington

Index

Acknowledgments

The publishers would like to thank
David Eldred who designed this
book and Ron Watson who
prepared the index. The following
agencies kindly supplied the
illustrations.

BBC Hulton Picture Library p 109
Bildarchiv Preussischer Kulturbesitz
p177
Bison Picture Library pp 17 (top),
85, 101, 102 (top), 136, 152, 174
Bundesarchiv pp 29 (top), 67,
68–69, 98, 99, 104, 107, 116, 117
(both), 129 (both), 140
Camerapix pp 243, 246
Charter Consolidated p 244
ECP Armées/Mars p 212
Fujiphoto/Mars p 135 (bottom)
**Heeresgeschichtlichen Museum,
Vienna** p 51
Robert Hunt pp 18, 44, 47, 59, 73,
74, 75, 96–97, 112, 114 (both), 115,
120, 121 (both), 123, 148 (both),
149, 207 (both), 208, 222 (top),
223 (top), 233 (top)
Imperial War Museum pp 31 (top),
32, 110, 125 (both), 169
Imperial War Museum/Mars pp
26–27, 31 (both), 33, 34, 35, 37
(both), 39 (both), 40, 42, 43 (both),
46–47, 48 (both), 49 (top), 50, 54,
55, 64 (left), 65, 148 (bottom), 151,
312 (left)
Imperial War Museum/Faces pp 1,
62 (both)
Keystone Press Agency pp 4–5,
194–95, 198 (top), 200, 201, 210,
211 (both), 213 (right), 214, 215
(both), 216 (both), 217, 218, 219
(both), 222 (bottom), 223
(bottom), 224, 225, 228, 229,
233 (bottom), 234, 235 (both), 236,
237, 238, 240 (both), 241, 242,
243 (both), 245, 246, 248
Mansell Collection pp 25, 60 (both),
71, 72
**Military Archive and Research
Services** p 102 (bottom)
Ministry of Defence/Mars p 232
(top left)
National Archives pp 78–79, 130,
139, 146 (top), 158, 159, 167 (both),
188, 203 (bottom), 204, 206, 207
(top)
National Army Museum/Mars
p 14–15
Novosti Press Agency pp 12–13,
17 (bottom), 125, 142, 143, 144,
146 (bottom), 154, 155, 163, 164,
178, 179, 185
Panama Canal Co./Mars pp 20
(top), 21
Personality Picture Library p 49
(bottom)
Popperphoto pp 23, 24
SADO p 129 (top)
Ted Stone p 128
Ullstein Bilderdienst pp 76 (both),
100 (both), 197, 198 (bottom)
United Nations/Mars p 70
US Air Force pp 160 (below), 175,
189, 220, 221
US Air Force/Mars p 170
US Army pp 6, 80, 95, 135 (top),
168, 173, 176, 180, 203 (top)
US Marine Corps pp 160 (top),
191, 192 (both), 205, 226, 227
US Marine Corps/Mars p 20
(bottom)
US Navy pp 2–3, 91, 93, 132, 138